Tribal Heritage

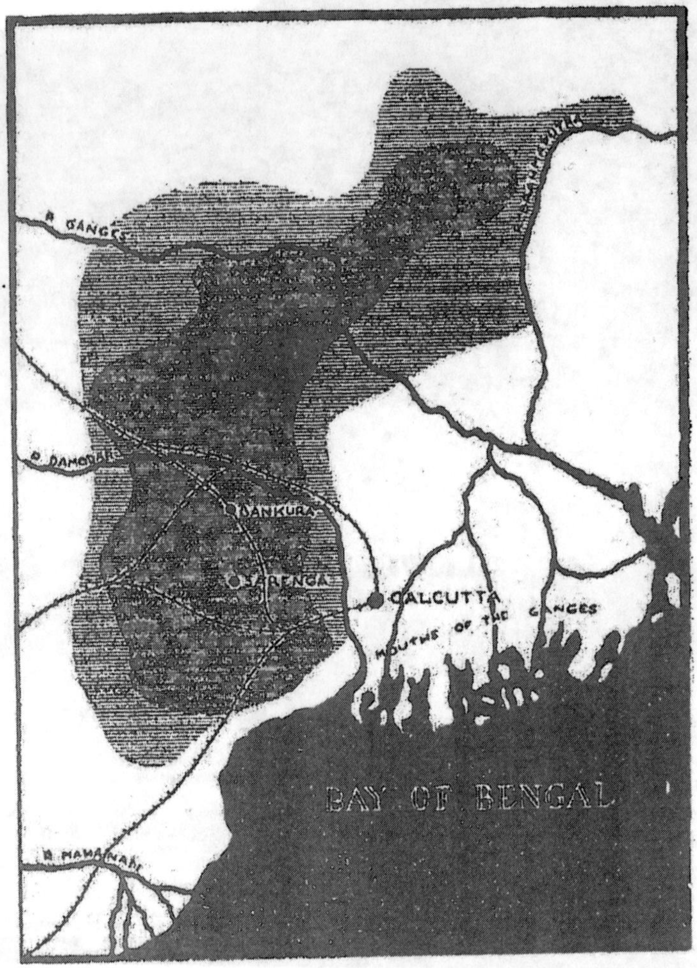

Santal Area of Eastern India

The heavy shading represents areas where the Santals form at least ten percent of the population; the lighter shading where thepercentage is smaller.

Tribal Heritage

A Study of the Santals

W.J. Culshaw

GYAN

Published by

GYAN

Gyan Publishing House
5, Ansari Road
Daryaganj, New Delhi-110002
Phone: 011-47034999, 9811692060
E-mail: books@gyanbooks.com

Distribution Network
gyanbooks.com
India, USA, Canada, UK, Australia, France

ISBN: 978-93-6280-231-6 (PB)

First Published, 2024

Printed at: Gyan Press, Delhi.

Tribal Heritage: A Study of the Santals
Author: W.J. Culshaw

PREFACE

THIS study represents an attempt to provide the kind of book that I wish could have been placed in my hands when I first began to work among the Santals. It is based very largely on material gathered during my residence in the village of Sarenga, District Bankura, between October 1932 and April 1943. Much of what is said is true of the Santals wherever they are found. The uniformity of Santal culture over a wide area raises questions of great interest to students, but no attempt has been made to deal with them here. Nor have I attempted to deal with the wider questions involved in the problem of the Christian approach to peoples living in small-scale societies, though I hope that I may have been able to supply some data relevant to the discussion. We missionaries are at times impatient of the strictures of anthropologists, but we would do well to heed the warning of such a missionary as Dr. Kraemer when he says: "Missions make the claim, on account of their religious aim, that Christianity contains the forces of moral and spiritual regeneration so sorely needed in this time of disintegration. It is encouraging to read twice, for instance, in Monica Hunter's *Reaction to Conquest* that Christianity proves able to supply a new invigorating moral basis of life. Yet missions ought always to be mindful that this does not result *mechanically* from the acceptance of Christianity, but that to achieve it there is need for a constant application to the task of religious, moral, cultural and social education—and this must be inspired by the desire *to serve the true interests of the people*."[1]

I count it among the more fortunate circumstances of my life that my first five years were spent at Pakur in the Santal Parganas; the investigations then begun perhaps helped to shape my outlook! During the years at Sarenga I came to owe a great debt to many individual Santals. Three men in particular helped by placing their knowledge at my disposal, and most of the statements in this book have been checked more than once in the course of many conversations with them. The late Ernest Soren was for many years headmaster of the Boys' School at Sarenga; he became a Christian in early manhood and was held in high regard by all who knew him, yet he never

[1] H. Kraemer, *The Christian Message in a non-Christian World*, London, 1938, p. 436. The italics are the author's.

forgot that he was a Santal. Another Christian who helped me was Babulal Hembrom of Barikul; a villager all his life, at my suggestion he kept a diary of life in Barikul for one year, and I have drawn freely on the material thus provided. The third name I wish to mention is that of the late Binu Hãsdãk', a *parganath* who lived in the village of Tantidanga. For some years he called to see me each week on his way to market; he used to accept a sum of two annas each time he came, not as a dole, but as the equivalent of the hospitality to which he was entitled as a visitor to my home. From him I learnt much about the ideas and customs that ruled his life, as they had done the lives of his ancestors.

A great deal has been written about the Santals, but most of the literature is difficult to find even when you know where to look for it. The bibliography contains a list of the works I have consulted, and acknowledgments have been made in footnotes. It needs to be said, however, that all subsequent workers must remain heavily indebted to that great Norwegian scholar and missionary, the late P. O. Bodding, particularly for his monumental *Santali Dictionary*, which is a veritable encyclopaedia of Santal life.

I wish to thank the Council of the Royal Asiatic Society of Bengal for permission to use material previously published in two papers in the *Journal of the Royal Asiatic Society of Bengal*, entitled "Some Notes on Bongaism" (Vol. V, 1939, No. 3) and "Some Beliefs and Customs relating to Birth among the Santals" (Vol. VII, 1941, No. 1). I owe much to the Rev. Edwin Smith, D.D., pre-eminent among missionary anthropologists, who spent Christmas at Sarenga in 1938, and has encouraged me since that time. I am deeply grateful to the Rev. Charles P. Groves, Professor of Missions at the Selly Oak Colleges, who has read the manuscript and saved me from numerous pitfalls, and to my friend the Rev. Wilfred H. Russell, who drew the map, as well as the illustrations on pages 24 and 49. I wish also to thank the Rev. Alec R. Spooner for preparing the Index. My wife has helped with many candid criticisms, constructive suggestions, and, above all, by her comradeship during the years at Sarenga.

W. J. CULSHAW.

BANKURA,
January, 1949.

A NOTE ON ORTHOGRAPHY

In spelling Santali words I have mostly followed the system of romanization developed by P. O. Bodding and described by him in *Materials for a Santali Grammar*, Pt. I (Second Edition, Dumka, 1930).

The following diacritical marks have been used:

A *circumflex* above a vowel, as in *ã*, indicates a nasal tone.

A *dot* below *a*, as in *ạ*, indicates a resultant vowel. The pronunciation is not uniform. Sometimes it resembles the pronunciation of the vowel in the first stressed syllable and sometimes the second syllable of such an English word as *worker* pronounced in the southern English way, the *r's* being silent.

A *dot* below a consonant indicates a hard sound; *t* and *d* without a dot are true dentals.

An *accent* with *n* (*ń*) signifies the palatal *n*; a *dot* above it (*ṅ*) is used for the guttural *n*.

There are four *checked consonants* indicated by an apostrophe, as *k'*, *c'*, *t'* and *p'*.

I have omitted the *dash* under the vowels *o* and *e*, used by Bodding to indicate the open vowel sound, in accordance with the latest recommendations of the Santal Christian Council on Santali spelling.

When Santali words first occur in the text I have endeavoured to explain the meaning, but a glossary has been added to facilitate reference.

CONTENTS

	PAGE
FRONTISPIECE (MAP)	iv
PREFACE	vii
A NOTE ON ORTHOGRAPHY	ix

CHAPTER

1. THE MAKING OF A PEOPLE	1
2. THE SANTAL AND HIS NEIGHBOURS	15
3. THE RHYTHM OF DAILY LIFE	25
4. DANCING, MUSIC AND POETRY	39
5. SOME FOLK-TALES	51
6. MYTHS AND THE CLAN ORGANIZATION	64
7. THE WORLD INVISIBLE—(1)	78
8. THE WORLD INVISIBLE—(2)	92
9. FESTIVALS	103
10. BIRTH AND INITIATION	120
11. MARRIAGE	134
12. DEATH	150
13. THE IMPACT OF CHRISTIAN MISSIONS	161
14. THE NEW COMMUNITY	175

APPENDIX

A. SANTAL KINSHIP TERMS	191
B. SANTALI TEXT OF SONGS	195
C. GLOSSARY	203
D. BIBLIOGRAPHY	207
E. INDEX	210

CHAPTER I

THE MAKING OF A PEOPLE

THE Santals are one of the largest of the tribal peoples of India; at the census of 1931 they numbered over two and a half million. Their villages are widely distributed over the area which lies between eighty-six and eighty-eight meridians east longitude and between twenty-two and twenty-six degrees north latitude. They are also found farther to the north-east, where some have settled in North Bengal and Western Assam. They are the most easterly of the great belt of primitive folk which stretches across Central India.

Where the Chota Nagpur plateau begins to give way to the Ganges plain the country is broken up into a series of ridges. Through the narrow valleys thus formed flow many streams which maintain a brief and furious life during the rains. There are few big rivers, and even these dry to nothingness in the hot season. In some parts there are ranges of low hills; in others conical-shaped hills rise abruptly from the undulating plain. The countryside is still for the most part well wooded, and the *sal* forests (*Shorea robusta*, Gartn.) contribute to the wellbeing of those who dwell in them. It is, however, a hard country in which to live, where the soil is rocky and the water supplies are scant.

Dr. B. S. Guha[1] has distinguished six main types among the races who inhabit India. The Santals belong to his second "main race", the Proto-Australoid, which he considers arrived in India soon after the Negritos. The name is given because of the similarity of racial type with Australian tribes. "We have no precise information as to when this race first came into India. It is found among the prehistoric skulls in the Tinnevelly district, and from references in early Sanskrit literature to 'Nishads', where they are described as noseless (*anash*) with dark skin colour and peculiar speech and habits, there can be no doubt that the Proto-Australoid tribes were meant."[2] The Santals are short in stature, and among them the broad flat nose with a sunken nose ridge is fairly common. They frequently have wavy hair; sometimes it is curly, though it is never frizzy. They share all these characteristics with other primitive tribes in the same group. Dr. Guha has cautiously attempted to state

[1] B. S. Guha, *Oxford Pamphlets on Indian Affairs*, "Racial Elements in the Population", 1944.

[2] B. S. Guha, *op. cit.*, p. 11.

those features which present-day Indian culture owes to the Proto-Australoid: "To the Proto-Australoid races may perhaps be attributed a large share of totemistic rites, exorcism, food taboos, and magical belief still obtaining in Indian life. The ban on commensality and intermarriage which forms the basis of the caste system must also owe its origin to them."[1] It is impossible to dogmatize on these subjects when one remembers how widespread each of the above factors is among primitive cultures in various parts of the world. The tribal structure of the Santals is totemistic and the clans are patrilinear, as among the other tribes of Central India. Many of the taboos and customs which have grown up round life's crises, many features in the tribal ritual, their attitude towards disease and towards the supranatural world, are fundamentally similar not only throughout these tribes but throughout the lower range of the Hindu social structure. The perusal of such a book as William Crooke's *Religion and Folklore of Northern India*[2] gives convincing evidence of the large stock of ideas that are held in common.

By the test of language the Santals reveal a high degree of social cohesion. Dr. J. H. Hutton's judgment cannot be gainsaid: "The extent of the survival of tribal languages is a better index than that of the survival of tribal religion to the social cohesion of the tribe, since the test of language is easier and more definite than that of religion, where the borderland of Hinduism is often vague and obscure."[3] The Santals have been more tenacious of their language than many of the other peoples to whom they are racially allied. They are the largest tribe in India to retain an aboriginal language to the present day. This belongs to what is known as the Austric or Austro-Asiatic family. It is closely related to Mundari as well as to Ho, Korku, Savara and Gadaba, languages spoken by smaller tribes. The relationship of the Santals with these tribes is racial and cultural as well as linguistic, and as they live in neighbouring territories it is very likely that they have a common origin. They have nevertheless been separate long enough to develop their individual languages and to possess distinct though allied cultures. Other representatives of the Austro-Asiatic languages are found farther afield, the Mon-Khmer branch being found in Indo-China, while Khasi, spoken in Assam, is another. The fact that Khasis are Mongoloid and that their society is matri-

[1] B. S. Guha, *op. cit.*, p. 28.
[2] Oxford University Press, 1926.
[3] *Census Report of India*, 1931, Vol. I, Ch. x, p. 348.

linear is an example of the danger in seeking to base racial history on linguistic affinities; but as recently as 1943 Professor S. K. Chatterji[1] speaks of the Austric race, in which he follows scholars like Schmidt and Hévésy.

The Santals first began to attract the attention of Europeans during the first half of the nineteenth century. The first book on the Santals, published in 1867, was entitled *Sonthalia and the Sonthals*. The writer, E. G. Man,[2] had by then been serving a period as an Assistant Commissioner in the newly formed district of the Santal Parganas. It is natural that the Santals attracted most attention in that district, where they were not only found in the greatest numbers, but where also they had risen in rebellion in 1855. Long before the rebellion the government had indeed become aware of their existence and of the special problems which they presented to the administration. An earlier report,[3] the result of an investigation into the land tenures of the "hill people", or Paharias, of the Raj Mahal hills, which had been written in 1819, could not fail to make some reference to the Santals, who at that period were engaged in a mass migration into the area and were driving the Paharias into the farther fastnesses of the hills. At an even earlier date Francis Buchanan's account[4] of the district of Bhagalpur in 1810–11 gives a short account of some "five hundred families" of Santals whom he found in the Dumka subdivision in 1809.

Another early account was published in W. W. Hunter's *Annals of Rural Bengal*.[5] The writer claimed little first-hand knowledge and based his description on information supplied by the American Baptist missionaries who began work among the Santals in the western portions of the Midnapore district and in Orissa. The first reference to the Santals in the papers of the American Free-Will Baptist Mission, as it was then called, is alive with all the excitement of a new discovery. In the journal of "Brother Noyes", under the date December 29, 1838, he records: "Came to a small village in the heart of a dense jungle. As soon as I came in sight of the houses, I felt persuaded I was coming among old acquaintances, they so much resembled the stick huts of the Coles of Cumbhulpore.

[1] S. K. Chatterji, *Oxford Pamphlets on Indian Affairs*, "The Linguistic Problem", 1943.
[2] E. G. Man, *Sonthalia and the Sonthals*, London, Calcutta, 1867.
[3] H. C. Sutherland, *Report on the Management of the Rajmahal Hills*, dated June 8, 1819, Deputy Commissioner's Record Room, Dumka.
[4] F. Buchanan, *An Account of the District of Bhagalpur in 1810–11*, Patna, 1939.
[5] W. W. Hunter, *Annals of Rural Bengal*, London, 1868.

When I saw the jet-black people, with a necklace of white beads about their necks, and their peculiar dress, if dress it might be called, I was more confirmed in my opinion. I immediately alighted from my horse and inquired if that was a village of the Coles, but was not a little surprised at being so soon transported from the Oriyas to a people who could not understand a word I said. I looked about with astonishment at the romantic change, till at length I found an old man who could speak broken Oriya, of whom I gained the following information. He said they were not Coles, but Santals."[1] The author of the *Annals* relied largely on information supplied to him by the Rev. Jeremiah Phillips, who was a pioneer in the study of the language. The following occurs in the Annual Report of the mission for the year 1846: "During the past year Brother Phillips has acquired some knowledge of the language of this people (the Santals), by which he has been able to commence efforts for their improvement, which it is believed will result in great good to this hitherto neglected portion of the inhabitants of Orissa. He has performed a journey of some two or three weeks among them, which was very serviceable and interesting to him. He has published a tract of 8 pages, which is the first work ever published in the Santal dialect."

The Santals have been living in South-West Bengal for at least three hundred years. It is probable that they have been there for about five hundred years. There is agreement among the authorities that they moved to their present sites from the more hilly districts of Chota Nagpur farther west. It has been computed that the village of Rangibari in Bankura district is over three hundred years old.[2] Such a long period of residence on the one site is exceptional; the great majority of the Santal villages of today cannot look back on so long a history. Wherever a tradition regarding the founders of a village has survived, one finds that the first settlers moved to their present abode from no great distance away. Regarding Barikul, we are told; "The one who tied the brown hen here was Haru Mạñjhi, whose family came first from Aurasuri in Bogri—a distance of about thirty-five miles. They say that formerly there were many wild elephants in Bogri, and for fear of the elephants many of the inhabitants fled to other parts. Sorup and Haru

[1] This and the following quotation I owe to the kindness of the Rev. A. A. Berg, who enabled me to see early reports in his possession.

[2] M. C. McAlpin, *A Report on the Condition of the Santals in the Districts of Birghum, Bankura, Midnapore and North Balasore*, IV (20), Bengal Government, 1909.

Mạṅjhi were two brothers. Sorup Mạṅjhi left Bogri because of the elephants, came to Raipur and settled. He had established himself well at the end of a year or two, so he told his younger brother: 'Leave Bogri, where the elephants are on the increase. Some day you will be trampled on and killed. Come with me.' Haru Mạṅjhi thought to himself: 'True enough, many men have been killed; perchance they will kill me.' Thinking thus, he took all his children, left Bogri and came to Raipur. From Rautora in Raipur they established a village in Barikul, Sorup Mạṅjhi saying to his brother: 'Go to, brother, put up your huts and stay at Barikul.' Then Haru Mạṅjhi went out with his children, his cattle and his goats, and built his huts there. He had four boys and two girls; the girls they brought with them from Bogri, and the four boys were born in Barikul. He obtained sons-in-law for his daughters to live with them, and one or two tenants came together. In this way the village increased to many houses." Wild elephants, of which there are not so many now as formerly, do still on occasion cause great damage to ripening crops. Barikul was founded five generations ago, a period of about one hundred years. At that time there was also a possibility that by moving his abode the Santal could regain a measure of independence. The Santals have been spoken of as formerly "nomadic".[1] It may be that in the strict sense of the word they were in some remote period nomads. For any period of which we have record, however, they have been agriculturalists, though food-gathering and hunting provide them with important subsidiary occupations. Their migrations have been due to pressure of one kind and another. They prefer to move to forest lands where they will have a hard struggle to establish new settlements than to remain where they have to defend their holdings and their livelihood against hostile forces, whether these be wild animals, malignant actions directed against individuals or the community from the unseen world, or the oppression of landlords and moneylenders.

The last cause operated to produce a great northward movement in the early decades of the nineteenth century, and finally goaded them into rebellion. The Santal rebellion has been frequently described.[2] It took place in an area remote from the Bankura district, but it has to be mentioned because it created

[1] P. O. Bodding, *Bengal District Gazetteers: Santal Parganas*, ed. L. S. S. O'Malley, Calcutta, 1910.

[2] J. H. Hutton, *Modern India and the West*, ed. L. S. S. O'Malley, Oxford, 1941. Chapter on the Primitive Tribes, pp. 417–44. Also bibliography.

a great stir throughout the Santal country. The story has become part and parcel of the consciousness of Santals everywhere, and the leaders are still celebrated in songs that are current far from the places in which they performed their exploits. The rebellion had no direct connection with the Sepoy mutiny. Both risings did, however, originate in the unsettled state of the country and the inexperience of the British authorities. The Santals rose against the intolerable rapacity of the moneylenders, with whom the subordinate officials of the government, and particularly the police, were in league. It became necessary to call out strong armed forces to restore law and order before the grievances could be redressed. The rebellion followed a pattern one might expect when ill-armed rioters faced armed and disciplined troops. The Santals gathered, sometimes numbered in thousands, and proceeded to plunder the nearby bazaar towns. In the first flush of indignation and excitement they sought out their enemies, murdering police officials and moneylenders, as also other hapless individuals who came in their way. The alarmed government dispatched strong military forces to the area and proclaimed martial law. The disturbances dragged on in sporadic fashion for over two years, at the end of which the constructive measures of the government began to take effect. A new district was set up with special regard to the need for protecting the land of the Santals, and their village system was used in the organization set up for maintaining order by giving a measure of responsibility to their tribal officials.

Since that date the history of the Santals has been peaceful and some measure of progress has been achieved. It was not however, until the second decade of the twentieth century that the Bengal Government passed an Act—the Bengal Tenancy Amendment Act, 1918—which endeavoured to protect Santals and other aboriginals in Bengal in similar fashion. It prohibited the transfer of land from aboriginals without the permission of the courts and prevented the attachment of their lands for debts arising out of causes other than the non-payment of rent. By that time most of the damage had been done, and consequently the Santals are now overwhelmingly in the position of under-tenants. The background of their economic life can be seen in the following example, which is typical rather than peculiar. In 1896 the villagers of Ramboni borrowed the sum of forty rupees from their landlord in order to excavate an irrigation tank on their land. In the year 1913 they were sold up for non-payment of the accumulated debt, which by then was a considerably larger sum. They were thus compelled to make new agreements with their landlord at an enhanced rent and with inferior rights. The later passage of legislation has done little to lift the burden of despair about the future which is an unhappy characteristic of Santal life today. Such incidents explain in no small measure the cry of the heart which is heard from time to time: "Give us back our land." It is some consolation that the Act of 1918, followed by legislation during the last twenty years aimed at improving the status of the peasantry in Bengal, has brought to a close some of the worst chapters in a long and sordid story.

The community life of the Santal centres in his village, and is so organized as to make common action inevitable in social, economic and religious affairs. The houses are built on either side of the village street, which must be left wide enough for two bullock carts to pass each other. This street extends from east to west, the eastern end being known as the upper end. The houses, set close together, have their main door opening on to the village street, and each household is responsible for the state of the road outside its own residence. It is here in the village that the Santal learns how to live; here he is initiated into the traditional loyalties of the tribe, and the village of his birth exercises a deep influence over him all his days.

The village headman, or *mạñjhi*, is the man of greatest consequence in the community. The post is hereditary, and it passes ordinarily to the eldest son of the former headman. When the direct line of succession fails through lack of sons or from incapacity on the part of the natural heir, the office passes on to a brother or near relative on the paternal side. The history of the village is preserved in the tradition handed down concerning the headman's ancestry. For example, at Sarenga they tell a story of the three brothers who were the founders of the village and divided the village offices between them. Among them Lokhon has acquired the greatest measure of renown, and he is commemorated by a shrine outside the present village. The story is told that he died suddenly, and before the news of his death had spread through the village his spirit took possession of a young man sitting in the courtyard of a house some distance away, and through him Lokhon told the villagers that they were to make a special shrine for him. There is a ceremony at the beginning of each new year which suggests that at one time the appointment of the headman, together with that of all the other officials, was renewed annually, but there is little reality in it at the present day and the post is held for life. He is the spokesman of the villagers in all matters affecting their temporal welfare. In the original settlements it was usual for two or three brothers to start the new village together. The eldest brother assumed the leading position, and all the lands cleared or claimed for the future were in his gift. The cultivable land was divided equally after some portions had been reserved for the officials in recognition of the services they would be called on to perform for the benefit of the community, and the headman received the biggest share of the reserved land. As the village grew, others came to settle. Some became the tenants of the headman, fleeing from the oppression of landlords elsewhere. Others came into the village by marrying daughters of the first settlers. So it comes about that the family of the headman is the most substantial in the village. During the course of years, however, even the headman has in the majority of cases lost his original rights to a non-Santal landlord and has himself become an under-tenant, in spite of which his family has maintained its favourable position in relation to the rest of the villagers. In some cases he has also been able to acquire the rights of other tenants who have defaulted for one reason or another in paying rent. In addition to land, the headman receives other payments which he can use for his own benefit. Thus, when an offender against tribal custom is fined the headman receives a fourth of the total amount. During the spring hunts he receives a part of the flesh of every animal slain by a man from his own village. During the marriage ceremonies he occupies an important position throughout, and when a new bride is coming to his village her father has to pay a rupee to him before the party sets out from her home. At all times he is treated with great respect, especially by the younger members of the community. A marriage party always pays its respects first at his house, and at festivals, when the young men go dancing through the village street, they start outside the headman's house.

In all matters involving the members of more than one village he is the acknowledged representative of his own people, whether it be the making of arrangements for a marriage or the fixing of dates for festivals and for hunts. In the settling of disputes he acquires considerable experience, being the chairman of the council in his own village and meeting with the headmen of other villages when the hunt council sits. Enjoying a position of great prestige, it is true of nearly all the village headmen that their whole bearing reveals a sense of dignity, and the exercise of their responsibilities has developed a practical wisdom in dealing with men and affairs that is not to be despised. It is unfortunate that the trend of policy under the British Government (except in the Santal Parganas district) has done much to undermine the authority of the headman, firstly through the development of a highly organized and centralized system of justice. When the aggrieved party in a dispute between Santals is able to seek redress in the distant district courts he is under a strong temptation to ignore the findings of the informal village and tribal councils. The temptation is all the stronger when the Hindu law administered by the court differs from Santal customary law, as it does in some important particulars. Secondly, the organs of local self-government which have been fostered in Bengal take no account of the Santal village system. It is true that some effort is made to secure representation of Santal interests by a system of nomination, but local influence has passed largely into the hands of the landlords. The government is aware of some of the disabilities under which Santals live, and since the passing of the Government of India Act, 1935, "Special Officers" have been appointed in several districts. It is their duty to watch over the interests of the Santals, but the success of their work depends largely on their own initiative, a factor which varies from one individual to another. In a few cases where Santal headmen have maintained their position in relation to dealings with non-Santals and with government, it is because they have secured some education and have been able to compete on more equal terms with their neighbours.

None of the other village officials compare with the headman for prestige. There is often a deputy headman, the *paranik*, who works as an adviser, but his main reason for existence is to function for the headman when the latter may be ill or away on family affairs, and he does not occupy a prominent place at other times. Many villages at the present day omit to appoint one. Next in importance comes the *jogmaṅjhi*, who is still found in every village. It is difficult to define his functions in a phrase; he is a kind of "censor of morals". As such he is the guardian of the morals of the young men in the village, and his wife exercises oversight of the morals of the young women. Unlike many of the tribes to whom they are closely related, the Santals have no dormitory system for the young people of the village. They have no memory of ever having possessed the institution, but a snatch of song once heard suggests that they did at some period abandon it. In a *Sohrae* song occur the words

> The young girls are sleeping in the girls' house,
> The young men are sleeping in the young men's cowshed.[1]

If, as seems likely, they once had such an institution, it is probable that the *jogmaṅjhi* and his wife were in charge. At some festivals the young men sleep at the house of the *jog maṅjhi*, and at the time of the *Sohrae* they go to him at the beginning of the festival and ask him in formal language to turn a blind eye to any of the faults they commit during that time. He is also called in to investigate allegations of immoral behaviour. The appointment is for life and it is hereditary, like that of the headman. In every village there are also two priests, who are responsible for maintaining right relations with the unseen world, but it will be more convenient to deal with their functions at a later stage.[2]

The humblest of the village officials is the *goḍet'*, the bailiff and messenger of the headman. When a child is born or a villager dies, it is the *goḍet'* who carries the news to all the houses. If it becomes necessary to summon the men of the village to a council to announce the near approach of a marriage party, or to collect dues from the houses for a feast in connection with a festival, it is the *goḍet's* duty to see that it is done. He is the errand boy, and consequently something of a butt for the wit of the village, as the following song (sung during the *Sohrae* festival) bears witness:

> Here comes the headman walking slowly,
> And here comes his deputy with wooden sandals,
> And also the *goḍet'* calling out to everyone.
>
> Put out a woven bed for the headman to sit on,
> Put out a wooden stool for his deputy,
> And put out for the *goḍet'* a broken bed.
>
> Pour out for the headman the first brew of beer,
> Pour out for his deputy the second brew,
> Pour out for the *goḍet'* the leavings.
>
> Give to the headman cakes of sifted flour,
> Give to his deputy some coarser cakes,
> And give to the *goḍet'* the lumpy bits.[3]

[1] See Appendix B, No. 1.
[2] See Chapter 7
[3] See Appendix B, No. 2.

The organization which binds groups of villages together is loose by comparison with the village system. The Santals distinguish between the various sections of the country in which their villages are situated, calling them *parganas*. Each *pargana* has a distinctive name, which may be either the name of a village situated within its borders or a general name. Over each of the *parganas* a *parganath* is supposed to have jurisdiction. McAlpin's report, the result of an inquiry instituted by the Bengal Government which led to the Tenancy Amendment Act of 1918, in addition to its main purpose of suggesting measures for the protection of Santal lands, dealt also with the condition of the Santal village system. McAlpin reported that the *pargana* system was far gone in decay, and it is not possible to question his conclusion. Binu Hãsdāk' of Tantidanga, late *parganath* of the Sarenga area, was typical of his class. His mind was well stored with the customary law of the tribe, and from time to time he was called in by nearby villages to help more particularly with disputes arising out of marriage tangles. He was personally popular and had some prestige as the possessor of valuable remedies against sickness, but on his own confession his authority was of a very limited kind. "What can I do", he once said, "unless the people of the village are agreed?" There is the crux of the situation; in the village, public opinion is a wellnigh irresistible force. Binu used, nevertheless, to go happily about his errands, for among other advantages which accrued he received a fee amounting to one rupee four annas when a guilty party was fined.

Kinship ties share with the well-knit village system the governance of the Santal's daily life, regulating his relationships with his fellows. The tribe is divided into clans, and each clan is again divided into sub-clans. The clan descends through the father, and when girls marry they are taken into the clans of their husbands. The clans have a totemistic basis and they are exogamous. Land is conceived of as belonging to the clan. Although individual and family ownership is now the rule, Santals will not countenance the transfer of land from one clan to another. The one exception for which allowance is made has been forced on them by economic necessity; it occurs in the case of a man without sons who brings his daughter's husband into his own house to carry on the cultivation, the son-in-law thereby acquiring rights in the property for descendants. The rights conferred by Hindu personal law on daughters in the property of their fathers or on wives in the property of their husbands are strenuously resisted by the Santals, and the fact that the civil courts administer the Hindu laws of succession leads to many cases of tension. In practice, certain rights are conceded to women for "humanitarian" reasons. To daughters who do not marry—a rare but not unknown phenomenon—and to widows, with or without children, the right to maintenance is given. Since the woman on marriage becomes a member of another clan, the succession to land cannot be carried through her.

Ties of kinship determine standards of behaviour to a great extent. Life in community is an art to be learnt, and the Santal has his own rigid standards of right conduct. The relationship between grandparents and grandchildren is one of deep intimacy and affection, which is no doubt fostered by the necessity for leaving the young children with the grandparents when both parents have to go out to work. The rules governing familiarity and its converse, avoidance, are based on kinship ties. The joking relationship, apart from grandparents and grandchildren, extends to his wife's younger sisters for a man and to her husband's younger brothers and her elder sister's husband for a woman. People within the circle of this relationship can talk freely with one another, indulging in jokes and calling each other names. Conversely, extreme care is called for in relationships which do not fall within this circle. A Santal child must behave with great respect to anyone who belongs to the same generation as his parents. Names are sparingly used between individuals, and relationship terms are the usual form of address. Husband and wife will on no account use each other's names, in distinction from the Hindu taboo, which is enjoined on the wife only. They behave circumspectly towards each other in public. A woman has to carry herself with care before her husband's elder brother. Her dress must at all times be properly arranged in front of him; she cannot sit with her legs dangling over the edge of a bed or the low veranda running round the house, her hair must be arranged, and she does not talk to him at all apart from the necessities of daily life. The rules extend to the finer forms of courtesy. Every Santal knows what is expected of him when he is meeting relatives—whether he has to make a deep obeisance to the ground before the person he has met, or whether he should wait for the other person to greet him first and then acknowledge the greeting by cupping his hands together and raising them towards his chest. A greeting between equals is performed by means of a salute with the right hand; this is raised towards the face, fingers slightly bent, the fingers of the left hand lightly touching the right forearm. When a Santal is meeting his co-parents-in-law, they embrace breast to breast, exchange jokes, and make use of the inclusive form of the dual pronoun. Honoured guests as well as relations are met with dignified courtesy. Few experiences can be more refreshing than to sit in the courtyard of a Santal home after a long and dusty walk. When greetings have been exchanged, one of the girls of the house comes forward to wash the feet and massage with oil the tired calves. This done, tobacco encased in the rolled leaf of the *sal* tree is offered and gratefully accepted.

ADDENDUM TO CHAPTER I

The following figures for the distribution of Santals have been taken from the Statistical Tables of the *Census Report of India*, 1931. Unfortunately, the figures for 1941 do not distinguish Santals from other primitive tribes, district by district.

Bihar and Orissa		*Bengal*	
Monghyr	26,742	Burdwan	101,522
Santal Parganas	754,804	Birbhum	64,079
Hazaribagh	129,103	Bankura	114,577
Manbhum	282,315	Midnapur	169,750
Orissa States	278,284	Rajshahi	25,591
Bhagalpur	30,799	Dinajpur	130,328
Purnea	46,995	Jalpaiguri	27,859
Balasore	15,444	Rangpur	7,410
Singhbhum	108,890	Malda	72,145
		Hooghly	38,013
		Murshidabad	22,725

(Districts from which only a few Santals were returned have been omitted above.)

In Assam, 101,949 persons were returned as Santali speakers.

The numerical and proportionate distribution of the population in the Bankura district was given as follows:

Total primitive tribes	139,063, 12% of the total
Hindus	920,456, 83% of the total

(Of the Hindus, 102,939 were Brahmin, while 353,675 were recorded as belonging to the Depressed Classes.)

The bulk of my data has been drawn from the Ranibandh and Raipur Thanas of the Bankura district. Unfortunately, I have been unable to obtain statistics of the distribution of the population in these two Thanas. The following statistics are of some interest:

	Sq. miles	*Houses*	*Population*	*Per sq. mile*
Ranibandh ..	166	8,952	47,823	288
Raipur	227	17,764	92,153	406

Ranibandh Thana has a much larger acreage of forest, and, although no figures were available, it is probable that almost 50 per cent. of the population are Santal, while in Raipur the number of Santals is unlikely to exceed 15,000.

CHAPTER 2

THE SANTAL AND HIS NEIGHBOURS

WHATEVER difficulty there may be for others, the Santals make a clear distinction between themselves and Hindus, whom they call *Deko*. The basis of distinction is race rather than religion. The prevailing Indian identification of race with religion has caused some confusion in their minds, but the fact that about 50 per cent. of Santals were returned in 1931 as Hindus and most of the remainder as followers of tribal religion indicated the heightened political consciousness of the enumerators more than any real division within the tribe. In many areas the returns depended entirely on the views of the enumerator and his reading of the issues at stake. The census gave rise to discussions in Santal villages, during the course of which one Santal said: "I am a Santal; I can become a Christian or a Moslem, but I cannot become a *Deko*." When speaking among themselves the Santals usually refer to Hindus as *Deko pusi*. *Pusi* in Santali means a cat, and the term is usually reserved for the higher Hindu castes. An old man explained it thus: "The *Deko* are very greedy and cunning, and that is why they are called *pusi*. Whenever a cat sees that someone else has milk, curds, fish or any bits of food, he roams around with his 'mew-mew', and as soon as he sees an opportunity he pounces on the food and finishes it off. The *Deko* go round like that, looking out for opportunities. They make friends with the Santals, give them beer and spirits to drink, and deceive them when they are drunk—for the Santals have no sense: they are like sheep. They will go wherever a *Deko* wishes them to go, for they do not have a good command of the *Deko* language." In this description many elements in the attitude adopted towards the *Deko* find expression. The Santal feels superior and gives free rein to his contempt; at the same time he has good reason to be afraid, and he accords a grudging admiration to the cleverness of the *Deko*. There is even a certain good-humoured acceptance of the situation in which the Santal finds himself, for cats are found in every Santal home, and they are valued for their uses, though not regarded with great affection.

Santals are not free from that common fallacy of mankind which looks upon one's own kind as superior to all others and the rest of the world as "queer". *Deko* smell different, and one particular caste smells more than others. Some day, they feel, the tables may be turned on those who lord it over them. In Bodding's collection of the Folk-Tales[1] there are two stories which turn on the fact that the bodies of high-caste strangers house the souls of animals, while the bodies of men of low caste house human and beautiful souls. (The means by which the real person can be discerned is to look at him through the wing feather of a vulture.) In common with other tribes of their group and many primitive peoples in other parts of the world, the Santals refer to themselves as "men" (*hoṛ*). A Santal once said in reply to a direct question as to whether any other race was superior to his: "No, there are no others who are greater than us. You can see that from the fact that even today our womenfolk will not eat rice that has been cooked by Brahmins. Formerly, when our menfolk ate Hindu rice they were made to sleep outside for one night; they could not sleep with their wives. When they brought rice from outside to the house they were made to eat it in the courtyard and clean up the place where they had eaten, and then wash their own eating utensils." Many Santals work as day labourers in the fields of well-to-do caste Hindus and receive payment in grain or sometimes in cooked food. The cooks in the homes of their employers are Brahmins, and so by refusing to acknowledge the supremacy of the Brahmin they hold themselves aloof from the Hindu social structure. Nevertheless, the complete aloofness of former days has been modified and is maintained only by the women. As one might expect, Santals share with others abhorrence of social customs which do not agree with their own standards of morality, and they exaggerate the iniquities practised by other peoples. The same person said: "When the *Deko* put out their lamps at night they have no sense of what is right and wrong. They respect no one, whether their younger brother's wife, elder brother's wife, their own sister or anyone else. Moreover, they do not respect any of their relations by marriage."

Many of the *Deko* make a living out of the Santal, as the cat finds its sustenance in his home. The analogy is by no means perfect, and its chief value for the Santal is that it ministers to his self-respect. In the Bankura district many of the landlords of the Santals are Sunḍis, who are themselves classified as an Exterior or Scheduled caste. Their hereditary occupation is the distilling and selling of spirits, and they are usually the lessees of the government liquor and drug shops. They owe their present

[1] P. O. Bodding, *Folk-Tales*, Vol. III, Nos. 74 and 77.

position of affluence to Santal habits of insobriety. Secondly, much of the land has been acquired by trading castes from Bihar who followed the Santals when the country was being opened up. They brought with them such things as salt and cooking oil, which they exchanged for grain. Clothing was added at a later date, for until within living memory Santals largely wove their own clothes from cotton grown on the lands surrounding their homesteads. Like the Suṇḍis, these traders provided credit facilities for their customers and so gained power over them. The monsoon fails on the average once in seven years in Western Bengal, and the traders import grain in times of scarcity. Formerly this was lent out at a recognized rate of interest amounting to 100 per cent. per annum. The only security which a Santal had to offer was a mortgage on his land, and, if the trader wished it, the almost inevitable result was an action in the courts, followed by an auction at which the creditor purchased the land. The third important class among the landlords are the Brahmins, descendants of the men who were brought into the country to act as priests and court officials to the local *rajas* or rulers. At the time when British rule was being established many of these *rajas* exercised control over tracts of country that were largely covered by forest and sparsely inhabited. They encouraged Santals and some other peoples to settle as cultivators, and they also rewarded the services of their Brahmin officials by grants of land. Brahmins are forbidden by caste rules to engage in cultivation, so they in their turn encouraged Santals to become their tenants.

The Santals have a proverb: "A *Deko* friend is like a thorn fence." In other words, if you stumble into it you are liable to suffer from scratches. They sometimes make fun of themselves and exaggerate the fear that they feel. Thus: "The elders used to run away and hide in the jungle whenever they saw an umbrella approaching the village." But in spite of the fun, the fear persists. A difficulty arose a few years ago in a village Santal church when the superintending missionary placed there as pastor a man who was a *Deko*. This resulted in a vigorous protest, and the leader of the villagers' delegation summed up their feelings in the following parable: "When a kite is wheeling overhead the chickens all take shelter under their mother's wings. After they have grown up they know that the kite can do them no harm, but nevertheless whenever a kite is overhead they quake inwardly and cannot get on with their pecking." In the company of non-Santals, a Santal is inclined to become tongue-tied. Even men who enjoy a wide reputation in their own tribe become ineffectual when engaging in a discussion with *Deko,* a factor which nullifies many of the advantages that they might otherwise gain by their representation on local self-governing bodies. The difficulty is not simply one of language, for those who reach such positions are men of some education who have a command of Bengali; it is caused by the old fear of the chicken for the bird of prey. Santals themselves complain that their own representatives are not "cunning" enough.

With certain of the lower castes who are cultivators like themselves the Santals claim a special relationship. Chief among these are the Kurmi or Mahato, who are looked upon as distant kinsfolk. "Formerly", said an informant, "they used to look on us as their younger brothers. At their weddings we used to carry away their baskets of sweets, and in fact without our presence their weddings could not take place. They sacrifice pigs at the time of the *Sohrae.* Our ancestors used to tell the story of how during the rule of the Moslems the Kurmi were oppressed. They had great trouble to survive. It is said that one day when we Santals were celebrating a *Mak' Mõṛẽ* festival, a band of Moslems was driving a group of Mahato before them. They came right into the place where we were sacrificing, but even so they did not lose caste. In this way they are co-sharers with the Santals." Here, however, is some Santal lore that is not altogether to the credit of the Mahato: "All the Mahato women have to learn witchcraft. If any of them does not do so, she cannot get married. For this reason when a Mahato party is seeking a bride the first question which they ask is, 'Has she learnt witchcraft or not?' "

There are other stories of related peoples, e.g. the Deswali, who are said to have resulted from the union of a local *raja* with a Santal girl, and there are a number of castes with whom they live in close contact. The most interesting of these is the Kamar caste, workers in iron. The Santals would appear to have been using iron implements both in agriculture and in hunting for a very long period, but they do not work in iron themselves. Until comparatively recently, iron smelting from ore gathered on the hillsides was common and the smelting was done by the Kamars. Modern industry has brought this to an end, but the sites of old furnaces can still be identified by the heaps of iron slag, which the Santals call "iron excrement". The Kamars, however, are still blacksmiths. Every moderate-sized village contains a family of Kamars who have been granted a piece of land from the village and who also receive payment in cash and in kind for their work. They are thoroughly familiar with Santali, but their mother tongue is the village Bengali of the area. They observe their own caste rules and do not intermarry with the Santals, with whom they live on excellent terms. They have no part in the Santal village cult, and they make no contributions when collections are made throughout the village for festivals. Their own cult is locally characterized by *Dharma* worship; in one village a post is planted in the ground at the end of the month of *Pus*. On the first day of *Magh* (mid-January) the village Kamar stands on top of this post with a white cock in his hands, and after bowing to the four corners of the compass in turn he releases the cock, saying: "Take, Dharma, we give it to you." There is then a scramble among the Santal spectators to catch it, and the man who does so is rewarded by the gift of a sheep. This ceremony goes on alongside the Santal festival which is taking place at the same time.

Occasionally there are in Santal villages isolated houses belonging to people of other castes. In one village one finds a Muci family, leather workers whose chief occupation is to make and mend drums; in another a Tanti family, who are weavers. The Santals do not have a great regard for the Bauri, the most numerous of the cultivating castes in the area apart from themselves. Their chief complaint about the Bauri is that the latter will eat food left over by anyone, a practice which fills the Santals with horror. On the other hand, there are frequently close friendships between individual Santals and men of other castes. The practice of sealing a friendship by a symbolic exchange of gifts is prevalent, and there are instances where Santals have entered into such friendships with Bauris and, indeed, with folk of other races who are of the same sex. The usual method of cementing such friendships is known as the "flower friendship", which takes the form of an exchange of garlands, followed by mutual salutations and sharing beer or food together. Friendships sealed in this way result in an intimate relationship, a real sharing of burdens as well as of joys.

While some forms of exploitation have been checked, there are still many who appear to thrive on the ignorance of the Santal. I witnessed a scene in the village street of Kuchliaghati when a *Deko* trader was having dealings with the women of the village. He had come to collect from them quantities of resin from the *babla* tree, a species of acacia, and he was paying them by exchanging equal weights of salt for the resin. The women had no notion of the market price of their resin and were quite content to be paid in this way. The same man had been dealing with that village for many years, and he must have made tremendous profits. Furthermore, on this particular occasion my companion, who was himself a sharp-witted *Deko*, soon realized that the scales were heavily tipped in the trader's favour. On this being pointed out, the latter decamped before his customers were aware of the reason for his haste. One finds also that it is, or has been until very recently, customary for the cultivator in Bengal to pay sums of money in excess of the legal rent to his landlord. The Santal is one of the worst sufferers from this practice, and he continues to pay more than he should for the sake of peace, even when he has been made aware of the fact.

Santals have not been caught up into the political activities of the last thirty years, for the Congress or nationalist movement is represented locally by those whom they regard as their worst enemies. They have shared some of the excitement engendered during periods of Mass Civil Disobedience, though their own contribution is liable to express itself in unorthodox forms. During the first such movement, in 1920–21, word spread that Gandhi rule had begun and it was Gandhi's order to boycott everything white-coloured. In some places Santals slaughtered large numbers of their poultry in consequence, and in one or two instances even goats and sheep were slain. Their political education has advanced since, and the disillusion which followed their "sacrifice" ensured that there would be no repetition of such tactics. The next great Disobedience movement, in 1930, made more impression largely because on that occasion the Congress programme stressed the boycott of the licensed liquor shops. The Santals welcomed this aspect of the programme, not from any zeal for temperance, but because they soon came to see from experience that the government staff available for enforcing the excise laws was hopelessly inadequate to its task. The practice of illicit distilling, which had previously been held in check by respect for the law, became widespread. Later the extension of the franchise under the Government of India Act of 1935 has shown them that their vote has power. Some of the more politically conscious, infected by the communal situation and influenced by the demand for a separate aboriginal province in Bihar, consider it a grievance that Santals are counted among the "Scheduled castes" on the electoral roll, and think they should be granted separate representation. In the elections to the Bengal Provincial Legislative Assembly which took place in 1946 a Santal offered himself for election for the first time from the Bankura Rural Scheduled caste constituency. He was a member of one of the rare well-to-do Santal families and had received education up to the Intermediate Arts standard of the Calcutta University at the mission college in Bankura. He stood as an "Independent" and he was supported by the Moslem League organization, but he failed to be elected. His rival was a non-Santal member of the Scheduled castes who was a Congress candidate. No Santal has yet been elected to the Bengal Provincial Assembly.

The fact that the dominant Santal attitude to their neighbours is one of suspicion and latent hostility does not mean that this has always been the case. There are some indications pointing to a time when relations between Santals and Hindus were more friendly than they are today. The story already related about the Mahato is one. It may well have been that during the period of Moslem suzerainty the aboriginals made common cause with the Hindus. To go back much farther, P. O. Bodding[1] has suggested that in the story of the *Ramayana*, one of the great Hindu epics, there is a hint of an alliance between aboriginals and the hero of the epic, Ram, when he made war against the King of Lanka. The reference is to the assistance given by the "Hanuman log", or monkeys, who, it has been inferred, may well have been in fact human beings of the stock from which the ancestors of the present-day Santals were drawn. In Santal folklore there are stories which describe the marriage of human beings with monkeys, and there is little doubt that such stories symbolize the results of interracial marriages.

Living as they do in close contact with their neighbours, the Santals have borrowed heavily from the ideas and institutions around them, and in some cases they have doubtless contributed to the common stock. It is almost impossible to isolate certain features in their culture and say that these have been borrowed from non-Santal sources. That which is distinctive in Santal culture is the way in which they have used a common background to conserve their tribal life and to provide themselves with the rudiments of a philosophy. The retention of their language as a vigorous element of their own culture must have preserved much from the ancient days of their own life, and has to some extent cut them off from familiarity with the epics

[1] *District Gazetteers: Santal Parganas.*

and legends of Hinduism. The linguistic evidence shows how their material culture has been vitally affected and has some bearing on the more elusive realm of thought and belief. The grammatical structure of Santali has little in common with that of the Indo-Aryan tongues. It is an agglutinative and not an inflectional language. There have, however, been large and extensive borrowings of words. An instructive example can be taken from their method of husking rice. The term *ḍhinki*, used for a foot-pedal rice husker, has been borrowed from Bengali, and a *ḍhinki* is found in almost every home. The rice that is husked at the time of making sacrifices must be prepared in the home of the village priest, and in its preparation the use of the older and more primitive *ukhuṛ* is obligatory. This is a wooden mortar in which the rice is husked by hand with a wooden pestle, or *tok*. Both these words are Austro-Asiatic in origin. It is likely that when the household adopted the new method of husking rice the tribe did not change over from the old method of husking the sacred rice for fear of a loss in efficacy. One reason given is that as the *ḍhinki* is operated by the foot, rice husked in the *ḍhinki* is unclean and so unfit for offering to the spirits. It may be that the association of a mortar and pestle with sexual symbolism enhanced its magical value. The symbolism in this case is familiar to the Santal mien, for one way of expressing differences of sex is to refer to boys as "pestles" and to girls as "mortars". The *ukhuṛ* has to be used by the medicine man in preparing remedies; it is also used at marriages, when the feet of the bridegroom's party are washed over an *ukhuṛ*, and an *ukhuṛ* filled with water is required during the death ceremonies. In Bengal the rice which forms the daily food of the people is boiled before husking, and the Santals follow the same method in preparing it; but the rice used in sacrifices, *adwa caole*, is never so treated, being dried in the sun.

Among their domestic animals, the fowl, the dog and the goat have non-Bengali names, while the names for pigeons, sheep, pigs and, most important of all, their cattle are borrowed. Fowls, goats and pigs are all used in their sacrifices. In the realm of wild life the Santal has found little need to borrow a vocabulary from his neighbours. Wild animals, birds, trees and shrubs, many fish and insects, also snakes, have Santali names. The same is true of most of the weapons used in hunting. Although the term for paddy is Santal, the names of all the implements now used in rice cultivation and the terms for the different kinds of rice fields are Bengali. Maize, a cereal that is important in their economy, has a borrowed name, but other lesser cereals retain their Santali names. In Bankura the Santals have lost the use of their own numerals beyond seven, though apparently these are known and commonly used elsewhere. Even so, in Bankura the Santal word for "twelve" is still used in phrases connected with the recital of tribal traditions, as in the phrase *gelbar paris*, meaning the "twelve clans". Iron has a Santali name, but other metals now in use, such as lead, copper and brass, have Bengali names. In addition to brass and earthenware utensils, the Santals make extensive use of the leaves of the *sal* tree (Santali *sarjom*), which they plait to form many varieties of plates, cups, pipes and cigarettes, and they possess a wide vocabulary to distinguish between the different kinds. Brass and earthen pots they buy from others.[1]

The difficulties of determining the extent of their borrowings in the field of religion may be illustrated by the fact that the language of spells and of prayers offered at the time of sacrificing contains a strong admixture of Hindi-Bengali words. This would seem to indicate that there have been many borrowings at this point; but it is also possible that the one who makes the prayers, wishing to put himself into a favourable relation with the spirits, uses a special vocabulary and so removes himself from the common run of his people when he is acting as a mediator between them and the spirit world. Many of the songs sung nowadays are composed in Bengali. There is a large stock of riddles, some of which are asked and answered in Santali, others of which are asked and answered in Bengali, while yet others make use of both languages.[2]

Only incidental reference has been made to the impact of Moslem culture on Santal life. Reminiscences occur of the period of Moslem rule, such as the following statement: "Concerning the *Turuk* (*Turuk*, or Turk, the name by which Santals refer to Moslems), it is said that they ruin our spirits because they cut the throats of fowls the wrong way. If we eat

[1] Another discussion of the linguistic evidence, giving many examples, and the whole stated from a somewhat different point of view, is to be found in Professor Sten Konow's introduction to Bodding's collection of Folk-Tales.

[2] In a suggestive article published in *Africa* for June 1946, Professor F. C. Bartlett has expanded his thesis in the Julian Huxley lecture of 1944 that each primitive culture displays both "hard" and "soft" points. The methods which he has outlined for determining, in the examination of any particular culture, what constitute the hard and soft points, and in particular the story method, may furnish valuable results when applied to the study of Santal culture.

the food of the *Turuk*, rice or other food, the spirits will run away. If anyone has fever or if we want to exorcize a spirit, we try to give him curds made by a *Turuk* to eat. They say that in olden times one Mirza Turuk drove us from the country we were in. On a certain plain we made ready twelve carts and fled away across the open country. Mirza Turuk searched and could not find us. He thought: 'I must search for the tracks of twelve carts.' However, as we drove the twelve carts one behind the other, we made only one track, and so he never found us." The local Moslem population is very small[1] and confined to one or two villages of weavers and cultivators, who are themselves deeply affected by the Hindu environment. No doubt the story is very different in those districts of Northern Bengal where the Moslems predominate, but even there the great dissimilarity between Moslem and Santal culture probably militates against influences passing from the one to the other.

Christian influence, the result of a sustained and conscious effort on the part of missions, is considered later. Of deliberate efforts to Hinduize the religious practices and beliefs of the Santals the area is ignorant.

NOTE TO CHAPTER 2

The relation of the aboriginal peoples to Hindu society has given rise to much controversy and discussion in India, not all of which is conducted in a spirit of scientific inquiry. An able presentation of many of the facts dealt with in this and the previous chapter, together with much else, and written from the Hindu standpoint, can be found in *The Aborigines—"So-called"—and Their Future*, by G. S. Ghurye, Ph.D. (Cantab.), published by the Gokhale Institute of Politics and Economics, 1943.

[1] The figures given for the local Moslem population in 1931 were as follows:

	Males	*Females*
Ranibandh Thana	238	190
Raipore Thana	358	278

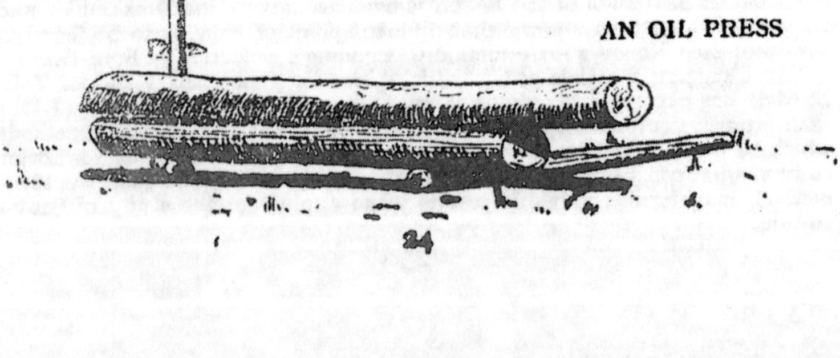

AN OIL PRESS

CHAPTER 3

THE RHYTHM OF DAILY LIFE

THE rhythm of daily life in an agricultural community grows out of the close relationship between the activities of man and the cycle of nature. Work and recreation depend upon the seasons and their contrasts of heat and cold, of dry and wet weather, of springtime and harvest. The Santals distinguish three seasons during the year, each possessing a characteristic climate. The "cold days" last from November to March. The rice harvest is gathered during the earlier part of this season; food is therefore plentiful and people relax. The skies for the most part remain clear, and the absence of movement in the air causes a blue haze to hang over the villages in the evenings, formed by the wood smoke of the cooking fires. The nights are cold; morning and evening the folk crouch over small fires in the open to warm themselves. Sometimes, when the wind blows off the distant Himalayas, the days are also cold. The new year begins at this time. Then come the "heat days", when the west wind scorches the skin during the midday hours and often the nights too are unbearably hot. From time to time a storm blows up from the north-west in the late afternoon, stirring the dust and then laying it and cooling the earth with welcome raindrops, while loud claps of thunder are heard and vivid flashes of lightning chase across the sky. During these days the forest trees shed their leaves and take on a garment of new green, flowering trees make gay patterns against the deep blue of the sky, while both men and women spend much time in the forests, the former hunting and fishing, the women gathering fruits, leaves and roots. Springs, streams and wells dry up, and many women have to go long distances to obtain water for domestic needs. Then come the "heavy-rain days", which last from the end of June till October, the time of the south-west monsoon on which so much depends. Eagerly the Santals watch the signs of the sky, working for long hours until all the rice seedlings have been planted out; then rain and sun are left to bring the increase, while men watch and tend the fields.

The year is also divided into two parts, one of which, the season from June until the new harvest has been reaped, is known as "hunger-time". This name is an eloquent reminder of the danger of starvation; even in normal years the Santal's holding of land is insufficient to support his family. The years pass, indistinguishable one from another except when famine or other calamity makes a landmark on which the memory will fasten in the years to come. Ten years ago many of the older men dated their birth according to whether they were born before or after "Seventy-two", the Bengali year 1272, when a disastrous famine broke up many families. Another memorable year was the year of the influenza epidemic that followed the close of the 1914–18 war, and young people today can calculate their age in relation to the year of the *maloṭ*, or epidemic. The division of the year into months is somewhat vague, for whereas the only names for the months now current are the twelve months of the Bengali calendar, the Santal reckoning is based on the moon. As one man remarked: "We sometimes have to slip a month." In 1939, when this statement was made, there was confusion in the Santal calendar between *Bhador* (the Bengali month extending through a part of August and September) and *San*, the month that precedes it. Names are given to the phases of the moon according to its shape. Thus I was told: "The *Ende* (the Ind festival which in West Bengal is associated with Dharma worship) is observed during the month of *Bhador*, when the moon is shaped like an open umbrella."

The days of the week also have Bengali names, and the day is divided into periods, the names of which relate in some cases to the meals taken, in other cases to the duties which have to be performed or to a more general association of the time. When Santals wish to make an appointment at a particular time it is sufficient to point to the position in the sky where the sun will have climbed. Some time before dawn it is "little cockcrow", and this is followed by "cockcrow". *Bạsiạm*, the time when breakfast is taken, is divided into three parts: "child *bạsiạm*", "*bạsiạm*" and "bent *bạsiạm*". The word *bạsiạm*, meaning "leftover", is a reminder that the breakfast consists of a small quantity of cold rice or rice gruel, cooked with the evening meal on the previous day and kept for the morning, when it is eaten with a little salt. The late afternoon is called the "time when women draw water". One way of describing a short period is to relate it to the time taken in boiling a pot of rice. Work is continued until the shadow of a house or a tree falls across a particular spot. It happens frequently that children draw a line outside their schoolhouse, so that when the shadow of the building falls across the line they know it is time to go home. A man who was in the habit of sleeping in his courtyard after the midday meal used to make sure of rising at the right time by telling his children to waken him when the shadows had reached a certain spot.

During the night the time is indicated not only by the position of the moon but also by the stars, and particularly by reference to the constellation Pleiades. There are at least two myths relating to the sun and the moon. In the one the sun is male and the moon female, while the stars are their children. The absence of the stars from the sky in daytime is explained by a story that they made a pact to eat their children. The sun carried out the bargain and so there are no stars visible by daylight, but the moon evaded her promise and so some of the children survived. The other version says that both the sun and the moon are male; they became related to each other by marrying each other's sisters. Only a few of the stars and constellations are named. The Pleiades have the same name as one of the clans; the Milky Way is known as the "cow track", and the Great Bear is the "old woman's bed".

Between the harvest and the Spring festival, a period which corresponds with the cold weather, the villages present a deserted appearance, due to the annual migration to the east for work in the harvest fields of the Ganges delta. This seasonal migration, dictated by economic necessity, plays an important part in the life of the area. Farther to the north many Santals work in the coal-mines round Asansol, while to the south labour is drawn to the great steel town of Tatanagar. In this area migration to industrial centres is rare; the Santals regard the conditions in industrial towns as highly dangerous to health, and they affirm that nothing will induce them to go there. The same reason, however, does not prevent them from leaving their own villages in a non-malarious tract of country for the malarious rice-growing areas farther east, in consequence of which the money earned is often more than spent in the expenses of protracted illness and long periods of idleness. Each village organizes its own party of migrants, who go to work for the same masters year after year. The wages they receive are more than double what is paid in their own locality, and so they earn the money required to pay rent, to meet social expenditure for marriages, and to pay off old debts. The homes are left in charge of the aged, and some of the children are left behind. The villages are denuded of able-bodied men and women, apart from a few who do not need to go. Family parties travel together, babies and very young children being carried by their parents. It is no uncommon sight to see a man striding along the road with a carrying pole across his shoulders; in the basket slung from one end he carries some of the family cooking utensils, while the youngest member of the family sits confidently in a basket at the other end. The immediate economic advantage of this annual migration, without which they might be forced to leave their present homes with dire consequences for their tribal stability, is secured at a heavy price. In addition to the toll on their health, tribal sanctions are loosened away from the village. Offenders against the tribal law, runaway brides, women accused of witchcraft, and many others who do not wish to submit to discipline can find a refuge away from their homes, and each year the number of those who elect to stay "east" is growing.

The older generation regard the yearly exodus as the prime cause of moral laxity because it flouts an old taboo. Formerly no Santal was supposed to cross the Damodar river, which forms the northern and eastern boundary of the Bankura district. When at first men were drawn away to work over the river the women were not allowed to accompany them. The reason given for this prohibition was that by crossing the river they would bring misfortune on themselves and their villages. The underlying causes may be connected in part with the fact that the tribal gods are forest gods and could not protect them on the other side of the river, where there are no forests; and partly linked with the fact that the Damodar has an important place in their customs for disposing of the dead.[1] Whatever they be, the old taboo is now ignored.

During the last few days of *Pus* (mid-January) and at each month's end till the Spring festival, parties of men, women and children can be seen returning along the roads in single file, the women always in front. They are bent on reaching their own villages before the festivities which mark the turn of the month. The old people watch for their return and the relieving of their responsibilities. They enjoy greater leisure and may be seen more often squatting on the narrow ledges that surround the houses, sunning themselves. As men and women return from the east they find employment chiefly in felling trees and in carting both wood and leaves to the railway. For many years the traditional attitude of the Santal to the forest has been to make clearings and begin cultivation. The forests of the area are privately owned by the landlords, and they are exploited

[1] See Chapter 12, p. 155.

for their timber. The *sarjom*, which predominates, is a valuable tree, but locally it has not been permitted to grow to any height. The trees are cut once in seven years and the timber is exported chiefly to supply firewood in the towns, while the leaf is used for the leaf plates required in city homes and food shops. This activity provides the main subsidiary occupation and is in full swing whenever work in the fields slackens, though it is not sufficient to keep the Santals at home throughout the year. Women share in the occupation; they help the men by stacking the timber as it is cut into lengths, and they collect the leaves which older women sew together while sitting at home. Other women, in the time they can spare from duties at home, collect the twigs and dry branches which they need for domestic fuel. Boys from about the age of seven are engaged in their occupation of tending the village herd of goats and cattle, for which they receive wages from the owners of one anna per month for each goat and two annas per month for each head of cattle in their charge. They are sometimes joined by the younger girls, but after the girls are nine or ten they stay with their mothers, look after the house or help to nurse the younger children.

Women play little or no part in the organization of social or religious life, but they are supreme in household affairs. Although men lay claim to superior intelligence and women openly disclaim any knowledge or interest in affairs outside the home circle, the attitude of the two groups towards each other is one of good-natured tolerance. In Barikul, at the close of a festival when there had been much drinking, the men were feeling unwell. Babulal reports: "Some of the men are saying: 'Yesterday I had nothing to eat, so give me something today.' To which the women reply: 'We have eaten all the food; you men are drunk!' And so they drank more beer and spirits, and became even more drunken than they had been the day before." In his diary entry for the next day he records: "Today all the drunks have begun to beg for some stale rice gruel. The women scolded them: 'You have earned a lot of food, haven't you? Why should you not go out to beg?' " After this chaffing the women relented and gave the men some food before they set out once more to their work. The Santal wife attends fairs and markets; she buys her own clothes and attends to the household shopping. The contrast between them and their non-Santal neighbours is heightened by the fact that they do not cover their heads. One end of the *saṛi* is thrown loosely across the breasts and over the left shoulder.

As the days lengthen and become warmer, other activities find their place in the routine. When the first rain has fallen the men begin to dig up the pits of rotted cow manure beside their homes, carry loads of manure to the fields, and first plough the beds where the seed rice will be sown. At the same period they carry out repairs to their houses, and the walls of new houses begin to rise. Some walls are built by constructing a screen of thin sticks on which a mud plaster is fastened, but most of the walls are built by adding a layer of wet clay to the layers which have previously dried in the sun. Timber for rafters and posts is brought from the forest, and is not always paid for. Bamboos are cut and sliced; they are needed as a foundation for the thatch. Home-made rope is prepared. Rice straw is the material commonly used for roofing.

At this time some men devote their energies to trapping and snaring. A party of men may be formed for digging out a colony of field rats which will supplement the diet. Many varieties of bird traps and snares are in use. Some have insects attached to them as bait, with birdlime to snare the birds. Others are set on the ground to catch partridge with ingenious arrangements of slip-knots and a captive bird in the centre to act as a decoy. Some of the operations call for elaborate preparation. Nets are taken down from under the rafters where they have hung since the previous year. The men seek out pools of water which may be still left in some shady hollow of the forest when most of the water has dried, for there the birds will come to drink. Traps are formed by nets, or by baskets attached by a string to where one of the men sits waiting to pull it and entrap the bird. On an April day in Barikul two parties of men set out on trapping expeditions. One of them went to a distant forest and returned with three peacocks. The other party spent the day near the banks of a nearby stream and gathered three-score birds, including doves, grey partridges, Indian drongos weaver birds and crow pheasants, all of which are eaten by the Santals.

At the same season the women find new employment. One of the commonest of the trees growing in the villages, the fields and the forests is the *matkom* (*Bassia latifolia*, Roxb.); it has thick sepalled succulent flowers during the spring. These flowers fall from the trees during the early hours of the morning, and the women and girls rise early to collect them. They are used in a variety of ways. When dried they provide either a nutritious cattle food or a supplement for human diet. They are used in preparing the cakes which the men take with them at the time of the hunt. The flowers have a high sugar content, and their most common use is in the distillation of spirits, the *paura* or brandy of the Santals. The work of distilling is carried on by one or two families in the village, and they sell not only to their fellow villagers, but they operate illegal liquor shops on market days. *Matkom* beer, a drink which is only slightly fermented, as it is prepared within twenty-four hours, is refreshing, but it is used chiefly for the purpose of counteracting the after-effects of a drinking bout.

The women prepare the rice beer which is brewed in all the homes. First they collect the roots that are used as fermenting agents from the forest. In this, as in most of their gathering activities, the women of the village work together. There is a certain ceremonial attached to the gathering of these roots. Parties sometimes consist of women from more than one village, and so a day for the expedition has to be fixed. The procedure suggests that this is regarded as the women's counterpart to the hunt. Before the wood is entered one of the older women invokes *Gõsãẽ* ("Lord", a general term used in addressing the spirits) and requests that they be led quickly to the places where they will find the desired plants. The first woman to light upon one falls on the ground, pretending to be drunk. These roots are known by the general name of *ranu ran*, "medicine of medicines". It takes three days for the beer to mature or "cook". It cannot be stored, so it is brewed fresh for festival occasions and also in the majority of houses as often as the family can afford. *Handi*, or rice beer, occupies an important place in the ritual as well as in the social life of the tribe. It is essential for all libations to the spirits. A myth relates how the secret of brewing beer was imparted to the first human beings by the chief spirit of the Santals himself. It is therefore the indispensable Santal drink. It is extremely difficult for a Santal to understand not only how a person can live without beer, but why he should try to do so. The case of Pitam, who lived near Benachapra, illustrates this. He was a man of great influence because of his powers as a witch-finder. He had, however, abandoned some of his tribal ways, and, influenced by Vaishnava Hinduism, he had given up meat eating and the drinking of intoxicants. During the annual tribal council some of his enemies charged him with undermining Santal society, and one of the counts against him was that by abstaining from beer he was doing harm to the spirits.

It would be a mistake to suggest that the attitude of the Santal towards intoxicants is one of simple approval. There are two standards at work. There is, on the one hand, the almost universal acceptance of the habit, reinforced by its sanction in mythology, the social function that it does fulfil and the fact that it is a form of food. There is also, on the other hand, a recognition somewhat grudgingly given to the undesirable consequences of the habit. It leads to a loss of working days, to quarrels and offences against the moral code. Most informants agree that the drinking habit has increased in recent years. Such a statement must be regarded with the suspicion appropriate to all attempts to glorify the good old days. It does, however, imply the existence of a critical attitude. The earliest records, which indicate conditions a hundred years ago, all mention the drinking habits of the Santal as phenomenal. It is probable that the drinking of spirits in preference to beer has grown during the time when the Santals have been drawn more completely into a money economy, and it is certain that the Congress boycott in 1930 gave more than a temporary impetus to illicit distilling. Nevertheless, there is further evidence of moral judgments being applied to drinking. The habitual drunkard is a figure of fun and regarded with contempt. The drinking of rice beer does not lead to much intoxication except during festivals. A woman who drinks to excess is considered to be loose in other respects as well. People frequently complain that whereas formerly only the old men and women used to drink, now everyone does so. It would be easy, however, to overdo the picture of a Santal conscience in these matters, for they are a pleasure-loving people and drink is associated with their pleasures. The common attitude was well expressed by an old woman who had been asked to sing when she replied: "I cannot sing without beer."

The annual hunt takes place during the hot season. This institution is still vigorous wherever there are Santals living within reach of a forest. Hunting is regarded as the characteristic activity of the male. When the date of a hunt has to be fixed, the responsibility for the arrangements and for making it known through the area rests with the *parganath*. The date may be fixed in different ways; each *pargana* follows its own tradition. In three adjoining localities the following three traditions are observed. In one the hunt is held always on the seventh day of the month of *Baisakh* (April-May). In the second it is held on the day of the full moon in the same month. The date of the third is arranged while the first hunt is in progress, and it is announced by means of a *gira*. This is a method of reckoning dates or announcing future events. It may be used in connection with a hunt, but it is also used to announce a forthcoming marriage or a burial feast. It consists of a length of string in which a number of knots are tied, each knot representing one day. A number of *gira* are distributed to the surrounding villages during the weekly market, and they are kept by the headmen, who untie one of the knots each evening until one knot remains, when they know that the hunt takes place on the morrow.

Although the ritual meaning of the hunt has been obscured in the minds of the Santals, it is implicit in much that accompanies it. A hunt is the activity of the whole adult male population of the area. Women are not permitted to take part, but certain taboos must be observed by them while the men are away from home, to avert the lurking dangers of the forest. The prohibitions are similar to those enjoined on mourners and widows. No woman may wear flowers in her hair nor use the vermilion paint in the parting of her hair which is a sign of her married status. She should also leave off wearing the iron bangle which is another symbol of her marriage, and she must not bathe. At the present day, although the first two prohibitions are observed, there is some slackness about the others. But the main responsibility for placating the possibly malevolent influences residing in the forest rests with the *dihri*, or hunt priest. This is a special office, and the name is evidently the same as the Khond *dehuri* and the Ho *dihiri*, or priest. Among the Santals the *dihri* is a priest only at the time of the hunt, and he is appointed for the *pargana*. On the morning of the day when the hunt opens he performs the sacrifice of a brown hen on the edge of the forest which will be entered, and the tribal spirits are invoked to protect the men from wild beasts. He is encouraged by the spectators, who remind him that if any of them comes to harm they will hold him responsible. At times a certain amount of mimic hunting takes place in connection with the sacrifice, during which the *dihri* plays the part of the hunted animal.

The hunt lasts through the greater part of the day. The forest is surrounded by parties from different villages and the game gradually driven towards the centre. Within living memory the stock of game in most parts of the area has declined, and some of the hunts are now poorly attended for that reason. Gradual deforestation and the absence of any effective protection for wild animals account for the present scarcity. Leopards, once present in great numbers, are now rare, though black bears are still relatively common. Some of the smaller kinds of Indian deer are found. It is many years since a tiger was killed in the Bankura district. Wild pigs are abundant, and so is the jungle hare, and there are many species of bird whose flesh is prized by the Santal. Every male of the tribe is an expert with the bow and arrow, and he is trained in its use from early childhood. The village parties hold together; they carry their own rations of rice and dried *matkom* cake for the night meal, and they are accompanied by their sleek and well-fed dogs. The men are dressed in loin-cloths, but they wear turbans roughly wrapped round their heads for protection against the heat of the sun. Some of the younger boys carry drums instead of weapons. The drums are used to swell the noise in the forest as the animals are driven closer towards the centre and to signal a kill, but they are also needed for the dancing that will follow. The flesh of the animals is distributed according to a regular code, though the rules are passing from use and now it is usual for the stronger of two parties to take the flesh of a kill when it is in dispute. The man who draws first blood receives the *madol*, consisting of one hind-leg, a part of which he must give to the headman of his village. If the man who first touches the animal belongs to a different village, he receives a shoulder; if it has been slain by yet another person than the one who drew first blood, the slayer receives five ribs, one fore-leg and the liver. The *dihri* receives the neck, and the remainder of the flesh goes to the co-villagers of the man who wounded the animal and not of the man who killed it. When the meat is distributed among the villagers, those who carry drums receive a double portion, and some of the meat is given to the dogs.

By evening several hundred men gather in the place where they are to spend the night. Camp fires are lit near some water-course, and the moon rises slowly over the graceful palms that fringe the water and the belt of *sarjom* trees beyond. For some it is a night of hard work, for others it is a night of revelry. The elders from all the villages are gathered together for this one night during the year and form the supreme council of the tribe. The disputes which have baffled their several efforts in the course of the year are brought forward. Complaints involving members of more than one village are voiced and range over a wide field, involving inheritance, marriages and instances of indiscipline. Members are allowed to appeal against decisions made in village councils. Punishments inflicted range from outcasting to fines, and crude punishments are sometimes exacted on the spot, as in a case of a youth who had transgressed the rules of behaviour towards a woman relative with whom he was not in a joking relationship. He was compelled to drag his nose along a line of urine provided by the village headman whose authority had been flouted. The hearing of cases continues till the small hours of the morning and the discussions appear interminable, with accusation and counter-accusation, the calling of witnesses and references to tribal law and custom. It is, however, one of the great educating and cementing institutions in the life of the tribe. It is known to them by the name of "high court", a name that has been naturalized in most Indian languages. It is also called the *sendra duṛup'*, the hunt sitting, and the *lo bir duṛup'*, the burnt forest sitting, the latter name being due to the fact that the hunt takes place when the undergrowth in the forest has been burnt to help the fertilizing of the soil.

Meanwhile, when the evening meal is over the young men gather in another part of the clearing and spend the night in revelry. There is much strong liquor in evidence. In some cases the place of meeting has become the site of a government liquor shop. The dances, of a class known as *doṅgeṛ*, are men's dances, and the songs, known as *bir*, or forest songs, are men's songs. They are frankly coarse and deal largely with the physical aspects of love, courtship and lust. Many of the songs that are sung on this night are never sung by the Santals in any mixed company, or, indeed, at any other time, a fact that indicates among them a standard of delicacy in sexual behaviour which certain modern schools of thought appear at times to deny to primitive people.

Towards morning some of the folk, young and old, rest for an hour or two of much-needed sleep, but when the sun has risen they take some breakfast and begin to disperse. They make their way to their own villages, hunting as they go; but on this second day the proceedings are apt to be unexciting. for they do not find much to kill. By late afternoon the men are home again with their spoils, and when these have been divided they work off their fatigue in sleep.

The supposed monotony of the struggle for a livelihood is broken by so many devices of nature and of man that it is doubtful whether the concept of monotony has any place in a Santal's mind. His love of a *porob*, or festival, is a byword in the tribe, and it is fostered by many occasions in the Santal calendar as well as by opportunities for "seeing", as they say, Hindu festivals. Some of these gatherings bring together the Santals from great distances. One of the most remarkable in the area takes place on the outskirts of Sarenga at the time of the Lakshmi Puja, at the full moon of the Bengali month of *Karttik* (October-November). This is a Hindu festival, and it is kept with due pomp and ceremony by the family of the local landlord, who is of a mercantile caste. This family built up the celebration by inviting their Santal tenants to come and dance on a field on the village boundary. For many years it has been of more than local significance. Villagers from ten to fifteen miles away turn up in force, and some come from much greater distances. Until the year 1930 they used to dance and sing throughout the night, and on one occasion a missionary counted over five hundred large drums. In the following year a small but determined group of Santal reformers, one of whose aims was to stop their womenfolk from dancing in public, practically brought the gathering to a standstill, but it was revived in 1932 in the modified form in which it continues. At about noon the air begins to resound to the beating of the drums as parties of villagers make their way along the roads and jungle tracks and approach the scene of the gathering. From the four corners of the compass they converge on the open field, men and women in festive attire, the women especially resplendent in new *saris* with gaily designed borders, their hair bedecked with flowers and their arms heavy with ornaments. The drumming intensifies as new parties arrive and more and more lines of dancers are formed. Finally the crescendo of sound from the drums batters on the ear-drums of the bystanders, and even at a distance of four miles it conveys an impression of continuous thunder in the sky. Then the clamour dies away as gradually as it began, and by nine o'clock the field is quiet once again. Since the night dancing was stopped the numbers have diminished slightly. Most of the parties return to their own villages and continue the dance there.

The weeks are enlivened by visits to the local markets. One of the entries in Babulal's record relates to a market day during the early hot weather: "Today was market day. From a very early hour everyone was preparing to go to market. It is very hot at the present time, and if we do not go early the sand on the pathways becomes unbearably hot for our feet. Pigs were killed at dawn, cut, and the meat was roasted first thing so that it would be ready when the people returned home. The day turned out to be very warm. Some men went into the village of G—— because of their thirst to get a drink of beer, and they said: 'One pice worth of beer from G—— is as good as six pice of beer from that other place.' " The market is the main shopping centre for the villagers. There are cloth stalls and stalls of imported trinkets and ornaments. Potters, weavers, blacksmiths, purveyors of "medicines" and many others display their wares. The Santals may have grain for sale in a good year; they sell fowls and vegetables and buy their salt and cooking oil regularly, with other commodities at need. The market is a great place for the exchange of gossip, for meeting friends and relatives; it is here that many flirtations begin and matches are set in hand.

Nevertheless, the main business of the Santals' life, round which most of their activities centre, is to wrest from the poor soil the greatest possible amount of food. The struggle leaves little time for philosophizing, but they do sometimes crystallize in a phrase some bitter lesson from experience, as when they say: "Rain in the morning, like a friendship that is easily made, does not last." They work as hard as their social obligations allow. There is nothing distinctive in their methods of agriculture, and for generations they have been accustomed to settled cultivation and the use of the plough. The division of labour between men and women, the taboo against women handling the plough, they share with the surrounding culture. They observe the same propitious days and seasons for sowing and reaping as their neighbours. A great authority on the Santals has said:[1] "They are on their way to becoming agriculturalists, but are, as yet, far behind. . . . They have not as yet learnt the need for and the benefits of weeding and manuring, or of changing the crops, and much more. For example, they do not take proper care of their cattle. These are mostly herded by children, who use much of the time for their own games and pleasures. When the paddy is harvested, the cattle are permitted to roam about. A direct result of this is that it is impossible for people to have any crops standing after the middle of December or thereabouts; the cattle would

[1] P. O. Bodding, *Studies in Santal Medicine and Connected Folklore*, Pt. III. "How the Santals live", *Memoirs of the Royal Asiatic Society of Bengal*, Calcutta, 1940, Vol. X, No. 3, p. 434.

eat all; and the Santals only very rarely fence anything in." The same statement could be applied to the backwardness of Indian peasant agriculture in general, and although it presents a recognizable picture it is somewhat unfair. It fails to take account of the formidable difficulties in the way of the Santals over which they have no control, and it ignores the fact that there is among them a fund of inherited practical wisdom and acquired skill of no mean order.

CHAPTER 4

DANCING, MUSIC AND POETRY

THE word *ṛaskạ*, meaning "pleasure", is often on the lips of the Santals, and it is dear to their hearts. They turn from their difficulties and sorrows to find solace in one or other of the many ways in which they can experience *ṛaskạ*. Among these dancing is one of the most important. Their word for dancing is the same as that used for the play of children—*enec'*—and dancing is indeed the play of the tribe. In every village there is a dancing floor, an open space that is well cared for. At festival times it is swept and freshly plastered with cowdung by young unmarried girls, and when it is not in use for dancing it is the place where the young men gather in the evenings to discuss their affairs and interests.

Some of the dances are connected with particular festivals, and they are performed only at those times or during the whole of the month in which the festival takes place. There are other dances that are suitable at any time during the year. Some are dances for women alone and others for men alone, while in a few both men and women dance. The chief element of variety is introduced by means of varying the rhythm; to the casual observer most of the dances look the same. A group of men or of women dance together, forming a line with their arms linked, stepping sideways or forward and then backward, keeping time to the beating accompaniment of the drums, moving either in a circle or from one side of the dancing-floor to the other, and from time to time breaking out into song. Whenever there is an occasion for rejoicing there will be dancing. It is much in evidence during the celebrations and ceremonies after the birth of a child or at his fuller reception into the tribe, and again during marriage festivities. The general type of dance on all these occasions is known as *doṅ*, which has within it many variations. At these times it is the women who do the dancing, while the men furnish an accompaniment with drums and flutes, and many of the songs refer directly to the purpose for which the folk have gathered together. During marriage ceremonies the *bapla*, or type of dance specifically associated with marriages, is also in evidence. The *doṅgeṛ* is the dance of the men on the night of the annual hunt. It is a wild type of dance, when there is much leaping in the air. Two of the young men stripped of clothing dance about in front of the lines, and the

SARPA

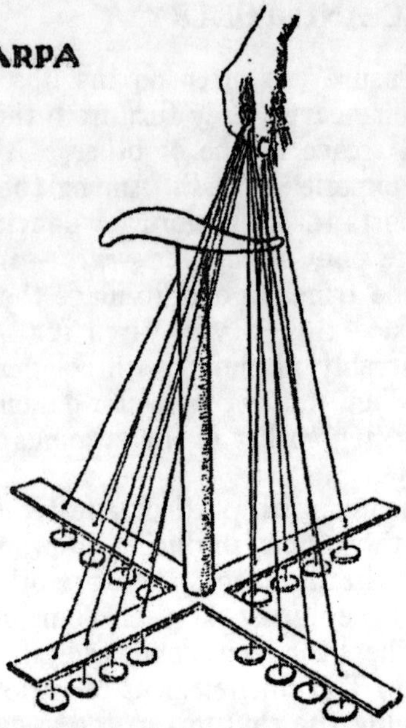

dances are preceded and ended by the shouting of obscene words. The Spring and the Harvest festivals possess their own cycle of songs and dances. During the latter the women make use of a musical instrument known as the *sarpa*, which is brought out only at this time. It is a percussion instrument that consists of a vertical pole about fifteen inches high fixed into two crossed horizontal pieces of wood. Holes are bored in the foot-long horizontal pieces, and through these holes pass lengths of string to the end of which are attached small circular wooden clappers. With the handle at the top of the vertical pole in the left hand and the upper end of the strings held in the right hand, the clappers can be drawn up sharply against the wooden bars, so producing a ringing sound. The workmanship of the *sarpas* varies; some are plain, while others display a handle carved in the shape of a dove and geometrical designs on the horizontal bars. The dancers form two lines; the older women form a line in front and sing and dance with their arms linked. Behind them comes a line of younger women, some of them beating the *sarpas*, some with small brass cymbals, while the two women at the ends of the line wave the end of their *saris* to fan the others.

The *buañ*[1] is a musical instrument associated particularly with the month that precedes that in which the Harvest festival is celebrated. This is the month known as *Dāsāẽ*, from the Hindi word *dasserah*. The *buañ* belongs to a type of musical instrument with a wide distribution in different parts of the world. Its prototype existed when men first plucked the strings of their bows in order to hear a pleasing sound. To the arc of the bow a large hollow gourd is attached, and this adds resonance to the sound of the plucked bow string. The gourd is

[1] See illustration opposite.

decorated with paper streamers. One of the songs sung to the accompaniment of the *buaṅ* is in honour of the instrument itself and recounts the birth and growth of the gourd on the manure heap. Some of the dances enact hunting scenes and fights with bow and arrow.

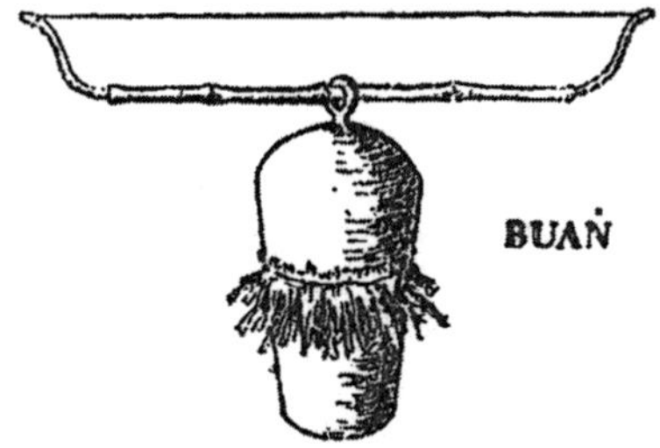

BUAṄ

During weddings and festivals the dancing takes place at night as well as in the daytime. Drink is plentiful, and the dance goes on until the moon is setting and the first light of morning appears in the sky. At these times dancing is associated with romance as well as with illicit flirtations and unions; amid the general rejoicing it is easy for couples to slip away unnoticed. Dancing, however, is not by any means confined to the more formal and set occasions. During the hot season in particular there is an almost nightly gathering in some part of the village, when the younger members of the community dance together. At these times the *lagṛe*, a simple dance, is much used. Of this there are many variations, and different varieties appear to be popular in different localities. One of the most popular in the area is a variety of *lagṛe* known as *porob*, which appears to be unknown elsewhere. These dances are suitable for any occasion.[1]

Santal music is largely but not entirely associated with dancing. The Santals are a musical people and find in music an outlet for the emotional and imaginative sides of their nature. From an early age boys begin to play on a whistle, the high and plaintive notes of which can be heard coming from the fields and woods as the boys tend the herds. Later most of them become proficient in playing the flute. The name *tirio* is used to denote different kinds of flute as well as the boys' whistle. Flutes contain six holes, and the usual type is the true flute that is held to one side—the instrument associated with Krishna in Hindu mythology. Some are beautifully made. One man playing at Sarenga during the Lakshmi Puja had a beautiful specimen; at the higher end there was a brass figure of Krishna playing the flute, while at the other end there was mounted a brass dove. Another type is shaped like an inverted T, the air being blown into the base of the T, while the arms,

[1] Bodding's *Dictionary*, Vol. II, p. 331, lists thirty-one dances.

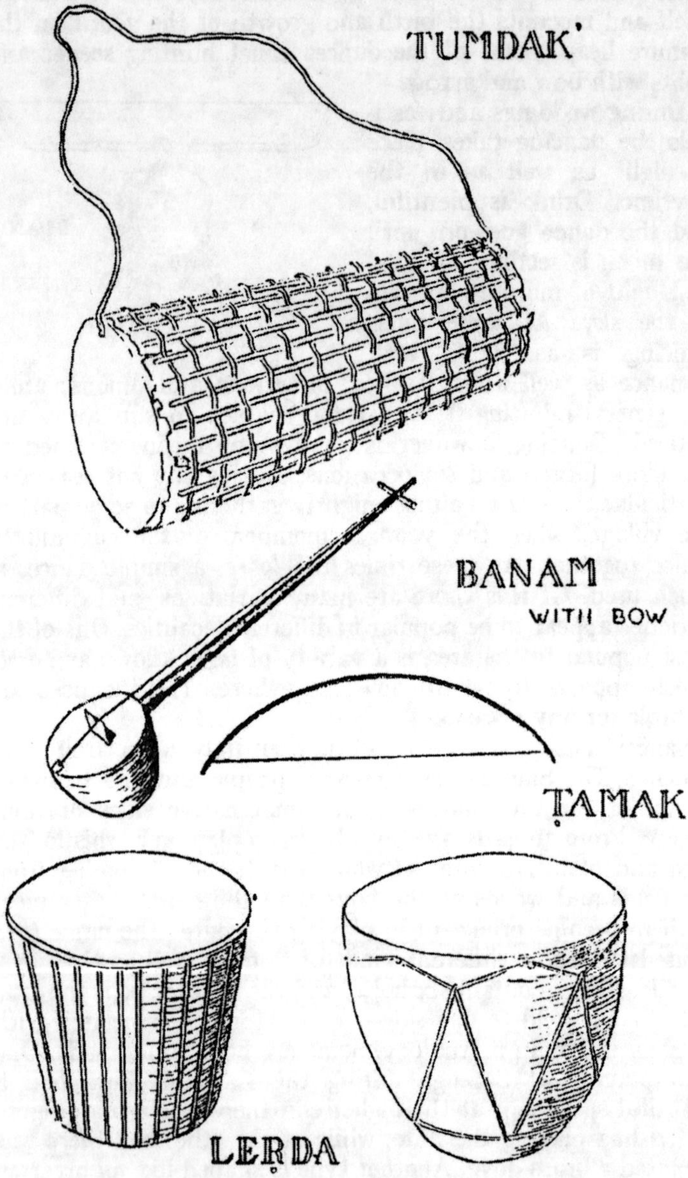
TUMDAK'
BANAM
WITH BOW
ṬAMAK
LEṚDA

which are longer than the base, contain the finger-holes. Another instrument in the use of which many of the men are proficient is the *banam*,[1] a one-string fiddle. The bowl is hollowed out from a piece of wood or formed sometimes from half a coconut, and it is usually covered with goat skin, though occasionally there are specimens covered with monkey skin, which is prized for the purpose. The bowl is pressed against the player's armpit and the bow is drawn across the string with the right hand, while the fingers of the left hand depress the string at the required point. The string of the fiddle is in these days generally a metal wire. The whole instrument is about eighteen inches long. It is a difficult instrument from which to produce a melody, and it is therefore used chiefly to accompany men's songs with a somewhat monotonous form of "seconds".

The most conspicuous of the musical instruments of the Santals, both for size and volume of sound, are the drums. The two kinds in common use are played together. They are known as the *tumdak'* and the *ṭamak*.[2] They are beaten at dances by the younger men, who drum and leap about in front of the lines of dancing women and girls. The *tumdak'* is made of burnt clay and is somewhat conical in shape. The narrow end is usually covered with goat skin and the wide end with bullock hide. These end coverings are kept in place by narrow leather strips running the length of the drum, and other strips are wound round the drum. It is suspended by thongs from the shoulders of the youth who is playing it. He beats out the main rhythm with his right hand on the narrow end, and the left hand beats a deeper note on the broad end to punctuate the bars. The *ṭamak* is a kettle-drum made of iron in the shape of a bowl and covered with bullock hide. In addition to being used as an accompaniment for the *tumdak'*, it is also the hunting drum. It is slung from the shoulders of the player and beaten with a pair of sticks. A variant of the *ṭamak* is the *leṛda*,[3] which has a flat bottom. The *ḍhāk*[4] is a large long drum hollowed out of wood. This drum is in popular use at weddings and also at large dancing gatherings. It has to be carried by two men and is slung from a bamboo pole which they carry on their shoulders. It is the reverberations of this drum which can be heard throughout the surrounding countryside.

With the exception of the *sarpa* and the cymbals, women do

[1] See illustration opposite.
[2] See illustration opposite.
[3] See illustration opposite.
[4] See illustration next page.

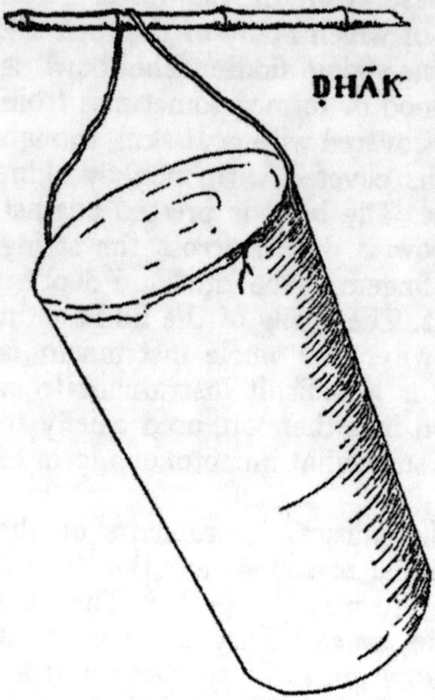

ḌHĀK

not learn to play any of these instruments. Young girls may be seen sometimes trying out their brothers' instruments, but they put them away with childish things. Their singing is, however, their peculiar glory. Not only do they sing while dancing, but on many other occasions. As the women of a village return home in the evening from their visit to the weekly market or after a day of gathering leaves in the forest, their high- and soft-toned singing can be heard coming over the fields. During the transplantation of the rice seedlings they sing as they bend over their task. Their songs during this activity are of a special class known as *heṛhet'*, a word which means the plucking of the seedlings and weeding. Men also sing, and when one is narrating the traditions of the tribe or relating a story he will often break into song to illustrate a point or amplify the story. Santal melodies are as a rule pitched high and in a minor key. The range of the tunes is meagre and rarely makes use of more than three or four different notes in the scale. One unfailing characteristic is a long-drawn-out succession of repeated single notes at the end of each line. Nevertheless, they afford scope for the expression of the dominant emotions experienced by the Santals, whose devotion to dancing and song has developed among them a high degree of musical aptitude. In order that they may easily and quickly memorize the great number of different rhythms with which they have to be familiar, they have invented a series of mnemonics which they repeat at the opening of a dance or a song. One example of such mnemonics, associated with the *doṅ* dances, is as follows:[1]

"Bhendaṅ netaṅ | dak' taṅ netaṅ | din dupuṅ | din dupuṅ—
bhendaṅ netaṅ | dak' taṅ netaṅ | dak' dupuṅ | dak' dupuṅ."

[1] Bodding's *Dictionary*, Vol. II, p. 112.

Poetry, like music, has to a great extent developed as the handmaid of dancing, though, again like music, it covers a wider range than the songs sung to the accompaniment of dancing. Much has been done in recent years to collect some of the wealth of poetry among the aboriginals of India.[1] A comparison would probably reveal that the store of the Santals in this respect is second to that of no other tribe in India. A great deal of the poetry is spontaneous in composition and therefore ephemeral. They delight in turning out new songs, and those who possess special gifts of song-making are not slow in exercising them. These new and topical songs give poetic expression to some new experience of the group. The coming of the railway was celebrated, as in the following *doṅ* type of song:

In the bazaar at Calcutta
The B.B. line carriages have fallen on the rails.
Send news to the Santals of Siuṛi,
Bring them here.
With a *hir hor khir khor kupi kol*
B.B. line train carriage *ho*,
Push it up once more.[2]

The beauty of a town lit up with electric lights did not escape notice in this snatch of a *lagṛe* song:

In Asansol
The electric lights
Look sweet, sweet.[3]

Love songs cover a wide range of expression, tender and passionate, as the following examples may serve to illustrate:

A *lagṛe* song[4]

The birds of the forest are crying,
They cry with different songs, love;
The fish cry softly, love,
My soul cries for you.

[1] W. G. Archer's *The Blue Grove* contains translations of Oraon poetry. *Folk-Songs of the Maikal Hills*, by Verrier Elwin and Shamrao Hivale, and *Folk-Songs of Chhattisgarh*, by Verrier Elwin, come from Central India.

[2] See Appendix B, No. 3.

[3] See Appendix B, No. 4.

[4] See Appendix B, No. 5.

At the four corners of the pond
Varied coloured birds have built their nests;
Some are on the wing and some are seated.
They cannot find their nests, they cannot find their nests at all.

porob[1]

Why went you to the water, my girl,
Why did you run away, my girl?
What, O mother, shall I say,
What, O mother, can I tell you?
In Rajaram's garden
The flowers are blooming;
In the flower shrubs
Have I been caught.

Sometimes in the songs there is an expression of the pathos of life and a haunting sense of the unknown and the unpredictable:

lagre[2]

The water has risen in the river;
O Bhagavan, help me over, help me over.

jhika[3] (a men's dance)

The life of man 'tis like a *jhinga* flower.
For what did you come into the world?
What will you receive but misfortune?
At the end Krishna will have you.

Here is the cry of a child in a harvest song:

In the corner by the plantain tree who is there?
In the corner by the plantain tree is the potter,
In the corner by the plantain tree is the potter.

You in there, potter, you turn the wheel;
My mother and my father have I none,
My mother and my father make for me.

[1] See Appendix B, No. 6.
[2] See Appendix B, No. 7.
[3] See Appendix B, No. 8.

I will make them, child, make them I will,
But the breath of life I cannot give,
But the breath of life I cannot give.[1]

Song and verse also serve to keep alive the memory of the past. Some refer to the dim past that comes within the scope of mythology and relate to the early days of the human race, as in this *Dãsãẽ* song:

Where, O *Guru*, were cows first born
Where, O *cela*, were men first reared?
In Hihiri, O *Guru*, cows were first born,
In Pipiri, O *cela*, men were first reared.[2]

Other songs keep alive the memory of more recent events, like those that commemorate the Santal rebellion. Others refer to local happenings of a past time, such as the following:

A *jhika* song[3]

There came to the yellow lake
Monilal Raja *ho*,
There came to Chaturpuri
Jadob Siṅ Rani.

Have you heard, Durjon Siṅ,
Raja of Tuṅ land?
Fight, fight,
Tighten your belts.

Poetic forms of expression are ingrained in Santal ways of thought, and appear not only in songs but in different kinds of rhythmic prose. The recital of the traditions brings out clearly the musical quality of the language used. This is true also of the formal conversation between the parties at marriages, in the marriage sermons and in the invocations to spirits. Here, indeed, there is a certain amount of rhyming, a device that plays but little part in the songs. Their speech is shot through with figurative allusions and they are fond of talking in riddles. A fourteen-

[1] See Appendix B, No. 9.
[2] See Appendix B, No. 10.
[3] See Appendix B, No. 11.

year-old boy who was once asked his name replied: "By my name I cannot do anything." Pressed for some explanation of his words, he said: "By my name I cannot walk." It was then explained by some bystanders that the name by which he was known was *Leḍha*, "the lame one". There is a large number of figurative and hidden names for common objects. These names are used in conversation between those who are in the joking relationship with one another and particularly at the time of weddings. "White horse" is beer and "red horse" is spirits; "sheep's *ghi*"[1] is salt; "jackal's horn" is pepper; "frog spawn" is water. "We are sweeping the courtyard" means that we are washing our teeth; "Have you taken the harrow over the field?" means Have you brushed your hair? "Have you married off your middle son?" means Have you eaten your rice? There are many phrases to describe the evacuation of waste products from the body, one of which may be quoted. A man excuses himself from the company of his fellows with the words, "I am going to pay my rent!"

The Santal love of colour and decoration also gives expression to their sense of the joyous in life. Men are sparing in the use of personal adornment, though youths wearing ear-rings or necklaces made from seeds pass without remark. Women are fond of ornaments. Most of them wear a small flower-shaped brass ornament in the left side of the nose and have brass ear-rings. They all wear a *ḥasli* of silver or brass, a large ring that hangs round the neck. Bangles of silver, shell or glass are worn. They delight to fix flowers of red and white in their hair, and they enhance the lines of their eyes with a dark paste. On special occasions some of the heavier ornaments are brought out—large bell-shaped ear-rings, silver ornaments for the hair, anklets and rings for the feet and toes. The women also decorate the houses with gay-coloured patterns. The houses receive a new plaster coat of earth at the end of the rainy season in preparation for the Harvest festival. The house plinth or veranda and the wall up to a foot or two above the plinth are plastered a very dark grey, the colour being prepared by mixing cowdung with straw ash. Above this dark colour, on a first coat of light earth, the housewives vie with one another to attract the attention of their fellow villagers and of passers-by. There is no uniformity and the colours used depend rather on the coloured clays that are available in the neighbourhood of the village, but red predominates. Some house walls give

[1] Clarified butter.

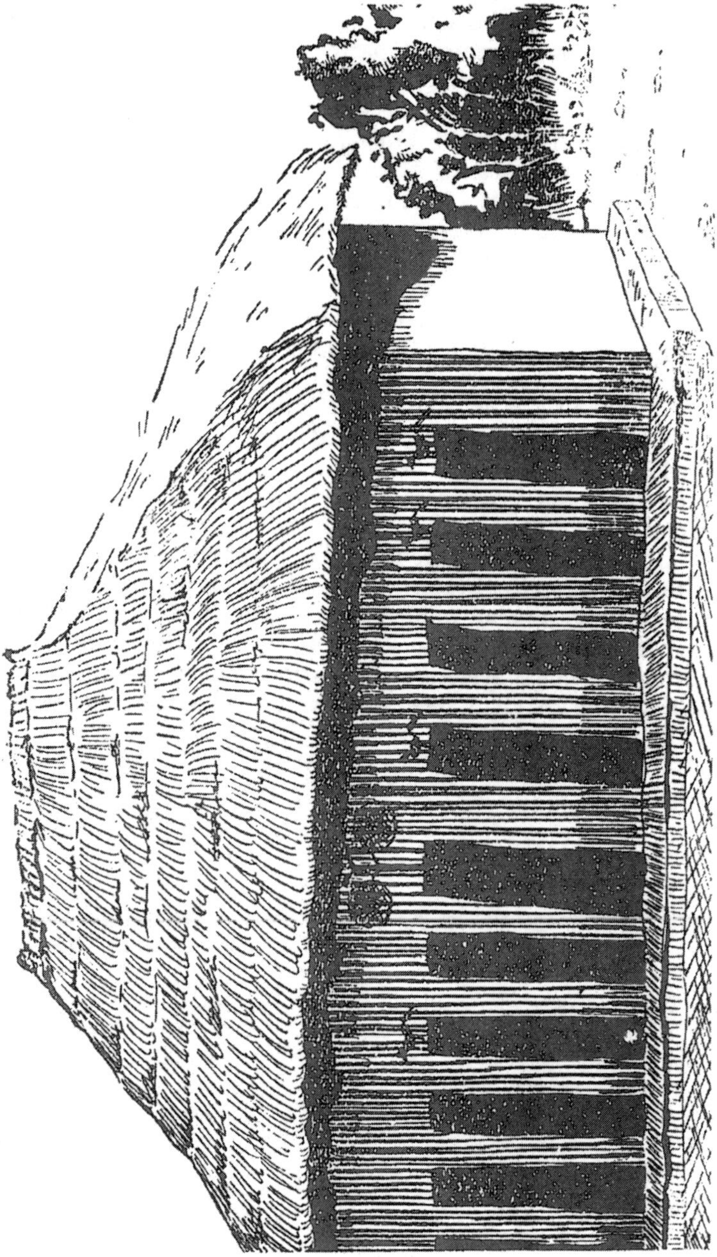

the appearance of a coloured chequer board, while others have rectangular blocks of colour—red, black and yellow. On some houses there are geometrical patterns, and a favourite design represents plantain trees. Imaginative artists find scope on some of the walls and draw designs incorporating flowers, birds and animals and stylized but animated figures of men and women; on one occasion I observed the figure of an aeroplane in blue, red and yellow earth, giving a tolerable imitation of camouflage paint. The forms are limited by the technique, the drawings being done with the fingers of the right hand dipped in the colours.

The decay of primitive artistic culture in India has attracted the widespread attention of students. Over wide areas tribes-people are being encouraged to be ashamed of their dances and songs, and their arts are dying out. It does seem, however, that at least in some areas the Santals are keeping alive their traditional arts and music, and that it is virile enough to find expression in the creation of new forms. Herein lies one of the greatest causes for hopefulness concerning the future of the tribe. It says much for their social life that they maintain these institutions in spite of their depressed economic condition and their status as a small minority in nearly all the areas where they live. Hitherto they have been spared from the dangers of a uniform national system of education, and it remains to be seen how much of their artistic life will survive the "planning" that is now in vogue.

CHAPTER 5

SOME FOLK-TALES

FOLK-TALES are meant to entertain, and only incidentally do they instruct. The stories current among the Santals do, however, reveal standards of conduct; they hold up certain types of character as admirable, others as ridiculous or contemptible, and so help to form the judgment of their hearers. Over two hundred stories told by Santals are available in English, for this is a field that early attracted the attention of Europeans living among them. The first in the field was the Rev. F. T. Cole, who in 1875 printed two stories in the *Indian Antiquary*. A further collection of tales was published in 1891, collected by the Rev. A. Campbell. The collection of C. H. Bompas, entitled *Folklore of the Santal Parganas*, was published in 1909, and this has remained a standard collection in the West. Bodding's monumental work in three volumes was not published until the years 1925–29. It contains ninety-three stories with Santali text and English translation, and the same plan was followed in his other publications, *A Chapter of Santal Folklore*, which contains ten stories, and *Witchcraft among the Santals*, which contains eight. The editor of this last work, which was published after Bodding's death, states that C. H. Bompas obtained the manuscript of many stories from Bodding.[1]

The field is far from exhausted. All collections that have been published up till now have been gathered either in the Santal Parganas or in the district of Manbhum, except for eleven stories published in a book that deals with the Santals of Mayurbhanj,[2] the extreme south of the Santal country. The tales included here are told in the Bankura district and serve to illustrate the Santal attitude towards many of the facts mentioned in other chapters.

(1) *The Grey Monkey and a Boy*

At the end of a certain bazaar there were a great many trees where lived a band of grey monkeys. Each day one of the

[1] Oslo Ethnographical Museum, *Skrifter Bind* 3, Hefte 5, p. 257: "Years ago most of these tales have been retold from Mr. Bodding's manuscripts by C. H. Bompas in *Folklore of the Santal Parganas* (London, 1909)." For some of the facts in this paragraph I am indebted to an article entitled "The Folk-Tale in Santal Society", by Mildred Archer, *Man in India*, December 1944, Vol. XXIV.

[2] Charulal Mukherjea, *The Santals*, Indian Research Institute, Calcutta, 1943.

female monkeys went into the bazaar, where she used to snatch at sweets from the sweetmeat shop and eat them up. And so the men used to drive her off, but they could never get hold of her, for she used to jump up into the trees. This continued for a long time. One day she went to the house of a wealthy man and saw that the folk, who were all busy about their work, had put down a baby to lie in the courtyard. She picked up the child and ran off with it to the trees where she lived. There she brought it up. She used to fetch all kinds of tasty food from the bazaar to feed the child, who grew bigger every day. He called the monkey his mother.

One day he said to his mother: "O mother, please bring me some parched rice and some pounded rice." On hearing his request, his mother went to the grocer's shop and brought the things. He continued to ask for things, until his mother had brought from the bazaar a *dhuti*[1] and shirt, shoes and stockings, a hat and various other articles of clothing. When the boy had all these things he was quite happy, but again he said to his mother: "O mother, you have fetched all these for me; now please buy me a horse." The monkey went one night to the house of a merchant, loosed a horse that was tied in the stables and took it back with her. The boy was overjoyed at this and started going for a ride every day. If he was going for just a short ride he would say to his mother, "I shall not go far", and if he was going for a long ride he would say: "I am going a distance today."

At length one day he said: "O mother, get me a bride." His mother took the necessary steps and arranged a bride for him at a far-distant place. For a long time after the marriage ceremonies had taken place the boy did not go to his wife's home, nor did he bring her to his own house, not even once after the marriage. Then at last the boy thought: "I shall go and bring my bride." He left home saying that he would be back at the end of two weeks. When he had not returned his mother went in search of him. At one place she questioned some cowherds:

> Say, O cowherds, say,
> Has a young prince gone this way?
> He had silver on his hands and feet
> And on his head a crown.

[1] The male garment. A Bengali word.

They told her that he had passed that way, and so she went on asking all the cowherds in turn as she met them. After a time she came to where some herdsmen were grazing elephants. In reply to her question they said: "Your son is behind seven-barred doors." She went on till she came to the place where her son was staying. She was given a welcome by her co-parents-in-law, but at the end of a couple of days she said that the time had come for her daughter-in-law to come away with them. The folk of the house took the boy away to have his bath, and they explained to his mother that they would make some water warm for her, as it was not fitting for them to give her a cold bath. They made some water boiling hot, seated her on a stool and, pouring the boiling water over her, scalded her so that she died. Then they propped her up at the back of the house under the eaves. When her son came back from his bath and asked, "Where is my mother?" they told him: "She is sunning herself out at the back of the house under the eaves." The boy went round to the back and pushed his mother over. He thought: "I have seen many kinds of death, but I never saw anyone die with their teeth clenched like this." To the others he said: "You have made a fine joke of me!"

Then he stayed in the house of his father-in-law.

(2) *Two Brothers and the Supreme Being*

A certain widow had two sons and one daughter. Her daughter used to stay with her and was fully occupied in all the housework, fetching water and washing the pots and pans. The two boys, who were older, used to take the goats out to graze. Each day they would take the goats out into the forest where the grazing was good, and there they used to play. One day they made a plough, and they began to play at ploughing. They continued to do so each day, and Father *Cando*[1] watched them at it. Finally, one day he took the form of a man and came to question them: "What are your names?" he said, and they told him. Then he asked them: "How many are you in the family?" The boys told him that they were two brothers and that their mother and sister were at home. *Cando* went away, but the next day he came again to them and said: "Keep me as a house son-in-law and husband for your sister." They told him that it was quite impossible for them to say anything about it, so he asked them to tell their mother. "Tell

[1] The Supreme Being.

your mother that a certain man proposes this, and you can tell me the answer tomorrow." When they told their mother she said: "We cannot support him, but if he is willing and able to work for his food he may stay." Next day they told him, and he agreed to come; he went home with them, saluted the mother when he arrived, and they all lived together.

One day the son-in-law said to his mother-in-law: "Mother, go to the landlord and ask him to give you a piece of land." She did as she was told, and the landlord said they could have a field that was covered with *sirom*[1] grass.

First they cut down the grass, and when they had prepared the land they said to their mother: "Ask the landlord for a pair of bullocks." The landlord gave them a pair of bullocks, so they ploughed up the land, and then they brought a measure of paddy seed and sowed a very big field of paddy. *Cando* gave them rain as it was required. The three menfolk worked hard in the fields, but when men were passing and looked in their direction they thought they could see a large number of men working there. Time passed, harvest drew near, and their rice became ripe. The three of them went daily to see how the rice was getting on, and all along *Cando* supplied just the amount of rain that they needed, but there was a lack of rain on the fields belonging to other men. Seeing this, the men of the village spoke to the son-in-law, saying: "Hey, son-in-law, we see your rice fields looking very healthy. How has that come about?" To which he replied: "Yes, it is true, for our crops have grown well by the mercy of *Cando*." When the time of harvest came they gathered in their rice with ease and threshed it. They had no troubles, but all the time while other people were cutting their rice or threshing it the rain continued and their grain was ruined.

These three, however, gathered in their crop, threshed it and stored it away in bundles made with straw rope. When all the other folk saw these bundles they were astonished and became most envious, saying to the son-in-law: "You folk have indeed gathered in a goodly crop." To which he replied: "Yes, indeed we have." And so they became rich. At last a day came when Father *Cando* left them—he became invisible, and so in the end they understood that he was not a man at all, but that he had been *Cando* come to them in the form of a man.

[1] *Andropogon muricatus*, Retz.

(3) *The Thieves and the Widow's Son*

A certain widow had a son of whom she was very fond. She was fairly rich, but the boy used to look after the goats all the same, and he used to take them out to graze, and grew big. When the boy had reached years of understanding he used to go about asking other people: "Is there anyone who can tell me about myself?" But no one was able to tell him anything. Every day he asked someone, and after a long time when he had asked a certain man the fellow replied: "Yes, I shall be able to tell you the story." He was, however, a very deceitful person, and he said to the boy: "If I teach you, what will you give me?" To which the boy replied: "It all depends on what you are going to tell me."

Then the man said: "It will cost one hundred rupees to teach you one word. Can you give so much money?" The boy agreed that he would give him the money, whereupon the man said: "Very well, then. Come here tomorrow with the money." The boy returned home and spoke to his mother: "Mother, give me one hundred rupees; I am going to learn a word." His mother asked him: "What word is this, my boy, for which you will have to pay a hundred rupees?" But the boy would only say, "Oh, please give it to me", and in the end she gave him the money. Next day he went back to the deceitful man; and when he had given him the hundred rupees the boy said: "Now teach me the word." The man taught him thus, saying: "For one hundred rupees, one word; that word is Ram."[1] The boy left him, and all through the day he repeated to himself: "Ram, Ram." In the end the boy said: "I must learn some more words." So this time he collected two hundred rupees from his mother and went once more to the man. He said to the man: "Teach me some more." The man said, "Bring the money", but the boy replied at once: "I have brought it with me." "How much?" asked the man. To which the boy replied: "Here I have two hundred rupees." Then the man told him: "Well, for two hundred rupees I shall teach you two words, as one of my words costs a hundred rupees." The boy said: "All right; if that is it, it must be so." The man then proceeded to teach him two words, and the words were these—*dui* and *tin*.[2] After the boy had learnt these two words he returned

[1] Ram, the name of the hero of the *Ramayana*. In counting it is usual for Hindus to say "Ram" in place of the number one.

[2] Bengali numerals, two and three.

home. For three hundred rupees he had learnt to say these three words: "One, two, three."

Now it came to pass that the boy kept on repeating "One, two, three" to himself all the time, whether he was out with the goats or eating his food or lying down to sleep. A few days later a band of thieves who had stolen three bags of rupees and a lot of ornaments from the house of some rich man came along in the night to the boy's house to steal some goats. They left the money and the ornaments at the door of the house, and some of them went into the goat-shed to pick out the goats. Just at that moment the boy roused from his sleep, and immediately he began to recite those three words for learning which he had paid three hundred rupees. Again and again he repeated the words: "One, two, three; one, two three; one, two, three." The thieves heard him and thought to themselves: "It may be that he is counting us to see how many there are." So what did they do but run away with all speed, leaving behind them the bags of money and the ornaments. The boy heard the sounds of men running away, tremblingly lit a lamp and went outside. What should he see but the money left by the thieves who had intended to steal their goats. When the boy saw three bags full of rupees he was overjoyed. He went and roused his mother and said to her: "Look, mother, because I learnt three words at the cost of three hundred rupees, today I have found these money-bags." They kept the money and the ornaments; the money increased, and in the end he and his mother became very rich.

The story is ended.

(4) *Seven Brothers and One Sister*

In a certain village lived seven brothers. They had one sister who was younger than them all, and they were very fond of her. She used to cook for them, but she was not made to do any other work. When she had grown up they arranged a marriage for her. The visits had been paid, gifts were exchanged and the bride price had been paid, so all that was left was the marriage day itself. In the meantime the brothers were excavating a tank. They dug very deep, but no spring appeared. The brothers were troubled as to how they could get water in their tank, and they asked everyone whom they met. One day a Brahmin came to their house, and they all asked him: "How can we get water in our tank?" The Brahmin told them: "If you want water to appear, there is one thing you must do. You will have to give that dearly loved sister of yours, and then you will get water." In accordance with the Brahmin's word they sent their sister down to the tank to draw water in a new brass pot. Try as she could, she was unable to get the mouth of the pot under the water, and as she tried she called out: "The water is up to my knees, brothers, but yet the pot will not go under." So it went on; at first the water came up to her thighs, then to her waist, then to her chest, her neck, her face, and she went on calling out in the same way. She could not get the pot under the water, but she herself was drowned.

The day of her wedding arrived and the bridegroom's party appeared. The brothers began to make all kinds of excuses. "Our little mother has gone to collect firewood", they said. But although they waited for the whole day she did not return, and so the party went away. As they were passing by the tank they saw on the water a water-lily. One after another tried to pluck the flower without success. As they approached it the flower moved away. After all the others had tried, the bridegroom went into the water, and as the flower was moving away he put out his hand suddenly, grasped and plucked the flower, carrying it to the bride's palanquin. When the party was still on its way the flower changed into the girl. The bearers felt the palanquin grow heavy, and looking in they saw that it was the bride. They continued their journey rejoicing, but the brothers were told nothing of what had happened.

Some time later there was a great famine, and the brothers came to that village to beg for food. When the girl saw her brothers she began to weep. Her father-in-law saw this and said: "Why do you cry, daughter-in-law?" She began to make various excuses; first she said: "I struck my foot against a stone"; then she said: "I trod on a cock, who pecked at me" and "I bumped my head against that rafter." Then they removed the stone, they killed the cock and they cut away the rafter, but she cried all the more. Seeing this, they asked her again, and at last she told them: "My brothers have come here like beggars, and it is all because they gave me up for a sacrifice." Her relatives told her not to cry any more, for they would give the brothers rice to eat. First they gave them oil and sent them to bathe, and when they had returned they gave them food, after which their sister made herself known to them. They were covered with confusion, and at the same moment great cracks appeared in the ground, into which they fell. The youngest brother had a knot of hair on his head, and this grew into a cotton plant, so from that day there was cotton.

(5) *Seven Brothers and a Bed*

There were seven brothers who lived together. Six of them were married, but the youngest had not married. The six brothers were very hardworking, but the seventh was exceedingly lazy and did no work at all. His brothers would tell him to do this, that or the other, but he never listened to them. If the brothers remained in the house he used to go outside; when he saw that they had gone out to work he would return, wheedle his sisters-in-law into giving him some food and then go out again. One day his eldest brother told him to do something, and that too he did not do. Then his brother said: "You eat, but you will not work. In future unless you work you can have nothing to eat." He told his wife that she was on no account to give him any rice. Next day the lazy youth came back to the house and abused his eldest sister-in-law so much that she gave him some rice. When his eldest brother came home he asked the youth why he had not done the work, but the youth remained silent, saying not a word. His brother then said to his wife: "If from tomorrow you give him any rice, I shall beat you. If he asks you for rice, give him ashes."

Again the following day the young man asked his sister-in-law for food. She did not give him rice, but placed a dish of ashes in front of him. Seeing this, the young man said: "My sister-in-law has actually given me ashes to eat because of what my brother said. I shall not stay here any longer, but find a home elsewhere." He left home early next morning, and coming to a certain village he stayed with a man there. It chanced that the man had a daughter for whom he could not find a husband, and so he planned to make the youth his son-in-law. Accordingly, he and his wife took great care of the young man, giving him plenty to eat, and at the end of two or three months he and the girl were married. He stayed on for a year after his marriage and never did a day's work, whereupon his father-in-law became enraged and decided that the young couple should set up housekeeping for themselves. He did not leave them empty-handed, but provided them with such things as an axe and a spade. Then on the day after they had begun housekeeping they had nothing to eat.

After a day had passed, the girl said to her husband: "How long are we to remain hungry? Take your axe and go to the forest. You can cut down some trees to make beds and stools to sell at the market. If you do not bring them by the afternoon, today also we shall have to go hungry." The young man went to the forest and was looking around at this tree and that when he heard some noises, for two of the trees were talking together. He cut down one of the two, brought it home and made a bed out of it, and then took it along to the market and sold it. The bed was bought by the king of that country. The king took the bed home and ordered his servants to spread his quilt on it, as he intended to sleep on it that very night. When night came the servants made the bed ready, and the king took his meal and then lay down on the bed. After a while he heard the legs talking to each other. One of them said to the others: "Look out, I am going to explore. Mind that you three hold up the bed properly!" He went off, and came back after a while, fixing himself into position. The other three legs asked him what he had seen, whereupon he replied: "I went to the king's apartments, and there I saw that his maidservants were helping themselves to food." The king was wide awake, but he pretended to be asleep and muffled himself up with his ear open to hear the conversation of the bed legs. After a short while another leg said: "Now it is my turn; I'll be off. Mind you three hold up the bed properly." When he came back he fixed himself on again, and the others questioned him. He told them: "I saw the steward of the household, and he was helping himself to his master's possessions." Later on another of the legs said: "Now it is my turn. Mind you three hold up the bed properly." He went off, and returned after a short time. Then he told them what he had seen: "Shame, shame, how shall I say it? The king's minister and the queen, I saw them sitting together and talking to each other. The minister said, 'You kill the king, and then we shall be able to live happily together', but the queen replied: 'No, no; let us go on in secret as we are doing now.' The minister got quite angry and struck the queen on her cheek; you can see the marks of his fingers."

When the king heard these words he became both sorrowful and angry and rose from the bed. If he had not done so, another of the legs would have gone for a walk. He went straight to the queen and saw of a truth that there were marks on her cheek. He did not rouse her from bed, but he asked her at once: "What have you done to your cheek?" The queen said:

"I scratched myself." But seeing the marks on the queen's face, the king believed all the things that he had heard the legs of his bed saying. He called the minister, he called the steward, he called his maidservants, and he punished them all. The minister and the queen were beheaded.

The king then made a proclamation throughout the kingdom to this effect: "Bring to me the man who made this bed." When the young man heard these words he became exceedingly afraid. He hid himself for a month or two, but in the end the king's men found him and brought him before the king. The king questioned him: "My boy, did you make this bed?" To which he confessed that he had done so. Then the king told him: "My life has been saved because you made this bed and because I bought it. I propose to give you a half of my kingdom and you shall marry one of my daughters." The marriage took place and the king built a house for them. The young man also brought his first wife, and they all lived happily together.

This is the end.

(6) *The Old Woman who had Itch*

They say that once upon a time there was a terrible lot of "itch" on the earth. All the people were continually scratching themselves to get rid of the pain. In the end they appealed to *Ṭhạkur*[1] to take away the itch. He came down to earth in human form and went round everywhere, gathering all the itch into a bag to take it away from men. As he went on his rounds he came to an old woman. It was during the cold season and she was warming herself over a fire. The warmth from the fire was giving her relief from her itch, and as she rubbed her limbs she said to herself: "Well, well, how lovely it is like this. I wish I could stay like this for ever and feel this sensation." Then *Ṭhạkur* came along and said to the old woman: "Give me your itch, old woman; I will take it from you and throw it away." She replied: "No, let it stay with me. Let it remain!" When he heard this, *Ṭhạkur* went off and left her with her itch. From her it spread again to others and increased; otherwise the whole earth would have been cleansed of it.

So far is the story.

[1] Another name for the Supreme Being.

(7) *The Story of the Potter Woman*

One day a potter woman went out to bring some clay from the clay pit, and while she was there she gave birth to a girl. She fell into a difficulty and wondered what she ought to do; should she take the clay home first or the child? She thought to herself: "If I take the girl away first, then we shall not have anything to eat today; but if I take the clay, then we shall be able to buy food." Thinking thus, she decided to leave the child. She wrapped her round with leaves from an *atnak'*[1] tree and carried home the clay. Then she returned to take the child home with her, but the child was nowhere to be seen, and so she went home again without her.

After the child had been left by her mother, a pair of vultures came and carried her away; the names of those vultures were Golden Vulture and Moustached Vulture. The two brought up the child, and they used to send her out to beg. They warned the girl: "When you go out begging, do not go into such and such a village, for the dogs in that village are very fierce." However, it came to pass in the course of her begging that the girl arrived at that very village. Just at that time the sky became covered to north, south, east and west with black clouds. The child did not dare to enter any of the houses, but stood outside and leaned against a horse-radish tree; but the sap began to drip on to her, and so she took shelter under the eaves of a house. There the water dripped on her, so that she became very wet and began to cry. The man and the woman in the house heard her crying, and immediately they understood that it was their own child. They brought her into the house, gave her food to eat, and told her that they were her own father and mother.

So the child stayed with them, but all the time the vultures were searching for her, and at last they discovered where she was. Her father and mother had covered her up in a basket, but the vultures came and were pulling her out from it. Then the father and mother began to pull the other way, and the child cried out loud; but no one listened to her cries. In the end she was pulled right apart into two pieces. The parents cremated one part of the body, and the vultures cremated the other part. While the vultures were carrying out their part of the cremation ceremonies, a part of the child's brain became stuck on the bill of the Moustached Vulture, and when she licked her bill

[1] *Terminalia tomentosa*. W. and A. Bengali, *Ashan*.

she found that it tasted very sweet. She called out to the Golden Vulture: "Here, Old Man, how sweet this human flesh is!" The Golden Vulture replied: "Whatever are you saying, Old Woman? I cannot understand you." Then the Moustached Vulture explained: "This child's brain stuck on my bill, and when I tasted it I must say that I found it very sweet." The Golden Vulture said: "I do not believe you, Old Woman." Whereupon the old woman vulture said to him: "Then have a taste, and perhaps you will see whether I am telling the truth or not." The old man vulture then put out his tongue and took a taste. A small piece of the brain got into his mouth, and the Golden Vulture said at once: "H'm, quite true; it is very sweet." The two of them proceeded to pick at the child and completely ate her up.

From that time vultures began to eat human flesh; they used not to do so before.

The above story, which is based on what might be called the "Sakuntala" *motif*, is well known in the area. A slightly different version relates the story of a boy who was born at the foot of a plantain tree. It used to be told in the villages by a blind beggar, and a part of the story would be sung in verse. Some of his songs are translated here:

In the Toregor tank, in the Bahagor lake,
My mother gave me birth,
My father carried me in his arms.

North, south, east and west, black clouds have risen;
I am an orphan from my birth.
Where, O mother, can I go?

I leaned against a horse-radish tree, but the sap fell down;
I stood in the shade of the eaves,
But the water dripped on me.[1]

After singing this song, the beggar was wont to break into a different melody and refer to his own condition:

Alas, alas! the sun; alas, alas! the moon.
The gift of life you gave me,
The gift of sight you denied.
Give me a handful for my stomach,
A little rubbing oil to keep me alive,
A wanderer I through all the countryside.[2]

[1] See Appendix B, No. 12.

[2] See Appendix B, No. 13.

The same beggar used to sing a song that referred to the second version of the story:

> At the foot of the plantain she gave birth,
> With leaves of the *ashan* she covered me.
> Vulture, vulture, the Golden Vulture,
> Vulture, vulture, the Moustached Vulture,
> They brought me up.
> O mother, give alms.[1]

[1] See Appendix B, No. 14.

CHAPTER 6

MYTHS AND THE CLAN ORGANIZATION

MANY of the social activities of the Santals are based on myths, and the strength of their clan organization is due in no small measure to its foundations in mythology. An examination of the intimate relationship between the two bears out the truth of such a statement as: "The sacred lore of the tribe is not a fanciful tale told in explanation of natural phenomena and inexplicable events, but a method of expressing certain ways of thinking and feeling about the facts of life and of regulating human actions."[1] When for any reason a piece of ritual associated with a myth falls into disuse, knowledge of that myth begins to die out; conversely, when the myth is looked upon as outmoded, the activity with which it is linked begins to lose its hold on the people's imagination. The Santal story of the origin of man and the division of the human race into clans does not appear to be known today in more than outline form, except by a very few, mostly of the older generation. It is recited in the village only on certain occasions—the *caco chạṭiạr* ceremony, at which a child is formally admitted into the privileges of full membership in the tribe; the *Jom Sim* festival, an occasional clan celebration; and the *Karam* festival, which is an affair of the village. None of these institutions has a vigorous life in the area; the *caco chạṭiạr* ceremony of today retains only a vestige of its ancient glory, the *Jom Sim* is very rarely performed, and the same is true of the *Karam* in its full form.[2] The village headman has to recite the myth, but not every headman now is capable of doing so. The decay of the ritual is leading to the disappearance of the ancient myth. It is nevertheless still true that these stories do reveal the Santal view of the world. When they are told they call forth assent, and frequently in ordinary conversation the myths are cited in order to point a moral or clinch an argument. Though there are few who are ready to recite the whole story, some part of it is still familiar to everyone.

The Santal story of the origin of man has been recorded in slightly varying form by different authorities.[3] It did not escape

[1] E. O. James, *Comparative Religion*, Methuen, 1938, p. 335.

[2] Further reference is made to these festivals in the chapter on "Festivals".

[3] The fullest account in English is in *Traditions and Institutions of the Santals*, translated with notes and additions by P. O. Bodding from the Santali text published in 1887 by L. O. Skrefsrud, edited (after the translator's death) by Sten Konow. Oslo, 1942.

the attention of Sir James Frazer, who quoted the account written by the Rev. A. Campbell in *The Journal of the Bihar and Orissa Research Society* (1916). Frazer found in the story confirmation of his thesis: "This Santal story of the origin of man combines the principles of creation and evolution, for according to it mankind is ultimately derived from two images, which were modelled in human form out of froth or damp clay, but were afterwards accidentally transformed into birds, from whose eggs the first man and woman of flesh and blood were hatched."[1]

The following account, written down in the Sarenga area by an old man who could not have had access to any of the previously published versions, brings out most of the essential features of the story.[2] He wrote:

"The sea was always there. *Ṭhạkur* said in the beginning: 'How shall we improve it?' Then *Ṭhạkur* called to himself many of the kings of the sea and asked them how it was possible for earth to be raised from the sea bottom, but not one of them was able to do it. So *Ṭhạkur* first of all called Crab and said to him: 'You there, can you raise the earth from the bottom of this sea?' Crab replied: 'Yes, I can.' Then he set about carrying it up from the bottom of the sea, but it dissolved and he could do nothing. After him, *Ṭhạkur* called Tortoise. When he came *Ṭhạkur* said to him: 'You there, can you raise the earth from the bottom of this sea?' Then Tortoise replied, 'I shall raise it', but he also did not succeed. Last of all *Ṭhạkur* called Worm. When he came *Ṭhạkur* said to him: 'You there, can you raise the earth from the bottom of this sea?' Then Worm said: 'Yes, I can raise it; but you call Tortoise here and place a golden plate on his back. I will eat the mud on the bottom of the sea, and then excrete it at the other end on to the golden plate on Tortoise's back. In this way I shall raise the earth from the bottom of the sea.' And so indeed it was done. But the earth that had been raised was very uneven, and *Ṭhạkur* harrowed it to make it level. During the harrowing the sea came up where there were hollows, and where there were high places these became mountains and hills.

Then *Ṭhạkur* said: 'The world is made after a fashion, but how shall we improve it?' Then *Ṭhạkur* made two birds out of *sirom* grass seeds. They were called *Hãs* and *Hạ̃sil*, goose and

[1] J. G. Frazer, *Folklore in the Old Testament*, Macmillan, 1918, Vol. I, p. 22.
[2] Durlob Murmu of Govindapur.

gander. The two birds laid two eggs in a clump of thatching grass. From those two eggs two humans were born, and they were *Pilcu Haṛam* and *Pilcu Buḍhi*.[1] They had twelve sons and twelve daughters, and at that time they were living at Hohelo Popelo. Once upon a time when they had all grown up they fell into difficulties over a famine, so *Pilcu Haṛam* took his twelve sons hunting, and *Pilcu Buḍhi* took her twelve daughters to the forest to gather edible leaves. Twelve years later they met again, and then they married each other, from the eldest son and daughter to the youngest. (This was sin.) There in Hohelo Popelo at the time of a food shortage they planted millet in the forest clearings. A certain female *murum*[2] took to coming every day to eat that planted millet, so the brothers went and fixed stakes all round it. As the *murum* could not get through the fence, it tried to jump over. It was pierced on the upright stakes and ran away, dying close by the place called Sangaṛiya. Next day all the brothers hunted it with bows and arrows. They followed the trail of its hoofs and blood, came upon it at Sangaṛiya, and there cut it up and ate the flesh.

At that time *Pilcu Haṛam* and *Pilcu Buḍhi* divided them into clans—*pạris*—and taught them also about the spirits. They propped up in one place a silken cloth, a golden umbrella and a pointed stick, and welcomed the spirits. After a time in that place they did not have enough to eat, and so they came to Campa Gar. But there too they did not have enough to eat, and so they repented in their minds and set out to find the right way to live.[3] For twelve years they searched for the right way to live, and as they went they carried on their heads a large pig, an uncastrated male goat and a basket of rice. In their searching they came first of all to the Twisted Banyan tree, and there all their words were twisted. From there they went to the foot of the False *Atnak'* tree, and there all their words were falsified; nothing came right. Thence they went to the Broken *Matkom*, and there all their words were broken into pieces; nothing came right. Thence they came to the Pasty Ebony tree, and all their words were made into a thick paste. Thence once more they went to a waterhole, where *Liṭạ* holding an axe was awaiting them. Near to that waterhole, therefore, they found the True *Sarjom* tree, and there they found the truth. It was while they were there that they said: 'O mother,

[1] Literally, "First old man" and "First old woman".

[2] A species of buck, *Portax tragocamelus*.

[3] A word exceedingly difficult to translate, *dhorom*, Sanskrit *dharmma*.

there a white hare jumped and passed along.' From there till the present day these words are used at weddings. All the festivals began from the time that they spent at the True *Sarjom* tree—the *Baha*, *Sohrae*, *Karam*, *Jom Sim*, *Bapla*, *Abge*, and many others.

At the time of their weddings they addressed *Pilcu Haṛam*, *Pilcu Buḍhi* and *Maraṅ Buru*:[1]

Greetings, Lord, Great Spirit, in the name of marriage
Two kinds of beer have we applied.
Here then we present them to you;
Here then do not importune us further, Lord.
Do not create either stomach or head pains.
So, Lord, may they laugh and talk together,
Accept our gifts and take them happily, Lord.
Today we are marrying these two, Lord.
May they live to a good old age,
May they become old man and old woman together, Lord.[2]

After cutting up the female *murum* and feasting and drinking, they two divided them all into clans while they were on their way home:

1. The original Hãsdãk' or Nij Hãsdãk'
2. The one who ground down the horn Mạrnḍi
3. The one who killed a sunbird .. Soren Sipahi
4. The one who carried a deer .. .. Hembrom
5. The one who killed an owl .. .. Ṭuḍu
6. The one who killed a kingfisher .. Kisku
7. The one who made a bundle of stale rice .. .. Baske
8. The one who carried an umbrella over his head .. .. Besra

[1] *Liṭa* is the "proper name" of the chief spirit of the tribe, who is also known as *Maraṅ Buru*.

[2] The Santali text of this invocation is given here. It is a good example of a sacrificial prayer:

Johar Gosãẽ, Maraṅ Buru, bapla ṅutumte
Jhardak' tapam dak' lagaogeya bajaogeya.
Tobekhan Gosãẽ ma tobe emam calam kanale
Tobekhan Gosãẽ abaṛte tobaṛte alom koeka ataṅka Gosãẽ.
Lac' hasu bohok' hasu alom sirjauk'a biḍauk'a Gosãẽ.
Ma tobe, Gosãẽ, landae baṛe kathaekin Gosãẽ,
Sukte saõãrte ataṅtale telaetale Gosãẽ,
Teheṅ dole baplayet'kina Gosãẽ.
Aḍharu buḍharukok'makin
Haṛamko buḍhiko makin Gosãẽ.

9. The one who killed a rough-necked iguana .. .. Cõṛẽ
10. The one who killed a dove .. .. Pauriya
11. The one who killed a bushy-haired monkey .. .. Ḍonka or Bhaduli
12. The one who restores us to tribal status .. .. Murmu

After dividing the clans, *Pilcu Haṛam* and *Pilcu Buḍhi* questioned their daughters and their sons thus: 'Who are you?' The daughters said: 'We are grown up, we can carry pots of cold water on our heads.' The sons said: 'We are hard and strong, ploughs made from the *rot*[1] tree and sticks made from the *hesel.*' "[2]

The above narrative is a literal translation of the original. A comparison with other recorded versions shows that many incidents have been omitted, including some that must have been familiar to the narrator. He has made no reference to the story of a great rain of fire in which all except the first pair of human beings perished. The references made to the chief tribal deity of the Santals are almost incidental and do not include the story of how he first introduced himself to *Pilcu Haṛam* and *Pilcu Buḍhi* as their "grandfather" and taught them how to make rice beer, whereupon they became drunk and lost their innocence. The story as here presented does, on the other hand, relate the myth in clear fashion to the clan organization. The name of the Santals' original abode is usually given as Hihiṛi Pipiṛi; Hohelo Popelo may be a local variant. The account given of the early wanderings of the tribe is much abbreviated, but serves as a reminder that they are accustomed to living in and near forests and their ancestors were driven by want from one place to another in what they now consider was a rather futile manner. There have been some attempts to find an historic basis for the names of the localities mentioned in the traditions,[3] but without confirmatory evidence from other sources it has not proved possible to put forward any satisfactory explanation.

The ancient story becomes real for the Santals of today at the point where it deals with the clans. It is worth noticing

[1] A forest tree, *Ougeinia dalbergioides*, Benth. A hard wood.
[2] A forest tree, *Anogeissus latifolia*, Wall.
[3] Cf. P. O. Bodding, *District Gazetteers: Santal Parganas.*

how the number "twelve" recurs in the traditions. Periods of twelve years are mentioned and twelve clans are named. Santal tradition is unanimous in talking of twelve clans, but there is little agreement about the names of the twelve. Santals using the clan suffix Ḍonka are unknown at the present day; local tradition says that they have changed their clan because of the odium attached to the murder of a monkey and the fact that they were reputed by some to sacrifice and eat monkeys. The conjecture of the narrator that the Ḍonka took the name of Bhaduli cannot be accepted. Two families in the area are known to have adopted the name Bhaduli, but they are members of a sub-clan of the Mạrnḍi. One of the Bhaduli could relate little or nothing about the myths of his clan, but he remembered a song that celebrated an old quarrel between the Mạrnḍi and the Kisku in which the former are referred to as Bhaduli and the latter as Koinḍa. The Bhaduli observe the same taboos as the rest of the Mạrnḍi. P. O. Bodding gives the name of the lost clan as Bedea,[1] a title that is not known in the area. The great interest that Santals themselves take in the determination of these matters was well illustrated by a lively correspondence initiated by a number of educated Santals and carried on for some time during the year 1944 in the pages of the weekly paper *Peṛa Hoṛ*.[2]

The clans are exogamous and, with two exceptions, the members of one clan may marry a person belonging to any of the other clans. The first exception to the general rule prohibits a marriage between a Mạrnḍi and a Kisku because of the quarrel in which these two clans were involved. The second prohibits the marriage of a Ṭuḍu and a Besra. The story behind this taboo was thus related by a member of the Ṭuḍu clan: "All twelve kinds of Ṭuḍu were exceedingly fond of dancing and singing, and they used to dance twelve dances in a single night. Well, one day two of the Ṭuḍu made a plan. Across the river from where they lived some girls of the Besra clan were engaged every day in grinding rice, and the youths thought to themselves: 'Tonight we shall get them out to dance the whole night through.' When they reached the river they found that it was in flood, and so they began to wonder how they would be able to get across. They walked along the bank looking out carefully till at last they found a creeping plant that stretched right across the river, its roots being on this side, while it was

[1] *Santali Dictionary*, Vol. IV, p. 596.
[2] Official organ of the Santal Mission of the Northern Churches, Dumka.

held fast in a tree on the farther side. They crossed over by clinging to it, and then they began the dance, which did not finish before cockcrow. Just before they were due to return home someone from the village cut the creeper, but not so that they would notice it. They had their dancing-drums and their kettle-drums slung round their necks, and they were swinging over on their way home when suddenly they fell into the river. Now, the Besra girls were seven in number, and they had placed some fish traps into position farther down the river; as the two youths were being swept away they became caught in the fish traps. They became entangled in the trap that belonged to the family of the youngest of the Besra girls. Her six sisters became very annoyed at this and said: 'No, we shall take them. You are the youngest, and you should not be married while your elder sisters remain unmarried.' When the Ṭuḍu youths heard all this quarrelling they became very annoyed and said: 'From today we shall never marry a Besra girl.' "

Another version of the origin of the clans bears rather obvious traces of the influence of the surrounding culture by dividing them on an occupational basis after the analogy of Hindu castes. According to it, the Murmu became the priests, or Brahmins, of the tribe; a hint of this is found in the list given by Durlob Murmu, who places his own clan twelfth in the list and describes it as the clan of "the one who restores us to tribal status". The Soren were the warriors, or Kshattriyas: hence the addition to their name of the epithet *sipahi*, or "sepoy". The Mạrnḍi were traders, the Kisku were *rajas*, the Ṭuḍu were drummers, and so on. This version, now widely current, is probably of comparatively recent date and may have arisen out of the need to compensate the Santals, or at least certain of the clans, for their low social status in the eyes of their caste Hindu neighbours.

The totemistic basis is very clearly marked, and in certain directions it still exercises a powerful influence on the habits of the Santals. The Hãsdãk' are always named first and they are the original clan. Their name is related to the goose and gander of the myth, from which the first human beings were born, and they do not eat either goose or duck. There can be no doubt in this case that descent from the totem animal is envisaged. On one occasion a member of the Hãsdãk' clan replied in answer to the question why they did not eat goose: "Because they are our brothers." Although presumably all Santals as well as the rest of the human race are also descended from the first pair, the prohibition against eating goose or duck flesh does not apply to the others. Some of the other clan names are either the same as that of the totem or are closely related to it. Mạrnḍi is the name of a weed that is common in the rice fields; Soren is the name of the constellation Pleiades, though there appears to be no knowledge of a myth connecting the two; Ṭuḍu certainly suggests the sound made by drums; Hembrom suggests *hotrin* for deer; Kisku is not unlike *kikir*, a generic name for kingfishers; Baske is one of the words that mean "stale rice", and Murmu suggests *murum*, the buck of the traditions whose flesh the Murmu do not eat. On the other hand, it is not possible at this date to explain all the names by this type of association.

Tradition says that each of the twelve clans, or *pạris*, are divided into twelve sub-clans, or *khũṭ*. The myth about the Ṭuḍu refers to "all twelve kinds of Ṭuḍu". At the present day in the case of most of the clans there are in fact many more than twelve sub-clans. These sub-clans do not affect the rules governing marriage outside the clan. Some of the sub-clan names are found in more than one clan, and while it is unusual for the member of a sub-clan in one clan to marry a member of the corresponding sub-clan in another clan, there is no absolute barrier preventing such marriages. Inquiries made in the Santal Parganas[1] led to the tabulation of two hundred and seventy-seven different sub-clans distributed among the eleven known clans. Many of them are found under more than one clan. All those which are common to more than one clan are found also in the Bankura district, but some of the other names are unknown there, while others that are found in the Bankura district do not seem to appear farther north. Each of the sub-clans possesses a distinctive myth and also customs that differentiate it from the others, while the same is of course true of the clans. These customs affect life at many points. Apart from marriage, the taboos determine in some cases the type of ornaments which may be worn, the type of houses that may be built, and the kinds of food which must not be eaten. They are also linked with the worship of the spirits, for there are special clan and sub-clan sacrifices.

In each clan there is a division that is taken to have been the original sub-clan, the word *Nij* being prefixed to the clan name. Here, for example, is an account of the Nij Mạrnḍi: "They are

[1] J. Gausdal, "The Khũṭ System of the Santals", *Journal of the Bihar and Orissa Research Society*, 1942.

one of the original twelve *khũṭ*. They are not allowed to have spots made on them and they will not be vaccinated, but they may be cicatrized; however, their daughters and sisters are not allowed to be tattooed until after they are married. The unmarried men are not allowed to wear any garment made from jute. They must not plaster their houses with any other than white earth; and they may not draw any pictures on the walls except plantain trees and date palms or figures that look like pictures of temples, drawn with three fingers only. They make their sacrifice at the time of the *Sohrae*; this is performed in the house, and they sacrifice a pig. One year it must be a male uncastrated pig and the next year a female, and if for any reason they cannot get hold of a pig they may sacrifice a black hen. They should sacrifice to their sub-clan spirit in the shelter of a white ant hill,[1] but in these days they bring some earth from the ant hill into the house and sacrifice there."

In a Sarenga schoolboy's essay on the origin of his own clan, he began by relating the creation of mankind and finally continued: "All the Sorens were the soldiers of the Kisku, who were the owners of the village at Campa Gaṛ. The Mạrndi lived at Cirunala, and between the two villages there flowed the Sitanala river. They began to quarrel with each other because the people of the two villages had to use the same river for bathing and for drinking water. Now, since the Soren were the soldiers of the Kisku, they are like the Gurkhas of Nepal. Just as the Gurkhas are fierce and do not fear death, so too the Soren." So is virtue inculcated by fostering pride in the clan. One of the sub-clans of the Soren is the Poita Soren. *Poita* is the word—as pronounced by the Santals—for the sacred thread of the Brahmin. They relate that in the very early days the ancestors of the Soren were celebrating the *Jom Sim* festival and some of the company began to prepare the food and cook it. In imitation of Brahmin cooks they put on sacred threads and served all the people. From that time they became known as Poita Soren. When they sacrifice to their sub-clan spirit they sacrifice to him alone, and the offering has to consist of a male uncastrated pig. The rite is performed at sunrise. They may eat the flesh at any time during that day and the following night, and if they are unable to finish it they must bury it before the following sunrise

[1] For references to the sanctity of white ant hills see *Religion and Folklore of Northern India*, by W. Crooke, C.I.E., p. 380. The belief is widespread in India. "From early times the earth from an ant hill has been regarded as specially pure, representing 'the savour of the earth', and it was, and is, used in building altars."

in the dung heap. Another Soren sub-clan is known briefly as the Sidup' Soren, and the name is connected with a custom followed when they are making their sub-clan sacrifice. The man squats on the ground in the courtyard of the house holding before him a sheaf of paddy. Meanwhile his wife squats nearby with her back to her husband. He passes the sheaf over his head to his wife, who receives it with her hands lifted above her head and takes it into the house. She may not perform this service if she has formerly been the wife of another man and is either a widow or has been divorced. The women of this sub-clan cannot wear a *campa*[1] flower in their hair.

There are two stories current concerning the origin of the Cilbinda Hãsdãk', or the Hãsdãk' who killed a kite. One of them states: "In the days of the early ancestors many very wonderful things used to happen. At that time kites were causing a great deal of trouble throughout the countryside. Every day they used to snatch away not only men's chickens but also the grown fowl, and in addition they used to take kids, young pigs and children. In this way they were the cause of much sorrow to men. Seeing this state of affairs, one of the Hãsdãk' brothers who was working out in the fields hid behind his clod-crusher and shot a kite through the hole in the middle, and from that time his family got the name." An even more suggestive version is more widely known. An old man belonging to this sub-clan told the story thus: "Formerly our ancestors fell into great difficulties. They were engaged in transplanting rice seedlings and had plucked them from the seedling beds, but there was no rain and so they could not proceed with the transplanting. Now, there was a kite perched in a tree adjoining the field. They shot it, and the blood moistened the land so that they were able to carry on with their work."

The claim to belong to the original sub-clan is made by many people belonging to various other divisions. Binu of Tantidanga made this claim for the sub-clan to which he belonged. He was a Jihu Hãsdãk' and he used to say: "They were the first of the lot." The name is derived from the fact that while their ancestors were hunting in the Khandarae forest they ate the flesh of the *jihu*[2] bird. Since that time they will never eat it, nor will they touch anything that is deep blue in colour, lest people say that

[1] *Ochna squarrosa*, L.

[2] There are two kinds of birds so named. The *Bhoṇḍa jihu* is the Bengal Babbler, *Malacoercus terricolor*, and the *Jạnum jihu* is the green Babbler, *Chaltorius striatus*.

they are touching the blue eggs of the *jihu* bird. The Hãsdãk' do not even touch a goose, and they will not take water from a tank in which geese or ducks are swimming at the time. Binu used to say that he had to perform four different sub-clan sacrifices. To two of the spirits pigs were sacrificed in the cowshed at the time of the *Sohrae*, to another spirit they sacrificed a goat in the house at the end of the *Sohrae*, and to the fourth they sacrificed a ram on the open land outside the village at the time of the Spring festival. The Kaṛwar Hãsdãk' tell the story of how long ago their ancestors were celebrating the *Jom Sim* festival and all the Hãsdãk' were present. They had performed the sacrifices and everyone had been served with rice and meat, but some of the younger folk present felt that they had not been given enough to eat, so they killed a buffalo and served that as well. The family of the one who slew the buffalo, or *kaḍa*, became known as Kaṛwar Hãsdãk'. They sacrifice a pig, a white hen and a brown hen at the time of the *Sohrae*; the rite is performed inside the house at sunset, and they must finish eating the flesh during the night, burying whatever is left over in the dung heap. The Hatibaṛi[1] Hãsdãk' sacrifice either a white hen or a ram to their sub-clan spirit. This should be done out in the open beside a white ant hill, but, like some others, they now bring a piece of earth from the ant hill into their cowshed. Like the Nij Mạrnḍi, of whom this is also true, they may not be vaccinated, but their womenfolk may be tattooed.

The Jihu Hãsdãk' are not allowed to brand their cattle. There seems little reason to doubt the fact that most of the clans use distinctive marks in branding their cattle. Bodding has affirmed of the *ḍhera dag*, or cross, that although it is used as a mark of ownership of cattle "it is not restricted to any sept or sub-sept".[2] (The word "clan" has been adopted in this book in preference to "sept".) In the Bankura district, however, many of the branding marks are definitely associated with the clans, and the marks correspond to those recorded by Charulal Mukherjea in Mayurbhanj.[3] The marks printed on the opposite page have been noticed in Bankura.

The Guạ or Betel nut Hembrom constitute one of the most numerous of the Hembrom sub-clans. Of them it is said that "a few days after the ancestors had been divided into clans, one of the Hembrom was born at the foot of a betel nut tree. When he

[1] Literally "elephant house", but the name may refer to a locality.
[2] *Santali Dictionary*, Vol. II, p. 272.
[3] Charulal Mukherjea, *The Santals*, p. 77.

grew to manhood he became a very important person and his sons were known as Guạ Hembrom. From that time they gave up the chewing of the betel nut. The women may wear any kind of *saṛi* and they may wear shell bracelets. They do not eat eels. It is said that their ancestors were great traders, and once upon a time when they were going on a trading expedition they were halted by a flooded river. At that an eel ferried them over the river on his back, and since then the Guạ Hembrom will not eat eels. They sacrifice pigs at the *Sohrae,* also one white and one brown hen." Another member of this sub-clan was able to throw further light on the origin of the name: "We are Guạ Hembrom, and this is how we got our name. During the first wanderings, one day while the ancestors were out in the forest a child was born at the roadside. They wondered what they could find to tie

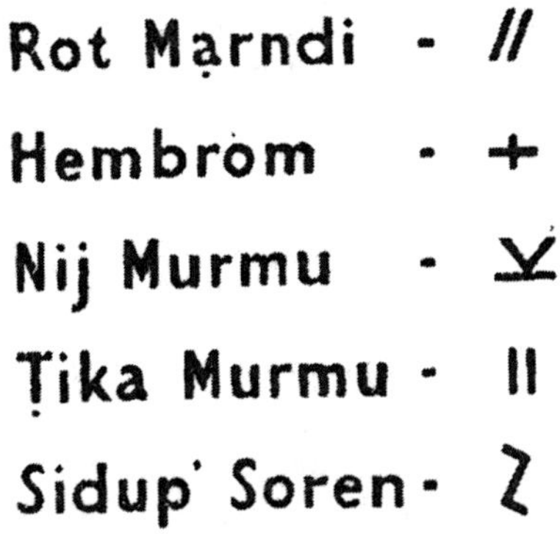

round the waist of the new-born child in place of the string. It was growing dark, so they quickly cut down the stem of a creeper, not knowing what it was, and bound it round his waist. Next morning they say that there was a betel nut on the end of the stem, and so the Guạ Hembrom began." The Nij Hembrom, like others already noted, perform their sub-clan sacrifices in the cowshed at the time of the *Sohrae,* with a piece of earth from a white-ant hill for the altar. It is set up in one of the corners. Another of their sacrifices is performed in the same month and has certain unusual features. No preparations may be made until after the sun has set and all the participants have already taken their usual evening meal, including the one who will perform the sacrifice. The rite is performed outside the village on a site that has been smoothed and plastered with cowdung. The person officiating draws a circle on the site with a paste made from flour and water. In it he first offers a red hen and then a ram. The blood is placed in a vessel and fixed on the ground, surrounded with small stones. Only men may eat the meat of the animals sacrificed. The girls of this sub-clan are not allowed to wear Bengali-style *saris* or shell bracelets at the time of their marriage, though they may do so after they are married. When the men of this sub-clan are bringing brides to their home they present them with a *hasli*, the neck ring, made of brass.

A whole range of the sub-clans is known as *Sada*, or "white". They may represent a reforming element, for their characteristic is a revolt against the use of red vermilion paint. When the first ancestors of the Sada Hembrom, so it is said, were going to perform a sacrifice they thought that they had with them all that they needed, but when they reached the spot where the sacrifice was to take place it was discovered that they had left behind their supply of *sindur*, the vermilion-coloured earth that plays a large part in the Santal cult. When they saw this they completed the sacrifice without the *sindur*, and since then their descendants have been known as Sada Hembrom and they have continued to observe the custom so carelessly begun! In other ways, too, they have abjured the use of vermilion. They make no use of it in the marriage ceremonial, though once their daughters are married and have become members of other clans they may put vermilion in the parting of their hair. The cloth which is a part of the presents given at the time of marriages must be white without any border, and their womenfolk are limited to plain cloth throughout life. The same pattern of behaviour applies to all the Sada sub-clans. The Sada Hãsdãk', along with some other sub-clans, when they perform their sub-clan sacrifices, first of all model a scorpion out of paste made from flour and water and offer it before going on to offer a hen, then a pig, and lastly a goat. This particular sub-clan has to eat all the flesh of the animals sacrificed and they are not allowed to throw any part of it away.

Some of the Murmu sub-clans are restricted in the type of dwelling-house that they may build. The majority of Santal house roofs are constructed on what is known in Bengal as the "charchala" plan. This consists of a thatch that slopes up from each of the four walls of the house. The main beam is set well above the four walls, being smaller than the length of the house, with four corner beams fixed two at each end of the main beam and going down to the four corners of the house to form the first stage of the framework on which the thatch rests. Most of the Murmu, however, have to build up the two end walls so that the centre forms the apex of a triangle. The main beam rests on these walls with rafters sloping from it down to the other two walls. The resulting roof has only two thatches, sloping to the front and the back of the house respectively. The Gar or Fort Murmu are able to provide but little information about their origin, but they maintain their distinctive tradition in the matter of the sub-clan sacrifice. It is performed during the month October-November out in one of their own rice fields. The one sacrificing has to observe the customary abstinence of priests during the previous night, and the sacrifice takes place just after the sun has risen in the morning. A circle of flour paste is made on a spot levelled and cleaned for the purpose, and a larger circle of white stones is constructed round it. All who are going to partake of the flesh have to remain within this enclosure. First of all they sacrifice a black hen, which can be eaten by men only. Next they sacrifice a pig, the flesh of which may be eaten by the women as well. After this they sacrifice a white hen and finally a brown hen, and again it is only the men who may partake of these. The gathering and the attendant feasting last through the whole day, and they return to their houses at nightfall, leaving no food. They believe that some misfortune will fall on them if they have not finished eating while daylight lasts.

There is a sub-clan of the Ṭuḍu known as the Kāṛã or Blind Ṭuḍu which is accounted for in the following way: "The first Kāṛã Ṭuḍu placed a torn cloth behind the fireplace in his house. In the evening when his wife went to cook she found the cloth there and cooked the supper herbs wrapped up in it. Then the man who had put the cloth down came to look for it, and not seeing it behind the fireplace he asked his wife if she had seen it. 'Yes,' she replied, 'it must be the one in which I wrapped the supper herbs.' They raked out the fire and the ashes and saw that she had in fact burnt that cloth."

Many of the points that have been raised in this chapter cannot be understood apart from matters that are dealt with in subsequent chapters. The stories have been gathered together in this way in order to bring out the fact that in the clan system of the Santals and in the myths that form its background there is a key to the understanding of nearly everything that is distinctive in their way of life. The clan organization regulates their behaviour within the tribe and their dealings with the spirits. They accept its rule without question, and so long as they live in closely knit village communities this system, with its manifold implications, will continue to control their lives.

CHAPTER 7

THE WORLD INVISIBLE—(1)

THE Santal village is organized to secure the greatest possible degree of co-operation not only in temporal affairs but also in dealing with the spirit world. The relationship between Santal society and some part of the universe inhabited by spirits is very close, and it is maintained by the society acting through its representatives. One of the most important officials in the village is the *naeke*, or village priest, whose business it is to maintain right relationships with the tribal spirits. A priest who was once asked whether he really believed in his work replied without any hesitation: "If I did not do my work the whole village would become sick!" His answer provides in effect a true summary of the Santal conception of the priest's work. He is a man apart, and he is conscious of his separation from his fellows. Alone of all the village officials he is not appointed by his fellow villagers, but by the *boṅgas*, the spirits that are worshipped. The investing of a new priest with the necessary authority occurs during the ceremonies following the death of his predecessor. The spirits take possession of the designated individual and so establish the identity of the new priest beyond any possibility of doubt. The marks of possession, the result of the process known to the Santals as *rum*, are quite familiar. *Rum* is the regular method by which the spirits reveal their wishes, convey comfort or warning, and assure the living of their fellowship with the spirits of the tribe and with their ancestors. The behaviour of a person who is possessed is similar to that of one who has suffered a sudden onslaught of insanity, and he speaks in the character of the spirit who has for the time being taken possession of his personality.

In spite of the supernatural origin of the priestly office, one finds that the spirits in making an appointment have been actuated largely by common-sense considerations. They usually ensure that the eldest son of the deceased priest assumes his father's functions, or, failing him, perhaps they will appoint a brother. One may discern two reasons why the succession is secured in this manner. In the first place, a son will have had special opportunities of watching his father at work, and having been brought up in the right atmosphere he is already familiar with the rules and customs that govern the office. Secondly, when the original distribution of lands was made in the new village, the first *naeke*, in common with the other officials, received a portion of land in recognition of his appointment, and land cannot easily pass out of the possession of a particular clan. The office therefore tends to remain in the family, for fresh lands are not obtainable after one or two generations have passed away.

The villagers recognize the priest's office, as they do those of the other dignitaries, by payment in return for services rendered. When one of the villagers is fined by the council, the priest receives his own share of the total sum. When game is killed in the hunt, the priest's share consists of a strip of flesh cut from the animal's backbone; it is formed into the shape of a cooking-place before it is handed over to him. He receives the heads of all the animals that are sacrificed by him on behalf of his fellow villagers. His duty is to make the offerings to the tribal spirits on behalf of the whole village at the time of the festivals. In order to prepare himself he has to separate himself from his fellows. Santals ordinarily sleep on string beds, but on the night before a sacrifice the priest sleeps on the floor, and he must abstain from sexual intercourse. On the morrow he has to fast until his work is done.

In addition to the priest, there is in every village a co-priest with special functions. This official is known as the *kuḍam naeke*. The word *kuḍam* refers to the area behind the dwelling-house. During village festivals, while the priest is making the main offerings, the *kuḍam naeke* sacrifices to the *pargana boṅga*, the spirit who is regarded as the guardian or perhaps as the personification of the wider territorial unit into which groups of Santal villages are formed. It may be that this particular spirit needs the services of the co-priest because the *pargana boṅga* was resident in the area before the villagers settled within its borders, while they brought the other spirits with them. The other function fulfilled by the *kuḍam naeke* reveals ideas which comprise perhaps a separate strata in the complex structure of Santal religion. During the festivals he offers drops of blood, which he produces by pricking his own arm with a thorn, to the boundary spirits, or the spirits of the outskirts of the forests. The name of this blood offering is *bul mayam*, *mayam* being the ordinary word for blood. The meaning of the term *bul* in this context is obscure, and Santals are unable to offer any explanation. *Bul* is a word connoting drunkenness; it can also be used as an adjective to describe an earthen pot that has become saturated with water, and it may refer to the saturation of the rice offering with the blood. In some incantations the phrase is coupled with one that refers to menstrual blood. The same practice of making an offering of his own blood is followed by the magician[1] when he is attempting to cure sickness. While the function of the priest is to deal with the tribal spirits, it would seem that his co-priest has to propitiate relatively unknown and fearful spirits; one might almost describe him as a kind of "minister for foreign affairs" in relation to the spirit world.

Santal worship centres round its sacred places, the most prominent of which is the *jaher*, the sacred grove usually to the west of the village. It consists of a number of tall, slim *sarjom* trees with perhaps one or two trees of other varieties, the whole having been left standing since the village was first founded. The surrounding forests have been cut down to form land for cultivation and for the homesteads, so the grove stands out from the landscape. Apart from festival occasions there is usually little to show the sacredness of the place, but the practice varies greatly from village to village. Two of the tallest trees standing side by side are thought to be the abodes of *Maraṅ Buru*, the national spirit of the Santals, and of his female consort *Jaher Buḍhi*, the Old Lady of the Sacred Grove. At the side of the former tree one sometimes discerns the blackened stones of the fireplace at which the village priest cooks—apart from the rest of the village—his share of the offerings. Other relics of festivals may be found, such as an ear of paddy still attached to its stalk, tied round one of the trees and left there since the time of the offering of first-fruits. Sometimes there are semi-permanent posts in the ground near the more sacred trees, two in front of the trees and two at the back, with cross-pieces joining them to form the framework on which a temporary thatch is placed during the festivals over the place where the sacrifices are performed. One of the trees is the abode of the "Five and Six", and near it a post standing in the ground represents the place of one *Laga Ṭhạkur*, who acts as their watchman. Removed to a little distance is the place where the food of the villagers is cooked: the meals eaten here are communal. There are other trees at which the *kudạm naeke* makes his blood offering to the boundary spirits, and these are indicated during the festivals by means of a piece of string. In some villages one finds indications of places at the edge of the grove at which one or other of the sub-clans performs its sacrifices. In some groves the space at the foot of the principal trees is tended carefully as befits a shrine. The ground is cleared and plastered regularly with cowdung and water, a cactus hedge is planted to

[1] The *ojha*. See Chapter 8, pp. 94 ff.

keep away marauding cattle and goats, and large earthen effigies of elephants and horses are set in position as worthy mounts for the spirits. The grove is not usually much more than a hundred yards away from the westernmost house in the village, but sometimes one finds that the dwellings of the people have been moved owing to sickness or some other reason and the grove remains in its original site. The determination of the site of the grove is an important element in founding a new village. Naturally there are few opportunities for observing the process at the present time, but the tradition is kept alive among the Santals, who tell that the choice of the site is made by the spirits themselves. They do so by taking possession of certain of the villagers and expressing their wishes through them. These men take stones and place them at the foot of three *sarjom* trees, which should be in a row, two for *Maraṅ Buru* and *Jaher Buḍhi* close together, and the third for the "Five and Six". Other trees are then set apart for a second female spirit known as *Gõsãẽ Era*, and also for the *pargana boṅga* and the boundary spirits.

Maraṅ Buru is the spirit who possesses the most clearly defined individuality. The name means "Great Mountain", but it is interesting to note that the word *buru* means not only a mountain but is also used for spirits in general, especially when it is coupled with the more usual *boṅga*. The use of *buru* combined with *boṅga* suggests that *buru* originally meant "mountain", that it was then used for "mountain spirit" and then as a synonym for *boṅga*. Another name for *Maraṅ Buru* is *Liṭạ*, which is a proper name and does not appear to refer to any attributes. The name *Liṭạ* is frequently used in stories and also in conversation, but it is not used in invocations. The Santal name for a rainbow is the "bow of *Liṭạ*". *Maraṅ Buru* is invoked on all occasions when offerings are made, and he is a complete sharer in all the fortunes of the tribe, good and evil. He seems to be regarded as a kindly but capricious old gentleman. The references to him in the mythology clearly indicate his dominant position. He appeared on the scene at a very early stage in the life of the first pair. He found them living in a state of innocence and told them that they had not yet learnt to taste the joys of life. After introducing himself to them as their grandfather and so establishing an intimate relationship between himself and them, he taught them how to brew beer and left them for a few days. When he returned he chuckled to see the change in their appearance, for during his absence they had become drunken.

In that condition they had for the first time experienced sexual intercourse and, realizing their nakedness, they had clothed themselves. He taught them that they must always offer beer to him when they invoked his name.

The Old Lady of the Sacred Grove, *Jaher Buḍhi*, is by contrast a shadowy person. Bodding reports[1] that her name is said to be *Ram sạlgi*, but except for the fact that offerings are made to her along with those made to *Marañ Buru* at festivals, little is known about her. The same may be said of the "Five and Six", who are thought of as a family of five brothers and one sister. It is only to the "Five" that offerings are made, and hence they are also frequently referred to as the "Five." One sacrifice suffices for them all. The "Five" are greatly feared because they are likely to cause some swift calamity when they are displeased.

The *Mạñjhi than*, the shrine of the spirits of the departed headmen, is the second of the sacred places in which the cult of the tribe is localized. The site is supposed to be fixed in much the same manner as that of the sacred grove. Local legends grow up round these shrines, and they exhibit many variations. Often they are situated somewhere near the centre of the village, to one side of the main street. In some instances the shrine consists of a raised mud platform over which there is a well-kept thatched roof supported on four corner posts and a central upright post about five feet high. In other cases it consists of a cleared space at the foot of a tree, and the roof of thatch is erected only at the times when sacrifices are offered. In some parts each departed headman is commemorated by a small stone which is placed in the shrine at the time of his death ceremonies, but in this area it is not possible to reckon the number of generations since the foundation of a village by the presence or absence of stones. Many of the villages have a history which extends back over more than six generations, and it appears that the stones which may have been placed in the past do not retain their sacredness over so long a period, and they have been removed. At the present time the immediate ancestors and also the original founder, revered as *Mạñjhi haṛam*, are honoured by setting up the clay effigies of elephants or horses in their names. Even the site may be shifted under the influence of new ideas. Thus in the purely Santal village of Jameḍia there is a shrine in the village street not far from the headman's house which has been in its present position for about fifteen years. The villagers referred to it as the *Mạñjhi*

[1] Bodding, *Santali Dictionary*, Vol. III, p. 228.

jaher rather than as the *Maṅjhi than.* Until recently the shrine had been in another place beyond the present limits of the dwellings, and the villagers had found such a site very inconvenient. They were encouraged to change the site by the fact that in the street there grew an *arjun* tree, one of the sacred trees of Hinduism, and they felt they should do something to signalize its presence in the village. On a cleared space at the base of the tree there were two miniature wooden seats which were used by the spirits when they came, and there were also a clay horse and an elephant which had been in position there since the establishment of the shrine. The duty of tending these shrines, of sweeping the floor and plastering it with cowdung, falls upon an unmarried girl from the headman's house. The headman officiates as the priest at this shrine, presenting the offerings to his ancestors as the representative not only of the family but also of the living members of the village community. Offerings are made during the *Mokor*, the festival that closes the month of *Pus* in mid-January, and also during the Spring and Harvest festival seasons. Animals are sacrificed, but there is a significant difference in the methods of killing the animals offered in the sacred grove to the tribal spirits and those offered to the spirits of the ancestors. In the case of the former the animal is beheaded, but in the latter the animal is struck by a heavy implement on the back of the head so that the blood is not poured out. It does not seem possible to obtain any explanation of this from a Santal, apart from the all-embracing statement that "it is the custom". There is here another indication of the complexity of Santal religion; it would be difficult to fit all the facts into a scheme that seeks to find the origin of sacrifice in a single or simple cause.

The spirit world is not only the concern of the whole community or of each village but also of each family, a fact that finds embodiment in the cult surrounding the third sacred place of the Santals. This is a sacred enclosure inside each dwelling-house known as the *bhiṭar*, an Indo-Aryan word that means "within". This is formed by constructing a wall across the breadth of the main dwelling-house and so dividing the interior into two rooms with a mud partition between. The *bhiṭar* is the smaller of the two. The wall may be carried as high as the average height of a man, but often it is only about four feet high. The opening through which members of the family may pass from one room to the other is left vacant without a door. There are no sacred emblems kept in the *bhiṭar*, and in fact it is used extensively as a storeroom, particularly for stacking the bundles of reserve rice. Any man may pass through this opening, but no woman may do so unless she belongs to the family living there. The daughters of the house are debarred from going into the *bhiṭar* after they have married. After marriage a woman belongs to her husband's family, and this prohibition is one of several that are enforced with a view to ensuring that she shall not bring calamity on her husband's house by continuing to have dealings with the spirits of her father's home. She has to remove herself from their influence. Within the *bhiṭar* dwells the house spirit, and it is also visited by the ancestors of the family. There offerings of food and beer are made to the immediate ancestors. In certain instances sub-clan sacrifices are made in this inner room. The names of the spirits to whom the sub-clan sacrifices are made are kept secret. The knowledge of these names is handed down within each family from the father to the eldest son or other heir, and under no circumstances should it be imparted to others. An instance was reported of a man who was in deep distress because his father had died without his having had an opportunity of learning the name of the *abge*, as this spirit is called. He hoped to learn the name from one of his father's brothers, but this person also died before he could pass on the information. Shortly afterwards his dead uncle appeared to him in a dream and revealed the name, and he confirmed the correctness of the information by visiting yet another uncle who knew the secret. This story shows that the rules of silence are not too strictly observed within the family circle. Women are not allowed to learn the name, and in most cases they are excluded from participating in the sacrificial meal. The same prohibition applies to sons-in-law, though one of the Soren sub-clans is allowed to leave a portion of the food from the meal for their sons-in-law. When they summon them to eat, however, they address them as they would the household dogs, which emphasizes their separation from the family and from the sub-clan.

Some features of the Santal cult, as well as an indication of the ways in which it may develop, can be illustrated by a description of the shrine that stands on the outskirts of the village of Sarenga. This village was at first a Santal settlement, but it is now a place of nearly two thousand inhabitants, most of whom are Bengali Hindus. The present-day Santal inhabitants number barely one hundred, but amongst them are some who claim descent from the founders of the village, who lived, so they say, nine generations ago. One of the first settlers was one Lokhon Mạṅjhi. Just before he died he had been paying a visit to the *boṅga than*, probably the sacred grove of that day. It occupied a site that is now taken by the landlord's rent-collecting office and has quite disappeared. He returned home, sat down on his string bed to have a smoke, then suddenly fell over and died. Almost immediately, and before the news of Lokhon's death had passed through the village, a young man in the courtyard of a house belonging to Lokhon's paternal aunt became possessed. He announced to the assembled company that he was Lokhon and that they must make a sacred place for him. They chose an old banyan tree to the north of the village. This tree has long since disappeared, but its place has been taken by an *atnak'* tree, which serves equally well. The fact that the village has become largely non-Santal means that the sanctity of this particular shrine is recognized by people belonging to many different castes, and its reputation has grown with the years. All the offerings there are made by the Santal priest in the village, a man who is descended from Lokhon. He is also the local Santal headman and combines the two offices in one person; such an arrangement is not unique and seems to have been adopted often in places where the Santals are living surrounded by other communities. He and his predecessors have adapted themselves to the new situation, and so this shrine, now utilized by many non-Santals, is still served by a Santal priest. Every market day people from the surrounding villages come to offer sacrifices, to ask a boon, or to leave their thank-offerings of money for blessings that have been granted. Some of the more unscrupulous of the local inhabitants defy the spirits by hanging around and picking up the coins left by the devout.

At the base of the tree is the shrine, formed by a raised earthen mound on which there are many burnt clay effigies of horses and elephants. In front of the mound a narrow path has been cleared for about eight feet, so that the tree is approached from the west, the direction in which all the effigies are facing. This path has been cleared through a jumbled heap of innumerable small clay animal effigies that have been left at the shrine by devotees in the past in the performance of their vows. Here there were many opportunities for watching the priest at work, and the chief impression that stands out is the dignity and reverence with which he performed his tasks. On a particular Thursday in 1941 he first of all cleared a small space at the base of the earthen mound and smeared it with his mixture of cowdung and water. He then took some vermilion paint from a leaf and mixed it with mustard oil in a small brass cup that he had brought for the purpose. This mixture he proceeded to smear on the foreheads of the larger animal effigies, and in doing so he used only the middle finger of his right hand. He then sprinkled some water over the effigies, and followed this by sprinkling some spice, of a variety known as *mithu*.[1] Up to this point all his actions had been performed in complete silence, and he was being watched intently by a small group of people who were waiting to make their offerings. He used the utmost deliberation and completed each part of the proceeding with great reverence. He next took up in his right hand a twig of the *sinjo*[2] tree and passed it in an anti-clockwise direction over the space that had been smeared with cowdung and laid it at the foot of the mound. Then he did an obeisance, bringing his right hand up to his forehead with the fingers lightly clenched, while the fingers of his left hand rested against his right forearm, the customary Santal salutation by an adult to his respected seniors. The process was repeated three times with three separate twigs, and as each twig was moved around he muttered his prayer. When it was over he told me that one had been for *Cando*, one for *Marañ Buru*, and one for Lokhon Mạñjhi.

All was then ready for the offerings, of which on that particular day there were three. The first was a pigeon that had been brought by the mother of a sick child. He accepted it from the mother, taking hold of it by his right hand and taking care—he was squatting on the ground—not to turn his back on the shrine. He smeared the head of the pigeon with vermilion and oil, sprinkled it with some of the *mithu*, and then held it to feed on a little parched rice that he had placed on a leaf on the smeared space. He then handed the pigeon back to the woman who had brought it. The same process was repeated with a black hen and a small black goat that belonged to others who had been waiting. As each of them took back the dedicated animals they paid a small money fee to the priest, this varying from one to four pice. He then placed his sacrificial axe on the ground to his left with the sharp edge uppermost. This axe, known as the *ṭangi*, has a curved blade. He took hold of the pigeon once more and severed its head by passing it swiftly

[1] *Trigonalla' Feonum-graecum*, Willd.

[2] The Bengali *Bel*, Aegle Marmelos, *Correa*.

across the axe edge, then held it so that the blood should pour on to the parched rice, after which he flung away the body of the pigeon with his left hand and placed the severed head with the parched rice. The hen was sacrificed in exactly the same way. He then rose to his feet for the sacrifice of the goat. This was of necessity a more elaborate proceeding. A little way off from the shrine, to the south-west, there stood a "killing-post" with a cleft at its upper end. The goat's neck was forced into this cleft, and it was secured with rope. Its owner held the goat firmly, clasping its front legs and securing them by drawing them up and backward over the goat's back, and the priest severed the head with one quick stroke of the axe. Immediately and with great speed he took hold of both the head and the body, so that the blood might drop on to the parched rice. This completed the offerings for the day, and he gathered up the heads of the animals and his other possessions and took them away in a small basket.

This Sarenga shrine affords a good example of the way in which Hinduism can take over the customs and use the beliefs of those who are not, strictly speaking, within the fold, but in spite of the eclecticism here apparent there is a point beyond which the Santals of the village will not go in accommodating themselves to Hindu society. The *Mokor* festival at the end of *Pus* is celebrated by all the lower Hindu castes of the area as well as by the Santals, and at Sarenga it is accompanied by a gathering near this shrine, when many different people, including the Santals, take part in the stick dancing. On the other hand, in 1930 a proposal made by the local Hindus of influence roused great indignation and had to be abandoned. A Santal couple from the village who had previously been baptized were persuaded, as a result of a mission by an agent of the Arya Samaj, to renounce the Christian faith. It was proposed that they should undergo the *suddhi*, or purification ceremony, at the hands of the Arya missionary at Lokhon Mạṅjhi's shrine. The Santals immediately announced that they would not recognize the validity of any such ceremony and that if it took place at their shrine they would cut down the tree and desecrate the shrine with their own hands. Many beliefs have grown up around the place. Binu of Tantidanga used to say that there were certainly times when the animals moved; he himself had twice seen them do so at the time of the *Pus* festival. He used to relate the local legend of how when Europeans had first tried to live at Sarenga they found it impossible to build a house. They were indigo planters, whose compound lay to the south of the shrine. Every time they tried to build the walls would crack, so in the end they offered a libation of their spirits to Lokhon Mạñjhi and all was well. In recent times a Bengali Christian has built himself a house between the old indigo compound, now the mission compound, and the shrine without so far having suffered any dire consequences, but Binu would stoutly affirm that he makes offering to Lokhon in secret!

The main intention of the Santal cult of sacrifice is to ensure the stability of the society and the wellbeing of its members. The usual burden of the prayers and invocations, the *bakheṛ*, is to threaten or cajole the spirits so that sickness may be kept away from the village and that the rains may not fail. The example of a prayer that has been quoted[1] throws light on the attitude of the worshipper and the language that he uses. The prayer is the accompaniment of certain material offerings, and a strong hope is expressed that *Marañ Buru* will find the gifts adequate; there is, in fact, more than a suggestion that he ought to find them sufficient and do his duty in return. While material benefits are mainly sought,[2] this particular example reveals that Santal worshippers do sometimes look beyond the needs of the moment, for it is a prayer for a blessing of long life and happiness to be bestowed on a newly married couple. The language of the prayers is rhythmical; doublet words with rhyming endings and frequent repetition convey to the ear an effect similar to that given by rhymed verse. Often the prayers are spoken in colloquial Bengali, though the language in this case is Santali. The words themselves are not conceived of as "magical" in the sense that any alteration in their form or the omission of particular words would nullify the efficacy of the formula. There is obviously an element of magic in the ritual employed in sacrificing, but the prayers are uttered as accompaniment to the actions in order to draw the attention of the spirits to the latter. Most often the one who is uttering the prayer uses a loud and threatening tone of voice.

There is no individual approach to the *bongas*. Fellowship with them is maintained through sacrifices that are offered on

[1] See p. 67 above.

[2] Cf. E. O. James, *Comparative Religion*, 1938, p. 278: "In a primitive agricultural community requests for ethical and moral virtues could hardly be expected, since, as Cicero remarks, 'men call Jupiter greatest and best because he makes us not just or temperate or wise, but sound and healthy and rich and wealthy'." The citation is from *De Nat. Deorum*, III, 36, 87.

behalf of a particular social unit, which is sometimes the whole village and sometimes as small as the family. Positively the goodwill of the *boṅgas* is retained by the observance of the due sacrifices, negatively by the observance of taboo rules. Many of the taboos operative in the daily life of the Santals can be directly traced to the necessity for safeguarding the interests of the *boṅgas*. The belief in the dangerous potentiality of women is reflected in the fact that all sacrifices are taboo for women in one sense or another. The fact that they may not eat the flesh of animals sacrificed to the *abge* has already been noted; they may not eat the flesh of any part of an animal sacrificed to *Maraṅ Buru*, nor the head of any animal killed in a sacrifice at all. Although they may help in the preparations for sacrifices performed in the house, they are kept away from participation in the sacred grove. No woman may climb any of the trees in the grove, nor may she be present when the sacrifices are made, nor eat of the flesh of any animal there offered. The one exception to this rule is that a portion of the flesh of sacrificed animals is reserved for the wife of the priest. Other taboos are related only indirectly to the belief in spirits. The code of behaviour between relatives is sanctioned by a belief that any infringement of its provisions will result in retaliation by the spirits, who cause such diseases as leprosy, or who will inflict dire punishment after death and make it impossible for funeral ceremonies to be duly carried out. Sometimes the retaliation acts swiftly, as in the case related by a Santal concerning an uncle. This relative was on a journey away from home. He stopped at a certain village to obtain a drink of beer, and in his haste, being exceedingly thirsty at the time, he omitted first of all to spill a few drops as a libation to *Maraṅ Buru* and his ancestors. This forgetfulness of a universal obligation was met apparently by almost immediate retribution. Soon after he had resumed his journey the man fell down—dead.

The *boṅgas* can be distinguished both from the Supreme Being and from various other classes of spirits by the fact that there is between them and the Santals some degree of personal relationship. Many of the *boṅgas* do not seem to have any very marked personal characteristics, but the Santal knows that in the normal course of events he will himself become a *boṅga* and will be dependent then for his happiness on those who come after him. Unless he dies in certain specified ways, once his funeral rites have been completed he will take his place among the ancestors, and his place in the hierarchy of the spirit world depends very much on his social status and correct behaviour in this one. The personality of *Marañ Buru* overshadows that of the Supreme Being in the consciousness of the Santals. The latter is universally acknowledged as the Creator, but he is far removed. *Marañ Buru* is the one who has made them what they are today. In the folk-tales there are frequent references to the Supreme Being in his character as the merciful provider, but these are stories of what happened "a long time ago". One example, in which the Supreme Being came and worked with the two sons of a widow and so altered their fortunes, has been translated above.[1] In another story which tells of a child who was left an orphan, he came down in the form of a man in order to comfort the child.[2] Sometimes in folk-tales extraordinary events are attributed to the action of the Supreme Being, as in a story that relates how a woman gave birth to a mongoose and one of her fellow villagers said: "This is indeed wonderful, that God should cause an animal to be born in the womb of a woman."[3]

Some of the names of the Supreme Being reveal the influence of the surrounding culture and reflect certain elements in Santal belief. The word *Ṭhạkur* in Bengali, meaning "one who is worthy of worship", is applied indifferently to a god, an image, a Brahmin caste and any Brahmin cook. Santals sometimes apply it to spirits in general, but they usually reserve it as a term for the Creator. It is so used in a saying that is current in the area which explains why the Santals may not celebrate their Spring festival until after the corresponding Hindu festival, the Dol Jatra or Holi Puja, has been held. If the Santals do not wait till the Hindu festival is over, they say that *Ṭhạkur* will be offered what has been left over from the offerings to the *boṅgas*. Here *Ṭhạkur* is undoubtedly regarded as the Lord of the *boṅgas* and is incidentally identified with Sri Krishna, in whose honour the Dol Jatra is celebrated. In some parts the name *Ṭhạkur Jiu* is used, *jiu* connoting "spirit" in the sense of the life principle. The word *jiu* is uncommon, the usual form of the term being *jivi*, but it is used as a suffix in the word *mae-jiu*, literally "mother spirit", which is the common word for a woman. *Ṭhạkur Jiu*, which should perhaps have been printed as one word, is the term used in the printed account of the Traditions, and as these were first published in 1887, its subsequent currency may be due in some measure to that fact.

[1] See Chapter 5, p. 53.

[2] Bodding, *Santal Folk-Tales*, Vol. III, p. 73. Finding out why the child wept, he caused the child's mother to appear to him, but first told him not to weep or he would die.

[3] Bodding, *op. cit.*, Vol. III, p. 80.

The most usual term for "God" is *Cando* or *Cando boṅga*, and this reveals a connection between God and the sun. *Cando*, which means the Creator, also means the sun and "a month". When used in conjunction with *siṅ*, meaning either "day" or "sun", *siṅ cando* means simply the sun; with the word *ṅinda*, "night", it means the moon. Occasionally the Santals talk of *Siṅ boṅga* as synonymous with *Cando boṅga*. This association of ideas—it would be unwise to regard it as an identification—is shown in the practice adopted when an oath is taken. *Cando* is called on as a witness, and at the same time the man taking the oath raises his eyes to the sun. Again, when a Santal is being reinstated into the tribe, he is made to stand at the entrance to the village with a brass vessel full of water held up in his hands. The elders of the village approach him, whereupon he first performs a low obeisance in the direction of the sun, after which he speaks to the elders and makes open acknowledgment of his guilt and his determination to make amends. Following this, the oldest of the men from the village takes the brass vessel from the hands of the guilty person and bows in his turn in the direction of the sun.

In spite of one or two apparent exceptions, it seems true that *Cando* cannot be appeased or influenced by sacrifices. The fact that the weekly sacrifice in the shrine of Lokhon Mạṅjhi at Sarenga includes one in honour of *Cando* illustrates the process by which modifications may appear in the general practice; it is not a typical shrine. It is said that a sacrifice is offered to *Siṅ boṅga* during the clan festival known as *Jom Sim*, which is hardly ever performed. For the most part, belief in a Supreme Being is not operative. He is frequently mentioned in conversation as the source of good and bad weather, and also of good and bad health; it is common to hear such expressions as "By the mercy of *Cando* we are well" and "If *Cando* has mercy we shall obtain good crops". By such means do Santals acknowledge that all their magic, their prayers and their hard work are an insufficient guarantee that they will attain their heart's desire and that God's ways are inscrutable.

CHAPTER 8

THE WORLD INVISIBLE—(2)

THE tribal *boṅgas* are the allies of the Santals in the struggle against adverse circumstances and untoward happenings, even though their influence is exercised mostly in a negative manner. Common interest as well as sentiment and tradition keep the human and the spirit partners together. There are, however, other kinds of spirits with whom society through its accredited representatives has no dealings. The belief in these latter spirits, the spirits of the malevolent dead and demons, is one which the Santals share with the peasantry of North India.[1] While there is much in the *boṅga* cult that is distinctive of the Santals, they seem to have absorbed the general beliefs of the region regarding spirits that are not worshipped but feared. They use the same terms as their neighbours and speak of *bhut*, *pret* and *curin*. These are the spirits of dead persons who have either died in some abnormal way or whose funeral ceremonies have not been completed. One Santal who was asked to describe the difference between the terms *bhut* and *boṅga* pondered his reply for a minute before saying: "Until the bones have been taken to the river all dead men are *bhuts*. These waylay people in the beds of streams. We fear them, and we do not look after them (*lit.* we do not feed them). We do look after the *boṅgas*, and they work for us." Santals do not seem to have made up their minds whether suicides automatically become malevolent spirits or not. Some think that they do, while one Santal affirmed that as death was rarely ascribed to natural causes suicide was not peculiar, being merely one of the ways in which evil influences worked on men's minds. Childless men become ghosts, and this belief is due to the fact that a son is desired who will light the funeral pyre. The *curin* form a special class of female ghosts with terrifying appearance. They are the spirits of women who died in childbirth, or while they were pregnant and after their child had quickened in the womb, and whose corpses had then not been disposed of in the right manner. Among the Santals, as among many other Indian peoples, the husband is required to cut open his wife's body and remove the foetus from it so that it may be buried separately. *Curin* haunt the beds of streams, where they lie in

[1] William Crooke, *Religion and Folklore of Northern India*, Oxford University Press, 1926, Ch. VII.

wait for men. Women are protected from the designs of these ghosts by the iron bangle which they wear.

Ghosts of the dead and other private spirits who are given the title of *boṅga* form part of the stock-in-trade of the two classes of people among the Santals who deal regularly with the occult—the magicians and the witches. They are bitterly opposed to each other's influence, and they clash for the most part on the battleground of sickness and disease. An exhaustive treatise on the Santal attitude to disease has been published, and shows conclusively that, as with ghosts so with sickness, the ideas of the Santals are common to all the lower strata of society in North India.[1] These ideas are not simple but complex, and range from the realm of the rational to the fantastic. Disease is sometimes ascribed to natural causes, particularly when the chain of causation is fairly obvious and can be repeated in a series of experiments; there is a whole class of food described as *batol*, which means that it is unwholesome. There are hundreds of remedies that require no supernatural aid to make them effective. Some remedies are the property of all, while others are the property of individuals and the knowledge of their ingredients is a closely guarded secret. Chaitan of Churimara began his career as a physician in response to a specific need. When he was a young man a friend had come to him in great distress and said that his boy was vomiting blood. He turned to Chaitan and asked him if he knew of any medicine that would be good for the boy. Chaitan was so sorry for his friend that he promised to do something, although when he said this he had no notion what he should do. As he was setting out for his friend's house he prayed to *Cando* and asked that he might be shown what he ought to do; at the same time he shut his eyes and kicked at the soil. As he opened his eyes again he saw a plant, which he immediately dug up. He ground the roots to make a medicine, and the boy recovered from his sickness. Since then he has applied the same remedy to many other cases. One of his patients had been extremely ill, he said, but was now the father of four or five children! He has been in great demand as a physician, and claims that *Cando* subsequently revealed many remedies to him. Sometimes it is claimed that remedies are made known in dreams. The plant that was first revealed to Chaitan was the *upel ṭaṇḍi* plant, which has a red flower.

[1] P. O. Bodding, *Studies in Santal Medicine and Connected Folklore, Memoirs of the Royal Asiatic Society of Bengal*, Vol. X.

There are many individuals famed in some degree as physicians. Some are equivalent to the general practitioners of the West, while others are specialists who possess remedies for particular diseases. There are others who might be described as veterinary physicians. When, however, an illness persists the patient and the relatives suspect that some supernatural agency is at work, and they then call in the *ojha*, or magician. The *ojha* is not necessarily a Santal, though there are now so many Santals who are learned in *ojha* art that it is usually possible for a Santal to be called. They are men possessed of special powers who have gone through a period of training, followed by an initiation ceremony at the hands of an *ojha*, and they in turn pass on their knowledge to their own disciples. Tradition says that formerly this training was strenuous and serious. It took the form of a course that lasted from May until October, the time of the *Dãsãẽ*, which is the same as the Dasserah festival of North India and the Durga Puja in Bengal. Throughout this period the disciples had to attend at the house of the *ojha* every evening until finally they were initiated. At the conclusion of this ceremony the *ojha* used to take his disciples on a begging expedition through the surrounding villages on three successive days.

These begging parties are a familiar sight in the countryside during *Dãsãẽ*, and they represent almost all that is left of the old initiation schools conducted by the *ojhas*. Every village has its bands of youths who meet each night for a month to practise the songs and dances and then go out to collect rice and cash from the neighbours. It is at this time that the *buaṅ* is used. When the young men sally forth they are dressed in picturesque fashion. On this occasion alone men are permitted to wear women's dress. They put on *saṛis* shaped like a skirt and a small waistcoat, a garment worn by the women in many parts of North India, though it is not normally worn in Bengal. They also don ear-rings, bangles and anklets, while on their heads they wear turbans in which they fasten peacock feathers.

These bands have little relation to the *ojhas* and they operate under their own leaders. One of the links remaining between this practice and the *ojhas* is the reference in some of the songs to the old *gurus* of the magicians, and in particular the original *guru*, a mythological person named Kạmru. The name may possibly refer to a person who came from the western districts of Assam, a region known as Kamrup, but he is now entirely mythical. He is regarded as the originator of magical knowledge and as belonging to the race of *bongas*. According to one version, he is a son of the god Siva.[1] In one of the songs sung by the *Dãsãẽ* youths at Sarenga the first verses are as follows:

> Which *guru* has a silver stick, sister, O sister,
> In the middle of the Kasai river, sister, O sister,
> The silver stick with a sound like tinkling bells?
>
> *Dhorom guru* has a silver stick, sister, O sister,
> In the middle of the Kasai river, sister, O sister,
> The silver stick which sounds like tinkling bells.[2]

The mention of *Dhorom* as the first *guru* links *Dãsãẽ* lore with a god who is prominent in the cult of the earth mother, a cult that is common among the Hindu lower castes and among many of the Central India tribes, for whom the Dasserah is one of the important festivals of the year. The song proceeds to repeat the same question twelve times in all—the number twelve here again symbolizes completeness—and the answer is repeated with a different name each time. The names of the *gurus* as they are repeated at Sarenga are Dhorom, Siba (Siva), Kạmru, Sidho,Ganḍu, Rohoṛa, Bạṭi, Buaṅ, Lokhon, Bhadu, Rạtu and Ramjit. The first eight names are mythical or symbolic, while the name Lokhon connects the song with local tradition, and Ramjit was the name of the last leader of the band before the present one. The names standing between these two also commemorate local *Dãsãẽ* leaders.

The practice by which *ojhas* are made today is informal and usually results from the attachment of a youth to an *ojha* as his servant for an unspecified period. There is a considerable amount of rivalry among the *ojhas*, who endeavour to steal a march on each other and especially to get hold of the powers of dead magicians. The following story, a literal translation of one that was current in the area, illustrates the nature of the power that they wield: "One day a man who had set out for his work in the jungle—he was a jungle keeper—saw three slender *sarjom* trees tied together and put down in the path at a cross-roads. He thought to himself: 'Now who could it be who was stealing trees from the jungle?' Saying this, he picked up the sticks and went on to the jungle. When he arrived there he thought: 'There is no need for me to carry these sticks round with me all the time; I will put them down here and pick them up when I am on my

[1] For a full discussion see Bodding, *Studies in Santal Medicine and Connected Folklore, Memoirs of the Royal Asiatic Society of Bengal*, Vol. X.
[2] See Appendix B, No. 15.

way home.' And so he propped them up against a tree, but as he did so a branch from the tree fell down with a crack, a branch as thick as a man could embrace. When he saw that such a thick branch had fallen he was greatly puzzled, for there was no strong wind and the branch itself was not rotten. He went on with his work, but when he returned home in the evening he related his adventure. An *ojha* of the village, hearing what he said, sighed and exclaimed: 'Ah, you have gone and spoilt all my work!' 'And what have I spoilt of yours?' asked the jungle keeper. 'In those three sticks which you picked up', replied the *ojha*, 'there was a *boṅga* on whom I had cast a spell. When he left the sticks he gave you a sign by snapping off that branch and making it fall. You are fortunate that it did not fall on you and break your neck!' The jungle keeper said: 'Impossible; there was no one there.' Then the *ojha* explained: 'All right, I shall tell you—listen! Recently an *ojha* was buried in that jungle. On the night of the new moon after his burial two of us went along to take possession of him. My companion made circles on the ground a little distance away from the grave, and I seated him there and protected him with spells. I told him not to be afraid, for I had also made myself safe with spells. Then I began to sing certain spells to make the *jiu* of the *ojha* come out. After a long time his *jiu* came out in the shape of the *ojha*, and I sent him over to the one sitting within the magic circles. He changed his appearance and took on the shape of a leopard, then a jackal, then a bear, in order to frighten us, but he could not even touch us, for we were protected by spells. Meanwhile by means of our spells we blocked the road back to the grave and so captured him. At length he returned to his own shape, and when we told him that he had to go home with us he made a great fuss and begged us, "First give me a meal of men" or "Let me eat some bullocks and some goats and then I will go with you", but we gave him no encouragement at all. Finally, he agreed to go with us if we would give him water to drink every morning, with sweetened rice and other sweets on festival days, so we tossed him the bundle of sticks and told him to get inside them. He vaporized and got into them, and then we cast a spell on the bundle. We had taken the bundle down to the cross-roads and had set it there with a spell to guard it. We intended to bring it to our home later, but when you picked it up you took it outside the circle cast by the spell and he evidently took his chance and ran. Oh, he is clever and never will come back! Now if you had ever been going about the work of an *ojha* and had taken one of those sticks in your hand, whatever you wished would have come to pass. You could have wound a string round one of those sticks and then if you had taken the string along with you to a cock fight you would have had good fortune, and the same would apply in hunting. But if you did not behave properly towards it and make offerings to it, it could finish you off and eat you. So that is what it is all about, and now that person will stay around anywhere at all and frighten people. He has become a *bhut.*' "

One of the methods by which it is possible to steal the powers of a dead magician, or rather to capture his "soul force", was explained in the following manner. It is necessary to go to the spot where he was cremated and there draw a picture of the dead man on the ground. If one made offerings to this picture and recited the appropriate spells, he could be brought under control. Some years ago, when a well-known *ojha* in the village of Bankadaha had died, his disciples kept guard over the spot where he had been cremated for some time after his death.

When the Santal *ojha* is called in about a case of sickness or of sudden death, his first function is to try to determine the type to which the particular misfortune belongs. He consults the oracles in order to discover whether natural causes are to blame, in which case it is called plain *rua̧*, or sickness, or whether it is necessary to lay the responsibility on a witch, a *boṅga* or a displeased ancestor. He sits down in the courtyard and waits until two *sarjom* leaves and some mustard oil in a leaf cup are brought to him. Holding one of the leaves in his left hand, he dips his right index finger in the oil and sprinkles some drops on the ground as an offering to the spirits. While doing so he asks for guidance in determining the correct cause of the illness or fatality. He then puts a drop of oil into each of the compartments of the leaf that he is holding, one drop representing one possible agency of evil. There is one for natural causes, three or four for different *boṅgas*, and other drops represent households in which there may be a witch, including the sick man's house, his father-in-law's house, the houses on the other side of the village street, and so on. When the drops are in position the *ojha* rubs the two leaves together and then holds the first leaf up to the light to discern the shapes that have been taken by the oil. He pronounces the cause of the disease in accordance with the pattern that he sees. If he decides that the *boṅgas* are displeased, he performs the ceremony known as *bul mayam* in much the same manner as the village co-priest does during the festivals. The blood which he draws from his arm, chest or thigh is mixed with some sun-dried rice until the whole is saturated. The *ojha* then proceeds to scatter the rice on the ground and prays to the spirits to spare the sick man from further interference. He confirms his diagnosis by oracle by examining the patient and in particular by feeling his pulse, and apart from his power with the spirits he has a stock-in-trade that includes many remedies, spells, and also powers of exorcism. This is resorted to at once in certain cases such as snake bite. The *ojha* squats down beside the sick person and takes in his left hand a peacock feather or sometimes one or two twigs from an old broom, and these he passes along the patient's body without touching it, moving from the head to the feet and chanting the correct spells as he does so.

The magician always warns his clients that there is a possibility of error in his diagnosis, for it is the common belief that witches can interfere with the process of divination in order to draw attention away from themselves. Sometimes at an early stage, but usually when the illness persists in spite of all attempts at a cure, the suspicion of witchcraft arises, and a second divination reveals that a witch is at work. Once the suspicion has been voiced the whole village is concerned in the consultation, and the headman walks through the village exclaiming in a loud voice near each house: "Beware, for if the sick man does not get well we shall deal with thee!" More *ojhas* are consulted, and once agreement has been reached that witchcraft is operating, then steps have to be taken to locate the witch. The villagers are as a rule reluctant to proceed to this step and only do so when other measures have failed, for no one can tell in advance whether the witch will be found in his own house or not. At times frivolous accusations of witchcraft are made in order to pay off an old grudge, but the fear of the real thing is very strong. The oil divination has to be confirmed by some other means, one of which is the ordeal of placing twigs in water. Some freshly cut twigs are placed in the mud at the water's edge of a pond and vermilion is placed on them. The twigs represent the various households and spirits, as the drops of oil do in the oil and leaf method. The twig that withers first helps to fix the direction in which the villagers must look for the answer to their suspicions. Another method of divination is to place some rice wrapped in a leaf in a white-ant hill; if the ants attack the rice immediately, then witchcraft is involved.

When it has been established that a witch is at work and that she lives in a certain house or village, the villagers of the sick person proceed to the *jan*, or witchfinder, who must give precise information about the individual who is a witch. None of the *jans* in the area are Santals, but the latter consult them quite freely. These men are notorious for having their scouts in the countryside, and they manage to secure all the information that they require before the party of villagers comes to them. They uphold their reputation not only by finding witches, but through being credited with second sight in other matters. They are consulted about lost and stolen property and about straying cattle.

All the witches of the Santals are women. This suggests that women find some compensation in a "private" cult for the fact that they are cut off from active participation in the tribal worship of the spirits. The general term for a witch is *ḍạn*, and ordinarily the *ḍạn* is reputed to be a member of a secret society with its own ritual and magic. Undoubtedly there are women who believe themselves to be *ḍạn*. The *ḍạn ḍhạkin* is one who possesses some kind of evil nature and is able to put the "evil eye" on others. The fear of these witches is responsible for the fact that Santal houses are built without windows. When sometimes they leave an opening in the wall, they see that it is very small and so placed that no person standing outside will be able to look at any of the individuals inside, especially at night. The *ḍạn jugin* are persons who use magic and know sorcery.[1] They acquire influence over certain *boṅgas*, and they make use of material objects in doing so. One of the tasks of an *ojha* who declares that there are buried *boṅgas* at work in a house is to locate them. He finds them buried in the house or the courtyard in the form of stones with human hair tied to them. The *ḍạn* can gain control of a person and cause madness, a point that is well brought out in a story that is related here in the form in which it was told. "There was a youth in our village about sixteen years old, named Monmotha. One day last year he was going through the jungle from Calta to Beltwala; he returned at about noon, and on his way he had to pass a *boṅga than*. As he was passing it he was struck with fear, and when he reached home he was out of his senses and began to talk a

[1] The distinction between witchcraft as an influence and sorcery as a magic art using material objects made by E. Evans Pritchard in *Witchcraft, Oracles and Magic among the Azande* (Oxford University Press) seems to find some correspondence here.

lot of nonsense. The people of the house consulted the oil oracle and found that a *boṅga* had possessed him. They did their best to exorcize the spirit, but the boy only became worse and began to wander about in the open. After a few days he left his home and did not return. Again they consulted the oil oracle and saw that he had been pounced on by a *ḍạn boṅga*; by trying to exorcize it they had only made him worse. From time to time the herd boys used to see the youth, but when they went to catch him he ran into the jungle. When he saw that the folk were trying to get hold of him he went over to Gurma hill, about seven miles from Calta, and lived there; he used to be seen there occasionally. His parents went there to try to bring him home; they stayed in the neighbouring village for three or four days, but they were unable to do anything. A few days later it came to be known that he was regularly visiting the house of a female *jan*. He went there at night to drink water from a brass pot that she placed for him. The boy's father heard about it and watched the place one night. Sure enough, the boy came and drank the water out of the pot, but when he saw his father he ran away. There has been no news of him from that time to this; no one knows where he has gone or where he stays or what he eats. His father says that he had become very thin and had long hair and long nails. They have not found him yet." The fear of witchcraft is a fact of everyday experience among the Santals; the possibility that evil forces can disrupt and disturb their lives, robbing them of the fruit of their labours and mocking at their prayers, is never far from the surface of their minds.

Although they fear greatly the influence of the *ḍạn*, they take vigorous action to rid their village of her presence once they have been convinced that a particular person is a witch. Very often they take some steps without going to the extreme of consulting the witchfinder. They act on the suspicions revealed by the oil oracle and confirmed by eccentric behaviour on the part of some individual who lives in the house that has been indicated. The nature of the action depends on the extent of the injury that has been inflicted, and is left at times to the initiative of the principal victims. It is extremely difficult to obtain authentic evidence of particular cases, but I can personally vouch for examples where women have been severely beaten, other cases where the whole house has been fined for "keeping" a witch, and some where all the members of a family have been driven from the village or have themselves preferred to leave. On one occasion I was informed that a woman had been killed as a suspected witch, but it was impossible to make a satisfactory investigation; and on another occasion I was asked to see the body of a young man where the villagers were convinced that witchcraft had been responsible for his death. It appeared to be a case of poisoning. Fortunately, some of the evidence relating to witchcraft and murder has been documented. Murder by Santals is comparatively rare, but fear of witchcraft is one of the most frequent motives at work. Statistics have been published for the Santal Parganas for the period 1931–40. During this period there were seventy-eight cases of homicide by Santals before the courts, and of the seventy-eight it was definitely established that sixteen were due to accusations of witchcraft.[1] It is reasonable to infer that the actual number was somewhat larger, for in most such cases the sympathy of the community is on the side of the murderers, and so it becomes a fairly easy matter to conceal the crime.

It appears that in other parts of North India the magician, or *ojha*, is a dealer in "black magic",[2] but among the Santals the order of *ojhas* might almost seem to have been called into being because of the need to defend society against the evil influence and the sorcery of witches who are the enemies of society. The *ojha* is a benefactor of society and seeks to overcome witchcraft by invading the territory of the witches and using their weapons. Each of the opposing camps is prepared to lay hands on any weapon that may serve its purpose.

The same truth is evident in all the Santal's dealings with things that he cannot understand. The attitudes summed up in the terms "magic" and "religion" are both in evidence. It is not usual in these days to distinguish sharply between them.[3] Magic is used by the Santal as a tool to accomplish many and varied ends. It is not absent from his dealings with the spirits, and it can be used for social as well as antisocial ends. It does

[1] S. M. Naqavi, "Santal Murders", an article in *Man in India*, September 1943, Vol. XXIII.

[2] W. Crooke, *op. cit.*, p. 423: "In Northern India the worker of black magic is the Ojha, a term derived from the Sanskrit Upādhāya, 'teacher', and the Syāna, 'cunning man', who follow the traditional methods handed down from their predecessors. Their stock-in-trade is a collection of Mantras or spells, many based on the magic of the Tāntras, 'rule, ritual', used in the cult of the Sakti or female energy, by which they are supposed to acquire the power of controlling spirits or demons, and of forcing them to obey the orders of the sorcerer."

[3] Cf. G. and M. Wilson, *The Analysis of Social Change*, Cambridge University Press, 1945, p. 72: "Magic for us, though it may not postulate any transcendent reality, is an integral part of primitive religion."

consequently overlap the sphere of "religion", which, however, covers experiences where the arts of magic do not reach, while magic also works independently in some situations. For the most part, the various approaches to the problems of living are simultaneously pursued, by individuals as well as by society. "Charms" are in almost universal use as a precaution against sickness; one finds the shell of a land tortoise hung in the cowshed to ward off smallpox, or cowrie shells worn as a protection against the evil eye, and amulets worn round the arm as a matter of routine and called *ran*, or medicine. A double attitude is most apparent in efforts to control the weather that plays so great a rôle in their life. In a period of great drought the Santals probably arrange for a special festival to be held, with sacrifices offered to the "Five". At the same time they busy themselves in other ways which are quite independent of the sacrifice. Unmarried girls plaster the dancing floor with cowdung, while the married women do the same to their own courtyards. An investigation is made as to whether any woman has tied a rope on any roof. It is taboo for women to climb on roofs in the ordinary way, but some of the cowsheds and outbuildings have low roofs on which it would be possible to tie the straw to a rafter without climbing up. If it transpires that any woman has done so, she is made to climb up on to the roof and undo her work, first removing her clothing. Other investigations are made too. It may be that someone has stored dried *matkom* on the floor in her house instead of placing it on a plank or on stones; or it may be that oil has been stored in a sealed pot, in which case the covering must be removed. Underlying all these activities is the conviction that the welfare of society and of the individual depends on establishing a balance between man, nature and the spirit world, and they witness to a faith that such a balance is possible of achievement.

CHAPTER 9

FESTIVALS

THE two great village festivals take place in the spring and after the harvest. The name of the former, *Baha*, means "Flower festival". It is held after the full moon in the month of *Phalgun* (February-March). The hot season is about to begin, sap is rising in the trees, and the *sarjom* is resplendent with blossom and tender green leaves. Until the festival has taken place the women do not gather the *matkom* blossoms which provide them with both food and drink. It is held on different days in different villages so that the celebrations can be accompanied by a round of visits to relatives. The opening day of all festivals is a day of purification, known as "bathing day". On this day at the time of the Spring festival two temporary sheds are put up in the sacred grove and the young men carry out a hunt in the woods near the village. The priest completes his preparations and bathes certain articles in the waters of the village tank. At sunset three hens are taken to his house by the villagers, who remain there to dance. Three of the young men become spirit-possessed. One impersonates the "Five", another the Old Lady of the Sacred Grove, and the third takes the part of *Marañ Buru*; they seize the implements which the priest has purified earlier in the day and make play with them. The priest receives them with respect; he washes their legs and, addressing the spirits, he asks for good fortune during the coming year. When this is over the young men are recalled to their senses by a series of sharp taps on their backs. Dancing is continued throughout the night in the village street just outside the priest's house.

In the early afternoon of the following day the priest is accompanied by the villagers in a singing procession to the sacred grove. On arrival there the same young men are again possessed and run away across the fields, being chased and brought back by the rest of the young men. The priest now assumes an attitude of great humility towards them. He receives them with a cloth tied round his neck in token of the submission of the village to the spirits. The hens are sacrificed and cooked in a hash with rice. The priest and his wife partake of one and the men of the village consume the rest of the food, after which everyone returns home except the priest. He has to remain in the grove until the young men return to escort him. He is then taken to every house in turn and received with great honour. His feet are washed in each house and he receives presents of grain and beer. The subsequent merrymaking dies down during the night. The celebration is completed on the following day, when the co-priest offers drops of his own blood to the boundary spirits.

The following account of the Spring festival held in Barikul in 1939 was recorded by Babulal at the time, and it conveys, as no outside account could, the atmosphere of the festival. He begins:

"*March* 17. Today is the bathing day for the Flower festival. Early in the morning the bailiff called everyone to make the booths ready in the sacred grove. The women were busy boiling their clothes. One young man from every house took part in the thatching of the booths; some brought *sarjom* branches from the jungle, and others made small wooden seats for the spirits. The priest washed all the things for the spirits' house—the bangles, the necklace, a bow and arrow, an axe, also basket, broom, bells and horns—and he brought back to his house an earthen pot of water for luck. The place of sacrifice was smeared with cowdung, and oil and vermilion were placed there in readiness. When the young men had finished the thatching they bathed, and then said to the bailiff: 'We go now to Sonadungri for the flower hunt; see that the drums beat and the horns sound at the foot of the banyan tree, for when we hear them we shall start. Do not delay, for we want to begin.' The bailiff completed his bath quickly, and taking four youths with the drums and the horns to the banyan tree by the stone fence he did as he had been requested. And so the youths went out hunting. They caught fourteen hares, thirteen jungle fowl, four partridges and ten squirrels. These they brought home hanging from a pole which was slung from the shoulders of two men. When they arrived back at the side of the large tank, the spoils were divided, and some we gave to the men of neighbouring villages who had joined in the hunt. The flesh was roasted and divided; some was given to the killers, some to the dogs, some to the villagers, and a special portion to the widows.

In the evening the bailiff called everyone to gather for the 'spirit possession'. We took three new winnowing fans and all collected at the priest's house. Three men were possessed, and each of them took hold of a winnowing fan. They were seated facing the east, and the priest put sun-dried rice on to the winnowing fan of *Marań Buru*. Immediately to his left sat *Mańjhi haram*,[1] and on the left of *Mañjhi haram* there sat the Old Lady of the Grove, and to them also rice was given. The spirits spoke and shook the rice in the winnowing fans. Then they began to shake their heads from side to side, and called out, '*His-sahăk!*' At this everyone called out, 'Greetings, Lords!' for the spirits had come. The Old Lady of the Grove placed the necklace round her neck, put on the bangles, seized the broom and put the washed basket on her head, and then ran away to the grove. *Marañ Buru* and *Mañjhi haram* went after her with the bow and arrows and the axe, and in the darkness the Old Lady lost her necklace and the bangles. When they all ran back to the priest's house and the loss was discovered we told her that she must find them again. So she went once more to the grove and brought them back. After this we said to all of them: 'The horses are weary; let the spirit riders descend!' The priest then applied vermilion on their cheeks, their chests and their backs, and they came to their senses. So it ended. Next the villagers began to dance, and the first song was this:

> High up in the *pipal*[2] tree
> Sings the crimson-breasted barbet;
> It wanders through the country,
> It flies over the land.[3]

Then they began the late evening dance and many other dances, such as the road dance, and they sang:

> Down in the valley blooms the *hat*[4] tree, sister;
> Come, let us make flower chains, sister;
> Come, let us wear the flowers, dangling.[5]

The priest spent the night sleeping on a bed of leaves, while everyone else, old and young, men and women, danced the night through. Next morning the priest told the bailiff quickly to collect the hens; he himself bathed and went to the grove, taking with him *sarjom* and *matkom* flowers, sun-dried rice, flour, oil and vermilion, all in a new winnowing fan. He also carried a brown hen and on his open upturned palm a small

[1] *Mañjhi haram* is the title that denotes the founder of the village. Possibly in Barikul he is honoured instead of the "Five", though it might be Babulal's mistake.
[2] Santali *hesak' dare*: *Ficus religiosa*, L.
[3] See Appendix B, No. 16,
[4] A small tree, *Holarrhena antidysenterica*, Wall.
[5] See Appendix B, No. 17.

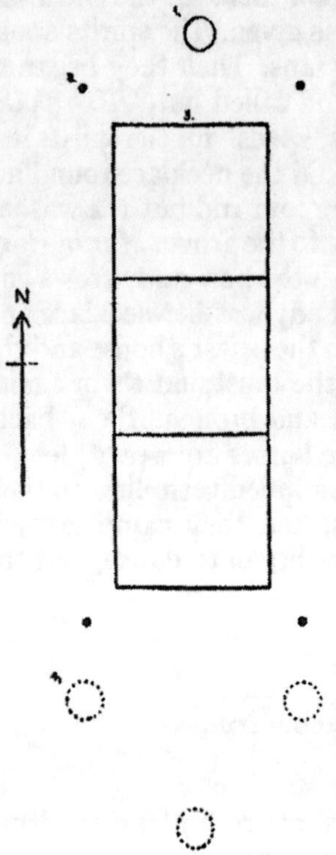

brass water-pot, while his wife carried the earthen pot of water brought for good fortune. Youths and maidens conducted him to the grove, dancing as they went, and there he began to make the sacrifice. The youths and the maidens danced in the grove, the young men singing only the Flower dance songs, and while the dancing went on the priest proceeded with his work. With the flour he made the circles and the squares. A hen was offered in each of the circles; the brown hen was slain in the Moslem[1] fashion, while the other two had their necks cut. Again each of the spirits took possession of a man, and they sucked the blood of the slain birds. One circle was for *Maraṅ Buru*, one for the Old Lady of the Grove, and one for *Mạṅjhi haṛam*. In the squares the priest sacrificed to the village spirits, and as we had brought many hens it was not possible to offer them all, so some were killed by knocking their heads on the ground. When it was all over, the priest cooked the heads of the first three hens with flour, making cakes of them, and then ate them and drank beer. This is called 'lifting the head'. Then the folk in the village who offer to the 'Five' took flowers from the trees of the grove, returned to their own houses and made mounds of the flowers. Near these mounds they offered either hens or goats. (Some of those who worship the 'Five' invite all their relatives at this time and make the sacrifice in the grove.) Meanwhile the priest drank beer and cooked a hash of rice with the brown hen.

Late in the afternoon the young men went to receive the priest back into the village. They went dancing to the grove and danced round the priest. Again the spirits took possession of the three young men, who danced with the others. The Old Lady again wore the bangles and the necklace and carried the

[1] This is Babulal's word. The offering to *Mạṅjhi haṛam* is strangled and not beheaded.

basket on her head; likewise *Maraṅ Buru* took the bow and arrows and *Mạṅjhi haṛam* held the axe. Just before sunset the men came to their senses, the priest gathered up all the things, and his wife carried the lucky water-pot. As before, the youths and maidens placed the priest in their midst and again the spirits came and danced with the others. Then in every house, from one end of the village street to the other, they washed the feet of the priest. He put *sarjom* flowers into the hair of the girls who washed his feet, and all the people sprinkled water on to each other. On that day we are free to sprinkle water on anyone else.[1] When we reached the priest's house he poured out two pots of beer and we all drank. Again the dancing began and went on till a late hour.

March 18. Yesterday was the full Flower festival day; today is the 'stale' day of the feast. Yesterday everyone was drunk, and again today they began to drink early. There were many visitors in the village, for we had invited daughters, sisters and sons-in-law to be with us. We had to feed them well, and we were busy with all the preparations. One prepared rice, another flour, while the men killed cocks or goats or pigs, for yesterday they had no time to feast well. Even so, in some of the houses a few people became drunk before they had time to eat. Those unfortunates had no meat either yesterday or today. Most of the time went in feasting, though there was some dancing in the village street, and the dancers sang:

> Let us gather, O elder sister, the *matkom*;
> Let us wear the *sarjom* flowers, elder sister, in our hair;
> Let us drink, O elder sister, the juice of the *matkom*.[2]

Most of the singing was done by a small band of old men and women who went into each of the houses and were given beer and *matkom* flowers by the people of the house. In our part of the village there was a fierce quarrel. Some of the men who went to stop the trouble were themselves beaten and returned very angry to their homes. Before midnight everyone was fast asleep, for all had been drinking heavily. I thought to myself, if anyone came here tonight with evil intent he could steal anything he wanted with the greatest ease; and, in fact, that is what happened. During the night someone stole from the headman's house five goats, male and female."

[1] Water "squirts" are made from bamboo and are used freely.
[2] See Appendix B, No. 18.

Having given his account of the festival, Babulal then proceeds with the following account of the myth which carries back the origin of the observance to the period of the wanderings:

"It is said that at one time our ancestors were moving from one place to another for fear of Mirja Turuk.[1] During that period they lost their 'religion'.[2] When it was realized, one man from each of the twelve clans went out in search of it. Now the names of those who went out on this quest, taking with them an uncastrated goat, a *Liṭa*[3] pig and some rice in a basket, were as follows: Ap'ṅambondak', Hutumṅambaṅjak', Narkakin ceḍe—these were two—Ote and Bole, and some others. They assembled in the Somoe valley in the forest of Siṅ, and there they remained for twelve years. The feathery grass of that place all died, but none of them wished to go on farther to look for their 'religion'. All of them held back; they said one to another: 'You go first.' In the end, Ote and Bole said in desperation: 'All right, we shall lead the way.' Going farther, they entered the Man forest. The other ten followed them, but when they came into the forest they could not find Ote and Bole. They searched the whole forest through without success. Some of them at length found some footprints, whereupon they sang this song:

> Look here, look at this,
> The footprints of the *nilgae*;
> Look here, look at this,
> The footprints of the wild buffalo.
>
> In what forest have they entered,
> The footprints of the *nilgae*?
> To what forest do they lead,
> The footprints of the wild buffalo?
>
> Into the forest of Man have they entered,
> The footprints of the *nilgae*;
> To the forest of Siṅ have they led,
> The footprints of the wild buffalo.[4]

[1] The now mythical Moslem ruler, mentioned also in Chapter 2, p. 24.
[2] An abbreviated account of this myth is given in Chapter 6, p. 66, where the word translated by "religion" is translated as "the right way to live".
[3] The meaning of this is not clear. *Liṭa* is the proper name of *Maraṅ Buru* (see Chapter 7, p. 81).
[4] See Appendix B, No. 19.

However, they could not find Ote and Bole; they searched everywhere, but they saw no tracks but the tracks of the *nilgae* and the wild buffalo. Nowadays the Santals say that the Ote and Bole who were then lost have become the ancestors of the 'sahibs'. One reason why we say this is that often when we are beginning to dance and at the commencement of songs someone calls out these words: 'Look, friends, the white hare has run away.'[1] This saying is the signal to begin the dance. The word 'sahib' is amongst us for a long time; in many ways our customs are the same."

This rather obscure piece of reasoning is in fact widely current among the Santals, at any rate among those who are unfamiliar with the origin of the word "sahib" and its currency in India during Moslem times. "White hare" is a term often applied to Englishmen. On one occasion I emerged rather suddenly from the waiting-room at a wayside station on to the platform near to where a group of Santal women were unloading a railway wagon. Unaware that I might understand their conversation, one of the women remarked, "The white hare has just come out of its hole!" greatly to the amusement of her companions. Babulal relates at this point how the brothers were met in the forest by *Marañ Buru* and led by him to the foot of various trees.[2] Babulal places the story in Moslem times. He makes the following remarks about *Marañ Buru* and his actions: "*Marañ Buru* deceived them so that when they wanted to offer sacrifices to *Ṭhạkur* they should do it in his name, afterwards to the Old Lady of the Grove, and then to the 'Five and Six'. In former days he used to be called *Liṭạ goḍet'*, *Liṭạ* the bailiff. *Marañ Buru* became the guardian of the ancestors. He used to take them out hunting and taught them how to kill iguanas, water-snakes, squirrels, mongoose and hares. On such days as they caught nothing in the chase he used to show them the dead cattle at the end of the village street, and would say to them: 'It is quite all right for us to eat these too; these are white deer.' And so we began to eat all these things."

He offers some more information about the Flower festival in his narrative: "In the prayer at the time of the Flower sacrifice we must use these words in addressing the spirits: 'If you are not pleased with the offering we shall dishonour your mother.' We consider that the spirits will listen to us if we use these words. We also say that if we urinate in a standing

[1] Another form of this saying is given in Chapter 6, p. 67.

[2] See Chapter 6, p. 66.

position the Flower spirits will be pleased. For this reason, if anyone sees us urinating in a standing position and scolds us for it we reply: 'We are making offerings to the Flower spirits!' The Flower festival is for flowers and fruits what the offering of new rice is for rice. Until the priest has placed flowers in the hair of the women and eaten some of the *matkom*, no one will wear flowers or eat the *matkom*. From the new year until after the festival the priest has to live very carefully. He eats nothing in other people's houses, because others may have been on a visit to villages where the festival has already taken place and then he might eat something that is forbidden. One of the songs that is sung when the priest is being escorted to the grove and again back to his house refers to the fact that the Dol Jatra festival of the Hindus has already taken place.[1]

'The Dol is over now, maidens, the *Pata*[2] comes next;
You must buy shields, maidens, for yourselves.

In the maidens' pubic region is the black bee's honeycomb;
You must buy shields, maidens, for yourselves.' "[3]

The second great festival is celebrated when all the harvest has been gathered in and there is plenty of food. The Santals say that for one month after the Harvest festival, known as the *Sohrae,* they eat rice without measuring it. Although it may be held at any time during the period between the dark night in October-November and the middle of January, in most of the villages of the area it is now celebrated at the earliest possible date, when Hindus are celebrating the Kali Puja. One reason is to enable those who are migrating for work to share in it before they depart, and some of the villagers distinguish between this fixed festival and a true *Sohrae* fixed in the traditional manner. In a bad year a Santal remarked: "This year we shall have no *Sohrae*. There has been no harvest, so what would we eat and how could we invite our friends?" The words were spoken while the village in question was actually celebrating the festival at Kali Puja time. Further, the celebration of Kali Puja amongst the surrounding cultivator castes, and especially the Bauri, has many features in common with the Santal cult, particularly with reference to cattle worship, and this factor has undoubtedly led the Santals to approximate the time of their celebrations to that of their neighbours.

[1] See Chapter 7, p. 90.
[2] The hook-swinging festival.
[3] See Appendix B, No. 20.

On the evening before the appointed day the village bailiff delivers the sacrificial hens, two white hens and one brown, to the priest's house. The priest observes his customary abstinence during that night, sleeping on the bare floor. Next morning the bailiff makes a collection of one hen from each house in the village, together with rice, salt and the various spices that are needed to cook a curry. It is the duty of the priest's wife to grind the flour that will be needed for "cakes"; his sister may perform this work only if she is unmarried. In the morning the priest constructs the sacred squares and circles on a piece of ground previously plastered with cowdung. The sacrifices are performed at noon, and these are in some cases offered in the sacred grove, but in some villages they are offered by the side of a stream or on the bank of one of the artificial lakes that abound. The sacred place is made from north to south, as in the case of the Flower festival, and the procedure is the same. First of all rice is sprinkled in the enclosures and some vermilion is placed on the rice. The birds are fed on the rice, water is sprinkled over them, and vermilion is smeared on their heads, their wings and their legs. When the sacrifice is complete, the priest eats the flesh of the heads, while the men of the village feast on a hash made from the rest of the flesh, and drink and sing.

The distinctive feature of the sacrifice is that, before the hens are offered, an egg is placed standing upright on a small pile of rice in one of the squares, and all the herdboys of the village are summoned to bring the cattle. The priest places vermilion on their goad sticks, and they drive their cattle across the enclosure in which the egg is standing until one of the cattle tramples upon and breaks the egg. This is the signal for an outburst of cheering and excitement. The cow or bull is garlanded and anointed with vermilion on its horns and its head. Sometimes the boy is carried shoulder high to the village headman, before whom he makes a deep obeisance, afterwards saluting the other men of the village. When the villagers return to the houses in the late afternoon they are supplied with beer in the priest's house, after which they visit the headman's house for the same purpose, and so on from one house to another. It is at this time that the youths and young women visit the home of the *jogmaṇjhi* and request him to turn a blind eye to their doings for the duration of the festival. The whole period is characterized by its freedom from traditional morality. The rules of avoidance are treated lightly, and many liberties are taken with members of the opposite sex. On the first night the young people go through the village conducting the ceremony known as "waking the cattle". There is much drumming and dancing outside each of the cowsheds, and the cattle are feasted and decorated; small white circles made of flour are painted on their hides, vermilion is placed on their horns and heads. When all the cattle in the village have been "wakened", the young men go round once more for the "blessing" of the cattle. They are garlanded and fed with sweetmeats, and the blessing is pronounced as a hope that they will be protected from the dangers of disease and witchcraft, from thieves and the depredations of wild animals during the coming year. This "blessing" is pronounced by the women.

Other ceremonies are performed on the following days. The whole celebration may last either for three or for five days. At one time during the festival the young men of the village lock the bailiff in his home, and he is not allowed to come out until he has promised to treat them all to a drink of beer. During the second day of the festival the sub-clans perform the sacrifices to their *abge* spirits. These sacrifices are also preceded by ceremonial bathing on the part of the members of the households concerned, and the men take to the waterside their hunting implements, bows and arrows, axes and spears. The head of the house officiates, and the sacrificial animals are set apart in the same way as for the village sacrifices, having vermilion in oil placed on their heads, their shoulders and their hoofs. The flesh of the animals is, however, cooked separately from the rice with which it is eaten. On the second day also the cattle are baited. A bull is tied to a post, and the group of men who gather round it begin to infuriate the beast by persistent drumming. One or two of the men at a time, holding before them the skin of a dead animal, engage in mock combat with the bull, leaping at it and inciting it to plunge at them with its horns. The pastime continues for several hours and sometimes results in accidents. It is a happy season for the herdboys; they receive presents of cloth and are well fed by their masters. On the last night of the festival the unmarried men and girls sleep at the house of the *jogmạṅjhi* in token of the fact that their period of licence is at an end.

The remaining festivals of the Santal year do not make the same stir throughout the countryside. *Mokor* is the name used in the area by Santals and non-Santals alike for the festival which takes place in mid-January. In some places it is called the *Sakrat.* At this time offerings are made to the ancestors in each house, and the celebration is accompanied by a display of stick dancing, which has replaced the former "sword and shield" dance. At the end of the following month the *Mag Sim,* the hen at the end of the month of *Mag,* is offered. In former times the village officials used to resign at this time and could be either replaced or reappointed, but the only relic of the old practice that has survived is that the headman has to treat the whole village to beer. Contracts with servants are renewed during the festival, and they receive the cloth that is always a part of the contract. In connection with rice cultivation there is the *Erok' Sim,* the hen that is offered at the time of sowing, and *Nãwãi,* when the first fruits of the first rice crop are offered in the sacred grove. Before this takes place the new rice must not be eaten. The village priest cuts the first handful of the crop and offers some at the foot of each of the chief trees. A sprig is also tied round the trunk of the trees and remains there. While the prayer is being said, milk is poured on the offering. After the priest has done his part, similar offerings are made in every house to the house spirits and the ancestors, the rice being taken from the crops belonging to the family. In varying degrees the Santals share in some of the festivals and practices of the low-caste cultivators around them. In the early monsoon days, during the period of *Rohini,* which is an auspicious time for sowing rice, they make a mark round their houses with cowdung as a protection against snakes. The snake goddess festival occurs in late August, and although its observance is not widespread among the Santals there are some local celebrations, especially when there is an *ojha* in the village. The *ojhas* all keep this festival, and others go to them at this time to ask for medicines against snakebite. Some Hindu festivals, as we have seen, furnish the occasion for large gatherings of Santals. At Sarenga, in addition to the Lakshmi Puja, a somewhat smaller gathering takes place during the hot weather in connection with the celebration of the Siva Gajon at a local temple. At this time the Charak, or hook-swinging festival, otherwise known as the *Pata,* takes place. The practice has almost died out within the last fifteen years. It had been prohibited by the government, but as long as the old generation, which was accustomed to the practice, remained it continued with gradually diminishing fervour. The Santals gather now to sing and to dance. They also join the throngs of pilgrims, sightseers and traders who collect at the Bogri *mela,* or fair, some thirty miles from Sarenga. This fair, which is one of the most famous in Western Bengal, takes place at the time of the Dol Jatra near a temple dedicated to Krishna. The last day of the *mela* is chiefly renowned for the fact that on that day there is a great concourse of Santals for dancing.

One festival which is shared with tribes living right across Central India[1] is the *Karam*. The fact that it is not peculiar to them is known to the Santals, and one informant once told me that they must have borrowed it from the Mahato. He had seen that the Mahato celebrated it and knew of the special relationship between the Mahato and his own people. Many of the songs contain references to Ram and Lokhon, heroes of the *Ramayana*. The festival is rather difficult to characterize, for its celebration takes different forms and arises from different causes. It is connected in all cases with the desire for prosperity, but it may be either a public or a private celebration. The *karam* is a tree[2] that is associated with the god Krishna in the *Vishnu Purana*. When a shoot of this tree is found growing in the land round a house or springing from the roof thatch, the head of that house is responsible for instituting an annual celebration of the festival. The fact that while it is celebrated annually in a great many villages it is not found invariably is perhaps accounted for by its accidental origin. The festival is also associated with certain other definite events. In some cases the leading celebrant is the local *ojha*, who holds a *Karam* festival at the beginning of the month of *Dãsãẽ* and before he sends out his disciples on their annual begging expedition. Sometimes it is celebrated in connection with the appointment of the new headman of a village, and sometimes in connection with the death ceremonies of a man of substance. Sometimes it is associated with the *Mak' Mõṛẽ*, an occasional sacrifice to the "Five". These spirits are peculiarly liable to become offended, and offerings are made to them to avert their wrath, which takes the form of inflicting a poor harvest or an epidemic. Whatever the occasion may be, the celebration of the *Karam* is regarded as an insurance either on behalf of a particular family or on behalf of the whole village. It may be either a way of enhancing good fortune or of warding off evil. Where in the area it has become an annual festival it is held at the full moon in the month of *San* (July-August). At sunset the un-

[1] References to Central India are to be found in *Folk-Songs of the Maikal Hills*, by V. Elwin, Oxford University Press, pp. 3–11.

[2] *Adinia cordifolia*, Hook., f. and B.

married men of the village bathe and then go to the nearby forest, from which they cut and bring back two branches of the *karam* tree. These branches, known as "virgin" *karam*, are set upright in two holes dug for the purpose. A piece of cloth is placed over the branches and a small light is lit in front of them. After the preliminary dancing one of the village elders recites the myth of the *Karam*, beginning from the creation myth; the story of the origin of the world is ordinarily referred to as the *Karam binti*. The recital is followed by another dance, which lasts through the night and is changed at cockcrow. The celebration continues till sunrise, when the branches are taken down to the water near the village by the same young men who brought them from the forest on the evening before. The youths immerse themselves, and the branches are floated away in a manner similar to that employed in floating away the bones of the dead.

The myth relates the story of the *Karam* to their own tribal history, and, as one finds in all Santal myths, memories of early wanderings are prominent. The following version was related by Durlob Murmu,[1] and it forms a continuation to the creation story:

"The name of Pilcu Haṛam and Pilcu Buḍhi's eldest son was Karmu Senor Siń. The eldest daughter was Hisi. They had two sons, who were called Karmu and Dharmu. Now Karmu was of the Hãsdãk' clan, and their maternal uncles were the Kisku *rajas* and the Mạrnḍi rich men. The Kisku lived at Campagor and the Mạrnḍi lived at Cirulagor,[2] and between the two villages flowed the Sitanala river. The people from both villages used to go to the river for their bathing and drinking water. There was a quarrel between them over a bride, and while the fight was on the Kisku killed the father of Karmu and Dharmu. After this they fell into great want. One day they went out to beg and were on the way to Campanagar. They came to the banks of a river, and Dharmu lay down at the foot of a *karam* tree and fell asleep. The name of the river was Tatijhari—it was the place where *Marań Buru* had first woven cloth garments. Below that place he had made a small embankment, and that place was called the Saḍoyar valley; just below it he had bathed, and so the place was known as Bathing river. That river had sprung from the Lope mountain hard by the Bell banyan tree, and its waters flowed towards the sunrise.

[1] See Chapter 6, p. 65, footnote 2. [2] Cf. reference in Chapter 6, p. 72.

At the foot of that tree *Karam Gõsãĩ* appeared to Dharmu in a dream. He spoke to Dharmu thus: 'Eya Dharmu, plant a *karam* tree. Make a drum from the leaves. Bow to it and salute it three times; then dance round it. By the side of the river there is a cow with calf; by a heap of stones near a clump of *sirom* grass there is a turban cloth, and in a hillock by the river there is a flute. Bring all those things here.' As soon as Dharmu awoke he planted the *karam*. Then he saw that a cow with calf had appeared on the spot. He fetched the turban and the flute, and putting the turban on his head he took the cow back to his home. When he arrived there his old mother told him to bring some turmeric and water in a pot and to wash the legs of the cow as well as her legs, and in that way he paid respect to the cow. He handed the turban and the flute to his mother and asked her to care for them, and then he tied up the cow. After that Dharmu went to the river every day, taking the cow with him. He used to plant a branch of the *karam* and dance round it. *Karam Gõsãĩ* blessed the family, and their cattle increased so that they became rich. One day the mother spoke to both her sons: 'Eya Karmu and Dharmu, a *karam* has sprouted in our thatch. The paddy seeds in the store are sprouting and *dhubi* grass is growing in the sun-dried rice. It wants but three days till the full moon of *San*. Fix a *karam* branch in front of our house on that day and invite all the neighbours.' When all the neighbours had gathered, Karmu asked two of the unmarried girls to plaster the earth round the *karam* branch with cowdung. Dharmu cut two branches of a *karam* tree, planted them in the ground, went down on his knees three times and saluted them. Their mother brought some sun-dried rice in a plate from the house, some *dhubi* grass, clarified butter and the piece of cloth dyed in turmeric. She placed the cloth on the twigs and swathed it round the branches. Then she also did obeisance three times and returned to the house.

Then the mother and the two sons spoke together: 'We have planted a *karam*, but how shall we dance?' Then they sang the following song:

An ape you will slay, my sons, then what will you do?
The ape that we slay, mother, we shall skin.

The skin you will take, my sons, then what will you do?
With the skin we take, mother, we shall cover a drum.

With the drum that you cover, my sons, what will you do?
To the sound of the drum, mother, we shall plant the *karam.*

Round the *karam* that you plant, my sons, what will you dance?
Round the *karam* we plant, mother, (the dance will be) *Goḍet' niphur ḍanḍahi mathayet'.*[1]

And so they danced from sunset till just before sunrise. Then two unmarried youths plucked up the *karam* branches. They carried them to the spring which was beyond the end of the village street and floated them down the stream after first immersing them under the water and offering them towards the rising sun. All who had taken part bathed and returned to their homes, and the cloth was given to a poor woman of the village.

Dharmu continued to dance round the *karam* every day and did not do his share of tending the cattle. At this his brother Karmu became annoyed. He plucked up the *karam* with his left hand and flung it on to a dungheap, and from that time their fortunes changed. At last they became so poor that they were working for a rich man, planting out his paddy seedlings. Whatever they gained for themselves disappeared at once, and so they could make no profit.[2] Their employer told them: 'Never mind, you will get some tomorrow.' But when the same thing had happened for three days in succession the brothers fell into a rage and said: 'Come on, let us pluck out all the paddy seedlings that we have planted.' While they were on their way to the fields they passed an old man, who stopped to ask them the way. When they had told him he asked them where they were going, and in reply they told him everything. He urged them: 'Do not do that, for it will make *Cando* very angry. All this has happened because of your sin. You should seek for *Karam Gõsãẽ*, whom you will find by the Condon mountain on the shores of the sea. He is a leper. Go and worship him. And mind, you will find that there are other holy men where he is; do not worship them.' They turned back in their tracks, and when they looked round again they saw that the old man had vanished, so they knew at once that it was *Cando* who had come to speak with them.

They set out forthwith on their journey. They came to a

[1] See Appendix B, No. 21.

[2] The method of payment for this work is for the labourer to receive a proportion of seedlings, which he can then plant in his own fields.

village, and before entering it they sat down to rest at the foot of an old jackfruit tree. The name of that village was Ujaṛḍi. Karmu told Dharmu to go and beg some food in the village, as he was hungry, so Dharmu went and fetched back some flour, but when they had soaked it they found that they could not eat, for it was full of worms. Then the jackfruit tree spoke to them and asked them where they were going. They replied: 'We search for *Karam Gõsãĕ*.' The tree replied: 'Then tell him about me. Some men have buried treasure here at my roots, and I am tired of watching it.' They went on and came to the Ajєy forest, where they found a cow with calf. Farther on they came to a mango tree, and Karmu told Dharmu to gather mangoes. They divided the mangoes out and took off the skins, but they were unable to eat the fruit, as it was full of worms. On they went and came to the village of Jhalḍa, where there lived a rich man. This man asked the brothers where they were going, to which they replied: 'We seek *Karam Gõsãĕ*.' 'Then', said he, 'tell *Karam Gõsãĕ* about me. I am tired of looking after all my possessions.' Later they arrived at the village of Khajepur, where there dwelt a rich man with very many head of cattle. When they had told him that they were seeking *Karam Gõsãĕ* he said to them: 'Then tell *Karam Gõsãĕ* about me, for I am tired of looking after all my herds.'

After many such happenings they came at last to the leper who dwelt by the Condon mountain on the shores of the sea, and they saluted the feet of *Karam Gõsãĕ*. He told them to salute also the good men who were around him, but they refused and said: 'No, we have come to you and we want to take you with us.' When *Karam Gõsãĕ* had heard everything that they had to tell him he blessed them and taught them thus: 'Never do things without consulting other folk. Plant a *karam* branch every day and do no sin.' Then they told him all the messages that had been given to them as they came along the road, and *Karam Gõsãĕ* then said to Karmu and Dharmu: 'Say this word to all of them. If they will give what is in their keeping either to a Brahmin or a Vaishnava, good fortune will attend them.' They set out on their return journey, taking *Karam Gõsãĕ* with them, and as they met the people they told them what *Karam Gõsãĕ* had said. Each of them replied: 'And where are we to find a Brahmin or a Vaishnava? You two are the Brahmin and the Vaishnava and to you we shall give what we possess.' And so as they returned to their home they collected many head of cattle, buffaloes, cows, goats and money. As soon as they reached home they did as they had been told by *Karam Gõsãẽ*; they planted a *karam* branch and once more they became exceedingly rich."

"Nowadays", concludes the narrative, "we do not set up the branch in that way, but even to this day in many villages the branch is planted on the night of the full moon of the month of *San*, and they do it because this was ordered by *Karam Gõsãẽ*."

Each festival, as it comes, serves to enliven the toil of the villager, and when it has passed it remains often as a signpost in the memory. Mothers recall that their children were born before or after a festival; the month is remembered even when the year has been forgotten. On the religious side the festivals bind the community to the tribal spirits and to the ancestors; the offering is shared by all the men and so makes each one conscious of communion with the spirits as well as with his fellow villagers. They also serve to keep alive the myths and songs, the games and dances, and so help the Santal to give full reign to his love of pleasure.

CHAPTER 10

BIRTH AND INITIATION

THE birth of a child is an occasion for rejoicing, and the event is announced by saying: "The new relation has arrived." Children are spoken of as the gift of *Cando*, which indicates that they are considered to be assets to the family. It is true that boys are rather more welcome than girls; every family desires that the first child should be a boy who will ensure the survival of that particular family within the clan. A boy can inherit his father's lands, and one day he will be required to assist at his father's funeral ceremonies and perpetuate the worship of his own ancestors. Girls are welcomed, though not to the same degree. Through their marriages they will in due course extend the range of the family's relationships, but they bring but a small economic return to their parents, and the bride price received at marriage is not comparable to the expense of bringing them to maturity. Where a family consists of both boys and girls in equal proportion the girls are well treated, and when later on they go to other homes their places will be filled by daughters-in-law. When, on the other hand, a woman gives birth to a succession of daughters she is likely to feel the displeasure of her husband's relations. A third or fourth daughter born into a home where the husband's mother reigns supreme does not enjoy much prospect of survival. Children are valued from the first because of their potential working ability. A villager, on hearing that a birth has taken place, responds at once with the question: "What is it? Does it carry on the shoulder (a boy) or does it carry on the head (a girl)?" Or he may say: "Is it a hunter or is it a water carrier?"[1]

There are Hindu shrines in the area to which Santal women resort along with others when other means of securing the birth of a longed-for child have proved of no avail. A spirit who can grant the boon of children resides near the village of Raniband at the summit of a hill which rises abruptly from the plain and is the highest point in the whole area. Cases have been reported of Santal man and wife making the climb together in order to present an offering. In most cases, however, the husband preserves an air of indifference; if his wife fails to bear a child he is

[1] Another way of referring to the sex of children, though not at the time of birth, is for a parent to say: "I have three *iṛi* and three *erba*", which signifies three boys and three girls. *Iṛi* is a cultivated millet (*Panicum crusgalli*, L.) and *erba* is a cultivated grain (*Setaria italica*, Kunth).

persuaded to take a second wife. Sometimes he may not be reluctant to take such a step for reasons quite unconnected with the need for children, though usually he is. In addition to supernatural aids there are known to be remedies for ensuring conception, and these are sought from the individuals to whom they belong. The secrets of these remedies are closely guarded. Bodding[1] has listed a number of those commonly known. My friend Binu was in possession of a remedy which had to be taken by the patient during a menstruation period and which ensured the birth of a boy. "No one", he said, "would ask for a medicine to ensure the birth of a girl."

Conversely, amulets are worn as contraceptives, and two different methods are used to induce abortion. One of these is to take drugs orally and the other is the highly dangerous method of piercing the womb with a stick inserted through the vagina. I have heard of the latter method being followed only by girls who wished to escape detection and who therefore could not ask anyone for medicine. Married women who resort to abortion are usually those who have already given birth to a large number of children. In one case which had fatal results for the mother she wished to avoid having a seventh child; another attempt which resulted in a serious illness for the mother, but which was otherwise successful, was made by a woman who had already had ten children.

Santals are fully aware of the connection between coitus and conception. From the time when pregnancy is suspected the child begins to exert its influence over the life of the home. A pregnant woman is called *poạti*, this being the common Bengali term, but here too the Santal love of figurative speech finds full play, and other common ways of referring to pregnancy are to speak of a "full body" or a "heavy body" or to say that the woman is now "two souls". Many of the restrictions enjoined on the woman are due to the physical dangers that surround her during the period and at its climax. These dangers may be brought about not only through natural causes but also by the action of malignant spirits. Thus it is dangerous for a pregnant woman to go anywhere when the sun is directly overhead, nor does she go anywhere alone at sunset. She should not cross a river, though some of my informants affirmed that this prohibition applies only during a first pregnancy. She may not sit on the narrow ledge surrounding the house with her legs

[1] *Memoirs of the Royal Asiatic Society of Bengal*, Vol. X, *Studies in Santal Medicine and Connected Folklore*, Pt. II, "Santal Medicine".

dangling or her hair loose or any portion of her clothing hanging loosely from her body. She must not walk over the straw rope that is used for binding bundles in which grain is stored. She may not take any life nor may she look upon a dead body. It is not good to look on the image of a god at a temple or in the home of a Hindu neighbour. Is this due to the fact that although the image has the semblance of life it is dead? She must not weep when a death occurs. If there should be an eclipse of the moon she must remain indoors, and she must not look at the moon even from the shelter of the house. All these restrictions are ascribed by the Santals themselves to the need for escaping the attention of ghosts, the unsatisfied souls of the dead.

Other actions are enjoined or prohibited because of their effect on the appearance or the character of the child who is to be born, and so illustrate the Santal reaction to the observed facts of heredity, the mysterious "law" which can be seen operating in the likeness of a child to its parents. Thunder is dangerous, and when the mother hears thunder she clasps close to her abdomen the cylindrical grinding stone used for the grinding of spices in the preparation of curry. By so doing she guards against her child growing up to be afraid of thunder. Turmeric roots, also used in the preparation of curry, are frequently forked. If the mother is cooking she does not break off a forked piece lest her child be born with forked fingers. If she sees an elephant her child may be born with large flapping ears. If she sees a monkey she fears lest her child will be born with the wide nostrils in a sunken nose that are a simian characteristic and one that is not uncommon among the Santals. If she sees a snake the child may develop the habit of constant spitting. Then again, the pregnant woman's taste in food must be humoured. If her whims are denied her child may grow up with a mouth always watering and be known as a "slobberer". These precautions furnish a useful means of determining many of the physical and mental characteristics that are displeasing to the Santals. One informant related a case that had occurred in his own family of a child who was born without an anus. The women of the village discussed the phenomenon and cast round for the reason. They put it down to the fact that the mother must at some time while she was pregnant have eaten the flesh of the flying fox, the reason being the belief that flying foxes are without this feature in their anatomy. In this case, which happened about forty years ago, the child was thrown away in the jungle while it was still alive.

Society takes little notice of the child before it is born, but, through the person of the father, the family and the clan begin to assert their interests. The restrictions enjoined on the father suggest that although his rôle in the heredity of the child is considered to be a relatively minor one, he is nevertheless an instrument through which the future child may be brought into danger and so hurt the interests of the family. During the period of his wife's pregnancy he must strictly observe the rule against taking life and he must avoid all contact with dead bodies. He is therefore excused from all participation in funeral ceremonies; he may not help to carry a corpse or even enter a house in which a death has taken place. If the annual hunt falls during the period he is allowed to accompany the men of the village, but he is not allowed to kill or to carry a slain animal or bird. He must not eat flesh from the head of any animal slain in the hunt or offered in sacrifices.[1] He is not separated from his wife, and my information suggests that intercourse is usual up to about the sixth month. There is a very strong sentiment against a man having sexual intercourse with another woman during his wife's pregnancy. There appears to be no rule as to when intercourse may be resumed after the birth of the child. The women speculate concerning the sex of the coming child. If the mother begins to look sickly, and especially if she becomes thin round the neck, it is a sign that she will have a boy. Although the "quickening" is not marked by any ceremonial, it is recognized as a definite stage in the life of both the new individual and of the mother. When a woman dies with child the procedure to be followed varies according to whether the death has followed the first quickening or not.[2]

Midwives are engaged for the delivery. They are to be found in every large Santal village, and they are generally old women, themselves grandmothers. They receive no special training, but they develop the "knack" for their work by assisting others, and they launch out on their own practice when they have established a reputation for being handy and capable. The midwife may be someone connected with the family, but, if so, she should

[1] Bodding, in the *Santali Dictionary* (Vol. III, p. 337), reports a custom in connection with the *Jom Sim* festival which accords a certain status to the child before birth. I have been unable to confirm his statement. He says that when the *Jom Sim* is observed in the family of a pregnant woman she is served with two platefuls of rice because she is, or rather she represents, "two souls".

[2] The procedure to be followed in the former event and the reason underlying it have already been described in Chapter 8; see p. 92 above.

not belong to the same generation as the parents of the mother. It is better for her to belong to the generation of the grandparents, because it is not fitting for the woman in childbirth to expose her nakedness before anyone who belongs to the generation of her own parents. Midwives are held in respect, and their work puts them in a relation of intimacy with large numbers of their fellow villagers. They are known as *ḍhạī*, the common word in most parts of North India, but they are also referred to as *ojha buḍhi* and sometimes as *dak'-dul buḍhi*, "water-pouring old women". The midwife is always a Santal, and being an inhabitant of the same or of a neighbouring village, she is not sent for until the pains begin. At the same time all the married women of the village are informed, and they gather at the house in order, as they say, to give courage to the mother now that her time has arrived. On one occasion I was called in to help in the settlement of a dispute in which a woman had been accused of infidelity by her husband. She had gone to her mother's home before the birth of her child—this being an action which is not in accord with Santal ideas—and the strongest evidence of infidelity offered by the husband was the fact that when the baby was born his wife's mother did not inform any of her fellow villagers.

The day of delivery is the mother's "sitting day", and the name describes the position of the mother at the time of birth. The mother may sit either on a mat which has been placed on the floor or on a string bed. There seems to be no rule as to which of these two places must be adopted, except that when a woman has been on the floor for the birth of her first child she will continue to sit there for the birth of later children. In either case she remains in the ordinary dwelling house. She is supported at her back by one of the women, who again must be either two generations removed from her or else be of her own generation. It is the duty of the midwife to cut the umbilical cord, and this is not done until after the placenta has fallen. The child is not put to the mother's breast until after the cord has been cut. This is cut with an arrow, having a coin placed beneath it. This is most usually a copper pice, but it may be a coin of higher value when the financial position of the family warrants it, and the coin is given to the midwife. They say that midwives are able to foretell the sex of children still to be born according to the position of certain irregularities on the surface of the umbilical cord which are caused, I am told, by the twisting or congestion of blood vessels. In addition, if they are desired to do so, they are able to determine the sex of subsequent children according to the place at which the cord is cut.

Special measures have to be taken when delivery proves to be difficult. An *ojha* is called in if he lives at hand. He may resort to consulting the omens with leaf and oil, but if matters do not appear to be so serious he proceeds at once to prescribe treatment. One of his methods is to take a square of bark from a plantain tree in his right hand and to prick it repeatedly with a needle held in his left hand. Or a dagger is held upright over a brass drinking vessel and water is poured down the blade of the dagger, this water afterwards being given to the mother to drink. Another method is to tie a root to the mother's hair. It is important that the strand of hair to which the root is tied should be cut off as soon as the birth has taken place, lest she should lose her entrails as well. No men are admitted to the room where the birth is taking place, and the husband has to remain at hand in the courtyard. When the delivery is difficult he comes in for some chaffing or abuse according to the degree of difficulty. Some action of his at the time when conception occurred is held to be responsible. One of his duties is to keep by him the materials for lighting a fire in the room after the child is born. No fire is kept lit during the process of birth, but the fire lit immediately afterwards is used for providing a dry-heat massage for his wife's abdomen and for massage of the infant. As soon as the child is born, the women cry out the news to the husband and any others in the courtyard, and the former takes a large stick with which he repeatedly beats the roof, crying out loudly at the same time to drive away any lurking ghosts. As soon as the floor has been cleaned and the mother is resting, the husband is admitted into the room. He then digs a hole in the floor with a ploughshare and in it he buries the afterbirth. It must not be buried directly beneath a rafter. The Santal does not talk of his "birthplace"; he refers to it as "the village where my afterbirth was buried".

One of the ceremonies that take place on the day that the child is born appears to relate chiefly to the wellbeing of the mother. She and the midwife sit facing each other on the floor of the house. The mother fills a leaf cup with distilled liquor and passes the cup to the midwife, who throws away its contents on her left side; this is repeated three times. The ceremony is known as *met' halañ*, or "lifting the eye", and no Santal has been able to offer me an explanation of the custom. It may be ascribed to the necessity for taking precautions against the evil eye. Most of the subsequent proceedings centre round the child.

The word *chaṭiạr* is used both in connection with birth ceremonial and the later initiation. It is connected with the Hindi *chut*, which means "pollution", but the ceremonial stands not only for the removal of uncleanness but also for the reception, of the new member into society. The ceremonial uncleanness resulting from birth is shared by the whole village, and no religious festival may be held until it has been removed. The house in which the birth has occurred is the centre of the pollution, and none of the other villagers will eat or drink there while it is in operation. If anyone is wearing a charm against illness he removes it before entering the courtyard of the house, lest the charm lose its power. Although all the ceremonies must be completed within a month after the birth of the child, the actual dates may be modified by a variety of considerations. If a festival is due the ceremonies will be advanced rather than delay or abandon the festival. During the cultivation season they may be either advanced or delayed in order to suit the convenience of work in the fields. The normal day for the *chaṭiạr* is on the fifth day after the birth of a boy and on the third day after the birth of a girl. The essential elements in the removal of pollution are shaving and bathing. The villagers all gather together in the courtyard, and first of all the barber—one of the villagers, a Santal—shaves the village officials, then all the men present and lastly the father of the child. The newborn child is then carried by the midwife to the barber, who cuts five locks from the child's head: two from the front, one from each side and one from the middle of the back of the head. These locks are placed in a leaf cup pending their disposal. When the shaving has been completed the men go to the nearest bathing place and bathe themselves. On their return to the house the midwife takes all the women down to bathe, and she carries the arrow that was used for cutting the umbilical cord. Two pieces of string are attached to the arrow; one of these is used to tie up in a bundle the child's hair, and at the bathing place the hairs are detached and floated away on the water. The second string is soaked in oil and turmeric and tied round the child's waist; there it remains until it is worn out, when it is always replaced by another. When the women return from the bathing place the mother sips some cowdung and water that has been prepared by the midwife and rubs some of the mixture on her head. Then three leaf cups are filled with a paste made from sun-dried rice and water. The contents of one are sprinkled near the four legs of the string bed in the house, of the second on the breasts of the men, and of the third on the breasts of the women. Then a brew of *nim*[1] leaves and water is brought out. This is very bitter, and the men to whom it is first presented generally make excuses to escape from having to sip it. All the women take some, out of sympathy, as they express it, with the mother, who drinks a cupful. She often continues to drink small quantities for several days, as it is supposed to aid the flow of milk. At this gathering beer is provided for everyone, and if the family can afford to do so they prepare a meal as well.

An essential part of the ceremonies is the naming of the child, whereby it acquires a definite status in the village and among the kinsfolk. In the area round Sarenga the naming is sometimes accomplished on a day different from that on which the shaving and bathing take place, and it is the naming ceremony that emphasizes the social obligations of the household. The villagers may bathe on the fifth day and gather at the house for the naming on the seventh day. The midwife receives her payment at the gathering, and she is paid in cloth and rice, receiving also a bangle for cutting the cord. She receives twice as much rice for a boy as for a girl. The name is chosen by the parents of the child and it is announced to the villagers by the midwife. Holding the child in her arms, she says to them if the child is a boy: "From today call him so-and-so when he goes hunting." If the child is a girl she says: "From today call her so-and-so when you call her to draw water." The first-born boy is named after his father's father and the second boy is named after his mother's father. The first girl receives the name of her father's mother and the second girl that of her mother's mother. When these names have been used, children are given the names of uncles and aunts, with a preference on the whole for the father's family. Before the naming the guests ask: "Of what country is this child?" When the name chosen comes from the father's family, the question is answered by giving the name of the father's village, the mother's village being given when the chosen name comes from her relations. If a child cries excessively it may be put down to the fact that it is unhappy over its name. Babulal of Barikul wrote: "Sometimes among us the children sleep happily right from birth and at other times they

[1] *Melia azadirachta*, L. For its connection with godlings of disease see W. Crooke, *Religion and Folklore of Northern India*, especially pp. 119 ff., and index.

cry like crows and kites! In that case we call an *ojha* to tell us the reason and we say to him: 'See what this child is up to; why does he cry?' The *ojha* asks for oil, reads the omens and then says: 'Such and such a dead relative is claiming that the child be named after him.' This usually happens when we want to name the child after someone on the mother's side. The dead ancestors on the father's side do not like to have it so." The above passage occurs in a part of his diary where Babulal was reporting the birth of twins, for whose naming there are special rules. Twins are known as *boṅga* children, and their advent is not regarded as a misfortune. He continued his narrative: "Today the babies did not cry at all, for they were to have *boṅga* names." One explanation is that *Maraṅ Buru* had twelve sisters who were twins, and I have been told that the children of *Cando* were twins. The pairs of names that are given to twins are drawn from Hindu mythology and they are, for girls, Cit̨a and Kạpuṛ, Dạṛgi and Poṛgi, Hisi and Dhụmni; boy twins are named Ram and Lokhon, Loba and Kisur, Cand and Bhạira, Sidho and Kạnhu. Most Santals when asked have denied categorically that dissimilar twins are posible. The only case met with in eleven years were twins born at the Mission Hospital in Sarenga, and it proved impossible to follow up their subsequent history.

The name given at the *chạtiạr* ceremony is known as the *bhitri ṅutum*, which means literally the "inner" or "private" name. Everyone knows what his own inner name is, but it is little used by others. In addition to his private name each person receives at least one nickname, which is called the "upper" or "outer" name. This is necessary in part because of the prohibitions attaching to the use of names by certain categories of relations. If a boy has been named after one of his grandfathers, then all those who are prohibited by relationship from pronouncing the grandfather's name, e.g. the grandmother, are equally prohibited from applying that name to anyone else. Even those who could pronounce the name do not do so while the grandfather is alive, in order to avoid confusion. The nicknames given in early childhood do not remain fixed but are replaced by others as the boy grows up. Some result from the same kind of easy intimacy and teasing affection with which we are familiar in English society and are bestowed by those who stand in a "joking" relationship with the boy. A new element has been introduced through the naturalization of many Hindu names, particularly among those Santals who have received some education. In many cases Bengali names that bear some resemblance to the form of the private name come into use. Thus Podo has become Padma Lochan and Kala has become Kalachand. Ernest Soren was known throughout the countryside by the name that he received at his baptism. At the time of his *chaṭiar* he was given the name of Singrai, this being the name of his paternal grandfather's elder brother. From the same time he was addressed as Jhongol, thus receiving not only the private name but the outer name of the same relative, who was not then alive. Before he could walk he was usually addressed as Ṭhenṭa, a name that signifies a restless bundle of mischief. Later when he was growing up he was known by his contemporaries as Ḍangṛa Sorkar, or Sorkar for short. The name Sorkar is often applied to those who are going to school, but he was known as the "bullock" Sorkar because he did not conceal his fondness for beef, whereas educated Santals are generally supposed to conform to Hindu custom and shun it. Names of relatives are bestowed without regard to whether the relatives concerned are living or dead.

The village community takes no formal notice of the growing child after the performance of the *janam chaṭiar* until he is ready for the ceremony of initiation, or *caco chaṭiar*. *Caco* is a word that means a toddler, one who is learning to walk. The ceremony, however, is not performed until the child is growing up. It is somewhat misleading to describe the ceremony as one of initiation, for in comparison with the elaborate ritual with which initiation is accomplished in many parts of the world it is a pale and colourless proceeding. In the Bankura area the performance of the rite is of an extremely casual nature. It is nevertheless the equivalent for Santals of initiation ceremonies in other societies, and it retains its importance not because of the intrinsic character of the ritual but because of certain consequences that follow from its non-observance. Unless the *caco chaṭiar* has been performed, no Santal boy or girl may be married, nor cremated after death. It may be that the custom has been drastically modified because of the expense involved, as the whole village should be feasted. It is now customary for families to wait until the ceremony can be performed for several children at the same time, and it is therefore delayed until the impending marriage of the eldest child makes it inevitable. In the village of Barikul, Babulal recorded a case in which the father and the mother had been living together for some years without having themselves gone through any marriage ceremonial. For both of them it had been a second marriage, and as they were extremely poor their plea to set up house together had been allowed and the marriage celebration that had been postponed was indefinitely suspended. The time came when they wished to arrange a marriage for their eldest son and they found themselves involved in a difficulty. Until the formal celebration of their own marriage had taken place their son could not marry because in its absence they could not carry out the *caco chaṭiar* of their boy. The problem was solved by going through one of the permitted forms of marriage themselves, after which on the same day they performed the initiation of their three sons. They were scolded by the villagers who gathered for the occasion, but again pleaded their poverty.

The whole of the population of the village is invited for the ceremony, and each person must at the very least be given two cups of beer for each child on whose behalf the ceremony is being held. The feast for the whole village is not practicable except for a very few, and it is regarded as sufficient if the village officials are presented with a meal of rice and meat or chicken curry. If possible, the midwife who presided at the birth of the children bathes them in the courtyard by pouring water over them; and if she cannot, this is done by one of the old women present. Water is also sprinkled over the assembled guests. The *jog-mañjhi* recites the myth of Santal origins; beginning from the account of the creation of the world and the founding of the clans, he brings the story up to date by leading to the birth of the children in the particular family with which the villagers are at that moment concerned. Then there follows a dance in the courtyard, and songs are sung in honour of the family. The event is neither preceded nor followed by any period of instruction. Such materials as exist for comparing the institution in different parts of the Santal country suggest that possibly its observance is of greater importance in the north, particularly in the Santal Parganas. Bodding has described the ceremony, basing his account on the published Santali account of the traditions.[1] Recently a long and full account of the ceremonial has been published in Santali, and this account comes from the same area but does not include a description of an actual observance.[2] On the other hand, Mr. C. L. Mukherjea's account of Santal culture to the extreme south in the state of Mayurbhanj[3] omits all

[1] P. O. Bodding, *Santali Dictionary*, Vol. I, p. 443.
[2] Stephen H. Murmu, *Karam ar Caco Chaṭiar*, Dumka, 1945.
[3] C. L. Mukherjea, *The Santals*, Calcutta, 1943.

reference to the *caco chaṭiaṛ*, which suggests that it is at the very least an inconspicuous element in the life of the area.

The universal custom among Santals of cicatrization of the boys and tattooing among girls may have been connected originally with initiation, though there is no evidence of any such connection in the past and it certainly does not exist at the present time. Boys make a number of self-inflicted burns on their left forearm. The resultant circular scars are usually five in number, but the only rule is that the number of scars must be an odd number, for the odd numbers signify life while even numbers mean death. There may be only one scar and there may be as many as seven. There is no ceremonial to accompany the practice, and boys burn themselves as soon as they are old enough to understand the shame of the cowardice implied by the non-possession of the scars. They usually do it when they are out in the fields together herding the village cattle. A fire is lit and a small piece of rag is rolled and set alight. Each boy then presses the burning rag on to the skin of his left forearm as often as he wishes to do so, and the marks remain for life. The operation is known as *sikạ*. Santals believe that they will be known by these marks in the after-life and if they do not show them to the guardians of the next world they will be eaten by worms as "large as a foot-pedal rice husker". The same explanation is given for the custom of tattooing the girls.[1] Apart from this motive there is no evidence for a magico-religious basis of the practice. The term for tattooing is *khoda*, and girls must in all cases be tattooed before their marriage. The whole operation may not be completed at once, but may be spread over two or three cold seasons during which the tattooers carry on their work. In this area the work is done by women of one of the blacksmith castes who come from districts to the west. During the cold weather they go from one village to another, and they are, of course, paid for their work. The operation is performed with a long needle, and the dye consists of lampblack which is mixed with human milk—if possible with the milk of the tattooer. There is no relation between the designs and the clan to which the recipient belongs. Marks are tattooed on the temples, also on the side of the nose, on the cheeks and on the chin. Designs to look like necklaces are common, and sometimes there is a decorative belt round the waist. Arms are decorated as with bangles and armlets, and there may be a design on the back of

[1] W. Crooke (*Religion and Folklore in Northern India*, p. 296) alludes to the practice among other tribes and castes.

the hand. The same is true of both legs and ankles. In fact, the decoration *motif*[1] appears to be uppermost and was well expressed by an old woman who said: "When I die I shall lose all my ornaments; but these at least I shall be able to take with me."

[1] See illustrations on p. 131 of tattoo marks from the left and right fore arms of a woman.

CHAPTER II

MARRIAGE

THE choice of a bride is limited firstly by the strict observance of tribal endogamy. No Santal who forms an alliance with a non-Santal can hope to be reinstated in society. The only cases that occur are found when individual Santals are away from their village community; Santal women working in " the east" do sometimes become the concubines of men of other races, but I have heard of only one man who had taken to wife a woman of another caste. He was a fugitive from the police who had been away from his village for some years, and he was living with a woman of *Haṛi* caste. The choice is further limited by the rules governing clan exogamy and also by the laws that regulate "avoidance" between certain relations by marriage. A man may marry the sister of his elder brother's wife with whom he is on terms of familiarity. On the other hand, he may not marry the sister of his younger brother's wife. All these restrictions are accepted without question; they are part and parcel of the religious and magical framework within which life must be lived.

Then there are many practical considerations that enter into the forming of any alliance between two families. Parents on both sides of the marriage make careful inquiries about each other's families. The location of the bride's home is of some importance. It is not advisable for a youth to marry a girl from his own village. "A hen and a bride from the same village run to their homes", says the proverb. Just as it is foolish to expect a hen from another house in the village to become domesticated in new quarters, one cannot expect a bride to settle down happily when her own parents are so near at hand. On the other hand, if the bride's home is too far away, the burden and expense of mutual visits become considerable, and so it is best to seek a bride whose home is within a day's easy walk from her future husband's home. Inquiries are made about financial stability and health. Particular attention is paid to signs of leprosy, which is widespread, and also tuberculosis. The qualities most admired in brides are a capacity for hard work and good health, cheerfulness and a steady disposition. In spite of the prevalence of pre-puberty marriage in India, it is extremely rare among Santals. In the only case that has come to my notice, an old man of sixty-five, whose only son had died, arranged a marriage for his granddaughter in order that she might be settled in life before he passed away. The girl was seven years of age and she was married to a boy of fourteen. Only a token bride price was received. Girls are usually married when they are about sixteen, while young men are generally between the ages of twenty and twenty-five. There is no test of a prospective bride's virginity. The fact that sexual experience of a kind is common before marriage is known to all, though it is not openly or actively encouraged, and a girl who is thought to be a wanton may have to wait for marriage through one of the more irregular channels that are open to her.

The initiative is taken by the parents of the bridegroom. Parents of marriageable girls are not always passive spectators, but any inquiries instituted by them are likely to be tactful and indirect. When the parents of a young man have made tentative inquiries and wish to begin negotiations they engage the services of a friend as a "go-between", known as a *raebaric'*, to visit the home of the prospective bride. He addresses the parents of the girl in some such roundabout manner as the following: "Have you found a place yet for your new cooking pot? I have some friends who are unable to cook their herbs and so they have asked me to find a new cooking pot for them." If the report of this first visit is satisfactory it is followed by an exchange of ceremonial visits. First a party from the bridegroom's village journey to the bride's home. The go-between is accompanied by the young man's parents and some of their friends, a party of five or seven persons in all. Omens by the way are noted, and they are not all left to chance. Before the party enter the bride's village the *raebaric'* goes ahead and tells the people to do nothing that will upset the auspicious nature of the occasion. When leaving their own village or on entering the girl's village, should they see fire, an axe, a woman with a load of wood on her head, a snake or a jackal crossing the path from left to right, they return home and the whole matter is dropped. If, however, they see a full water pot, a cow, a new brass plate, a panniered bullock, the pugmarks of a leopard or a jackal crossing the path from right to left, the omens are good. If all goes well, details of the bride price are fixed, a time is arranged when the bride's relations will pay their return visit and all is sealed by the proferring and acceptance of tobacco and beer.

On their way home from the bride's house the members of the party sing:

O go-between, how far have you been
In search of good omens?

To which he replies:

Far away across the hills
Where *Cando boṅga* appointed.

Again a question is asked:

O go-between, how big is the bride?

And the reply comes:

Not big nor little,
Like a broom with bells in the handle,
She is firm when used for sweeping.[1]

On the return of the party the bridegroom asks eagerly for news and his mother tells him:

I looked at her with my hand covering my eyes,
I tested the new pot by striking it,
I will choose you a sound earthen pot.[2]

When the bride's folk pay their first visit to the bridegroom's home the go-between sings to them:

Look well at the bridegroom, look well at the house,
Raise the sheaves of straw and look well.[3]

Behind this song there lies a story. It happened once that a party were visiting the home of a prospective bridegroom. They were well pleased by the condition of the house and went away satisfied with their welcome. During the whole time of their visit the young man whose home they had gone to see was seated on the veranda. His legs covered by straw, he busied himself plaiting straw rope. The next time they saw him they found that he was lame and they had been tricked. The warning serves a useful purpose, for cases where defects have been concealed are not unknown.

The party sing also about the bridegroom. They ask:

O go-between, how far is the bridegroom's home?

[1] See Appendix B, No. 22.
[2] See Appendix B, No. 23.
[3] See Appendix B, No. 24.

And this is the reply:

> Neither far nor near,
> There by the plantain grove it can be seen.

Again they ask:

> O go-between, how big the bridegroom?

The answer comes:

> Neither big nor little,
> He herds the cows on the banks where the *kasi*[1] grass grows,
> Playing sweetly on his flute.[2]

During the month of March 1939 Babulal recorded: "Eleven people from our village, men and women together, went today to Ambritpal to see a bridegroom. When they came to our village there were seven of them. As we were going to see the bridegroom our party was larger by four; it is our custom that more should go to see the bridegroom than come to see the bride. The party returned in the evening, singing songs as they came, for they had been drinking. The girl's relations asked them: 'Well, and how was the bridegroom and what did you think of the house? Were you pleased?' They replied: 'We are satisfied. The lad looks well enough and the house was in good condition, only we saw no "elephants' eggs".'[3] One of the men said: 'I sat so that I could see right into the inner chamber, but I could see nothing there.' A fortnight later a similar party went from Barikul and returned at an earlier hour. A number of people said: 'Why have they come back so soon? It looks as though they were not satisfied about the bridegroom. If they had been they would not have returned before sunset.' Others, however, said: 'No, they must have been pleased because they have been drinking!' "

Tradition enjoins that a further set of ceremonial visits follows these first visits in order to ratify the "engagement", but when the families are already well acquainted both time and expense are frequently saved by going through with the engagement on the first ceremonial visit. The ceremony is known as

[1] *Saccharum spontaneum*, L.
[2] See Appendix B, No. 25.
[3] Another example of figurative speech. A name for bales in which grain is stored. Their presence would indicate prosperity.

horok' cikhna, the "putting on of a sign" in token of the agreement. When the bridegroom's party arrive at the home of the prospective bride they are welcomed as honoured guests. String beds are placed in the courtyard for them to sit on, their feet are washed and massaged with oil and they are served with beer. This over, they are taken into the house and given parched rice with molasses to eat. Their hands are then washed by their hosts and they are served with more beer before emerging from the house. Then the guests adjourn to bathe, and on their return they are seated on mats in the courtyard to eat a meal. This meal consists of rice and curry. Unless food consists of rice and curry it is never considered to be a full meal. While the menfolk eat, the women prepare themselves by dressing their hair; they put vermilion in their hair parting and also on both sides of the forehead, the marks going up from the outer end of the eyebrows in the shape of horns. When all have eaten and washed, the guests sit down once more and the bride-to-be is brought out by a married woman to pay her respects to the visitors. When she makes a low obeisance before the bridegroom's father he invests her with the "sign". This is either a necklace, a piece of cloth or a pair of bangles. When she bows before him she places at his feet a small brass vessel full of water, and in it he drops two rupees.

In the conversation that follows, all outstanding details of the wedding arrangements are completed. First there has to be agreement about the bride price. This is known by two different terms, both of which are of Indo-Aryan origin. The first term, *gonoṅ*, is from a root meaning to count or calculate, and the second, *poṅ*, is from a root meaning earnest-money or a pledge. The amount is variable, and this leads to some bargaining. Thirty years ago seven rupees used to be considered a high figure, whereas now the sum varies from eleven to twenty-one rupees. The *jogmạñjhi* of the bridegroom's village asks the bride's father to declare his wishes. He does so, not in words, but by placing the correct number of cowrie shells in leaf cups, whereupon the cups are passed over to the visitors. When a small bride price is agreed upon, the bridegroom's father understands that he cannot expect any gifts at the time of the marriage and he will have to bear the expenses of his own party for new clothes. Ordinarily, however, the bride's parents present the cloth to be worn by the bridegroom during the marriage ceremony. In addition, his family are entitled to receive the present of a cow or a goat, according to circumstances. The bride's family expects, in addition to the bride price, to receive a cloth for the bride's mother, one for her father's eldest sister and one each for her two grandmothers.

Some agreement must also be reached about the time of the marriage. This must not take place in the month in which either the bridegroom or bride was born. Formerly, I was told, there was no other prohibition regarding the month. Nowadays, however, the general practice of Hindus in Northern India is followed. Astrologers are not consulted, but marriages may not take place during the rains, and the most popular months are during the spring when the harvest has been gathered in and food is abundant. When the time is approaching, the actual date of the wedding is arranged by the go-between, and the *giṛạ* is used to mark off the days remaining.

The whole community in both villages is vitally concerned in the due celebration of the wedding, and this fact is emphasized by the rôle of the village officials. The *jogmạñjhi* of the bride's village acts as the master of ceremonies from the time when the marriage booths have to be erected until the end. The headman of the bridegroom's village does not take part in the preliminary visits by virtue of his office, but when the two families immediately involved are satisfied that they wish to proceed, both headmen are called in. They have to be present when the engagement is confirmed, and they are consulted about suitable dates. The final "contract" at the climax of the wedding celebrations is entered into by the people of the two villages, and it is made by the respective headmen. The village priest also plays a part, for the community involved in the marriage includes the spirits, who are guardians of the welfare of the tribe, and the ancestors, guardians of family and clan. Their blessing has to be sought. In an interesting passage Dr. Verrier Elwin says of the marriage ceremonial of the tribes of the Maikal hills: "There is little religion in it." On any definition of religion it would be difficult to maintain this thesis with regard to Santal marriage. The whole passage is quoted here, for the rest of what is said does apply in most of its detail to the Santal form of marriage: "We have already spoken of this ceremony as a work of art. There is little religion in it, but it has great social and symbolic value. It is hard to conceive of a better way of impressing on a man and woman their social and sexual union. The tying together of the clothes, the exchange of rings, the first meals together, the ceremonies by the river that symbolize mutual aid in domestic, sexual and food-obtaining activities, are of great significance.

They are all the more important because some of them are things that a boy and girl would never do publicly together."[1] Among the Santals many of the symbolic acts cannot be truly interpreted apart from their relation to the unseen world. The invocations used in addressing the spirits at the time of marriage come as near to true prayer as any used at other times.[2] Before the wedding party leaves the bridegroom's village for the home of the bride, the bridegroom's father provides a hen for the village priest, who offers it in the sacred grove. He prays: "We offer to you a hen because of the marriage booth. Accept it, enjoy it and grow big. Now we are about to go as a marriage party to such and such a village. Guard us so that on the way through the forest there may be no sudden fright, no tripping, no tumbling, no spells, no enchantments. Clear the way for us to right and to left, O father spirits. There we shall eat and drink. May we suffer no stomach pains, no head pains. Guard us also so that there be no quarrels, no bickerings, no divisions, no disturbances, no ruin, no spoiling between relations."

Before the marriage, booths are erected in the courtyards of both homes, and all the villagers assist in the work. Straw ropes are strung from side to side in the village street with mango leaves inserted through the strands, and the courtyards are decorated in the same manner. The posts of the booths are made with branches of the *matkom* tree. In the floor a hole is dug in which some fresh turmeric mixed with sun-dried rice, five cowrie shells and three leaves of *dhubi*[3] grass are buried. These are covered in and then the whole floor is plastered with cowdung The young men who build the booth are feasted and provided with beer. On the day before setting out for the bride's village the bridegroom's party go to the village bathing place for the "water marriage". One of the young men digs a small hole at the water side into which the water can seep and three arrows are planted round the hole. Vermilion is placed on the arrows, while at their base are placed some cowrie shells and a hen's egg. One of the women shoots at the water with an arrow, while another strikes it with a "sword", generally a stick. Then libations of beer are poured out to *Maraṅ Buru* and the ancestors before all present partake. Finally, water is drawn in pots and taken to the home. Again when they reach the courtyard another hole is dug, the arrows are placed round it and the water

[1] V. Elwin and S. Hivale, *Folk-Songs of the Maikal Hills*, p. 205.
[2] One example has been quoted in Chapter 6, p. 67.
[3] *Cynodon dactylon*, Pers. Reg.

is poured into the hole. The "anointing girls" are tied to the arrows by a thread fastened to their left wrists, and they have to husk a grain of rice in their fingers without breaking it while the bridegroom is shaved and bathed preparatory to being anointed. The anointing ceremony is carried out in the evening by unmarried girls who anoint the assembled company with a mixture of oil and turmeric. The village priest and then his wife are first anointed, after which the remainder of the officials, then the villagers, then the father and mother of the bridegroom, and lastly the bridegroom himself.

A similar ceremony is carried out in the home of the bride, beginning with the "water marriage". The bride is led out in procession from the house to the courtyard holding the hand of her *hili*, or elder brother's wife, and accompanied by two unmarried girls, the "anointing girls". In her right hand the *hili* holds a brass pot full of water which she sprinkles to right and to left. The other girls bear plates in their hands on which there are several leaf cups. One contains a small lamp that has been lit, and others contain turmeric and sun-dried rice and sprigs of *dhubi* grass. The women in the courtyard sing:

> Round and about
> The guinea fowl flies;
> Round and about
> The black cow's house.
> It fell in the water hole, a golden chain;
> It fell in the spring, a silver anklet.
> Who picked up the golden chain?
> Who has gathered the silver anklet?
> Kạru[1] picked up the golden chain,
> Kạru has gathered the silver anklet.[2]

The procession moves round the booth three times, after which the bride is seated under its roof. The anointing follows, and the bride is anointed after the *dhubi* grass has been placed on her head. When the ceremony is over the bride is led back into the house and the older folk dance and sing:

> In whose courtyard has water sprung forth,
> Water sprung forth and is now flowing away?
> In a Hembrom[3] courtyard has water sprung forth,
> Water sprung forth that is now flowing away.[4]

[1] Here the name of the bridegroom is sung.
[2] See Appendix B, No. 26.
[3] The clan name of the bride.
[4] See Appendix B, No. 27.

If the distance between the two villages be great, the party of the bridegroom will have arrived on the outskirts of the bride's village on that evening and are accommodated in a special shelter for the night. They do not enter the village, but at the first sign of approaching morning the go-between comes from the bridegroom's camp, bringing with him a small quantity of the oil and turmeric left over from the bridegroom's anointing, and with this the bride is once more anointed.

Meanwhile the bridegroom's party make ready to approach the bride's house. The *jogmạṅjhi* and *goḍet'* of the village meet them at the end of the village street, where they are asked to wait awhile. Mats are placed for them to sit on and they are given tobacco to smoke. The bridegroom's party always enter a village from the west end and leave from the east end. The officials who greet the party are accompanied by a band of young folk from the village who sing and dance and who in the course of their songs make insulting remarks about the bridegroom and the village from which he comes. These insults are expected and have to be accepted in good part. When they at length set out for the bride's house, the bridegroom is carried by a woman who lifts him and carries him on her hip as she would a child. On first arriving at the bride's home, some of her friends pretend that the bridegroom is not properly groomed, so they proceed to shave him again with a leaf for a mirror and a rough piece of wood for a razor. When he greets his future father-in-law he places a necklace round his neck while his father-in-law winds a turban cloth round his head, after which they sprinkle water over each other with a spray of mango leaves. They exchange *pan*[1] and embrace each other. When the bride is brought out of the house she is carried in the same way as the bridegroom, and first of all they sprinkle sun-dried rice over each other (this is called "sowing" the rice), and follow it by sprinkling water with the sprays of mango leaves. The bride is seated in a basket and made to face the west, while the bridegroom faces towards the east. Then he takes from a small wooden box that is wrapped in his waistband the vermilion which he proceeds to place on the bride's head, and as he does so the assembled company make the air resound with shouts of "*Horibol*". This is sheer Hinduism, for it is the invocation of Hari, one of the names of Vishnu the Saviour. The bridegroom helps the bride down from the basket, places an

[1] The leaf of the *Piper betle*, L., rolled with lime, the nut of the areca palm and other spices wrapped inside it. Rarely eaten by Santals except on ceremonial occasions, but very generally used by others in Bengal.

iron bangle on her wrist and iron betel nut crackers in her hand. Then they are led inside the house, where they are set down and fed on a dish of black beans and rice. The bridegroom has to make a show of refusing to eat until the bride's father presents him with a rupee.

The party outside begin to drink beer that is variously named by the different groups. The bride's fellow villagers drink beer "in honour of the guests", while the bridegroom's fellow villagers drink "in honour of the new relations"; the young people are permitted to drink "dew beer" that will help them to avoid the chill they might otherwise contract by dancing and drumming through the whole night. While a feast of goat's meat curry and rice is being prepared the guests sit around and talk and sing. The headmen of the two villages, however, have some work to complete. The presents from the bridegroom's family are handed over by their headman to the bride's headman. These are for the most part clothing. The *boṅga iṭaṭ'* is a cloth of twelve cubits for the sister of the bride's father. *Iṭaṭ'* is a word that ordinarily means food left over on the plate of one who has eaten; perhaps it is applied to these presents in the sense that they are left over when the bride price has been given and received. The bride's mother receives a cloth of eleven cubits. The grandmothers receive cloths of ten cubits known as the *heṛe iṭaṭ'*, or husks. The bride's father may receive a cow, and her maternal uncle is given a money fee, it is said, instead of a cow. The amount given is small, usually a few annas. The headmen themselves receive a half-rupee each, the *jogmaṅjhi* receives a loin-cloth and the *goḍet'* one anna, while the anointing maidens receive a half-anna each. In this way the special duties and responsibilities of various parties to the wedding are acknowledged. The bride's maternal grandmother is made to "pay" for her cloth. She does so by presenting five small measures of rice, five sticks of turmeric and five rolled cheroots to the bridegroom's headman, all being wrapped in a bundle together. The bride price that is paid at this time is also paid through the headmen. Many of the presents and fees are known by hidden names. The bride price is called the "milk tree", a term that is also used sometimes for a mother; the fee received by the headmen is known as the "tree of the sacred grove"; the cloth for the bride's mother is called "hot water".[1]

When the feasting is over the bridegroom's party gets ready to leave and the members are escorted to the end of the village street. There once more they sit down and a final beer-drinking

[1] See Chapter 4, p. 48, for other examples connected with marriage.

takes place. This is drunk only by the headmen of the two villages. Water from a brass pot is spilt on the ground and the headman of the bride's village delivers a marriage sermon. Here and there the words of the sermon may vary slightly, but the form is fairly well established. The bridegroom is addressed: "Well now then, from today we have tied a wooden cow bell round your neck. When you go out to hunt and when you go to collect fruits in the forest you may eat a half of whatever you find, but you must bring a half of it home." The bride is told: "Well now, until today you have been able to go about just as you wanted to, but from today we have tied a wooden cow bell round your neck; you can no longer go about to markets and festivals as you please." The headman of the bridegroom's village is told: "O father headman, from today our two villages have become as one. When the girl has any illness or when she dies, it is for you to see to it. Up till now you have not been responsible, but from today we shall require of you blood of the head, blood of the ear. If any mishap befalls and you cannot spare a man to send the news, then you must send word by a dog. Formerly you were strangers and you used to pass by our village. Now if any of your people is passing this way going to hunt or going to market and he is thirsty, he must stop and ask for a drink." The headman of the bridegroom's village makes a suitable reply acknowledging the new ties that bind them together.

The comparative freedom of association between youths and girls in markets, fairs and other gatherings of Santals gives rise to situations that cannot be dealt with as normal marriages, and so other forms are recognized. When an unmarried girl becomes pregnant, providing there are no barriers to the marriage on account of clan and family relationships, she is encouraged to go to the home of the youth involved in the case. Bride price is paid, but the ceremony of putting vermilion on her head has to be postponed until after the birth of her child. Sometimes the village has to take cognizance of a situation arising out of the disagreement of the parents of either a girl or a boy to a marriage which they both desire. It may be that the boy and girl have run away together. Then the village officials call a council to regularize the situation. The father of the bride can claim only half the usual amount of bride price and the only cloths provided by the bridegroom's father are for the bride's mother and maternal grandmother. The third cloth is not given, I was told, "because it has been eaten by white ants", i.e. when the young couple lay out on the ground of the forest together. There are two ways open to a youth to force the issue on unwilling parents or an unwilling bride. Marriage by capture is still recognized as valid, provided that the girl expresses her willingness to stay with her captor. In such cases all the usual presents have to be given and a double bride price must be paid. The second method open to an impatient bridegroom is to waylay the girl of his choice and forcibly place the vermilion on her head. This is usually accomplished with the aid of his friends and often with the secret connivance of the girl concerned. Marriage by this means has to be recognized, but the fellow villagers of the outraged girl's parents do not accept the situation without protest. They march to the young man's village and if on their arrival they receive a friendly welcome and are asked to be reasonable they sit down to talk and make arrangements, which include an enhanced bride price by way of compensation to the girl's parents. If, on the other hand, they are received sullenly and the young man hides from them they become angry and do all the damage they can to his home, from pulling down the roof to killing any animals that may belong to his family.

Occasionally it happens that a girl takes matters into her own hands and forces her way into the home of the young man whom she wants to marry her. This, according to Santals, is only a ruse, for no girl would go to such a length unless she had very good reason to suppose that she would be welcomed. When this has happened marriage does not necessarily follow, but the girl must not be turned out and sent back to her own home until a council representing the two villages has met and sanctioned such a course. If marriage is decided upon, the girl's father has to forego the bride price. Another type of concession is made when the parents of the bride are considered to be too poor to pay all the expenses of the full ceremony. The wedding then takes place in the home of the bridegroom and it is known as a *ṭunki dipil bapla*. *Ṭunki* is the name of a small basket in which the presents, including a cloth for the bride, are carried on the head—the meaning of *dipil*—to her home. These things with the bride price are taken to the bride's home, but the party return on the same day to the home of the bridegroom, taking with them the bride and her relations, and there the main ceremony is performed.

A second marriage, whether it be the marriage of a widow or a widower, a woman who has been previously divorced or a man who is taking a second wife, conforms to a simpler pattern than a first marriage. The bride price paid is only a half of the usual amount. The man and the woman are seated on the ground facing each other. The man takes a flower in his hand, and applying the vermilion to the flower and not direct to the woman's head he places the flower in her hair. Afterwards he places on her arm the iron bangle. As one would expect, widowers are usually anxious to marry again as soon as possible, for they are greatly dependent on the help of the woman in the home and in their fields. In the spring of 1941 I was passing through a village in which a wedding was in progress between a widower and a girl who had been previously married and deserted by her husband. In that year marriages were scarce in the countryside because the previous year's rice crop had been a failure and not many could meet the expenses of a wedding. This bridegroom explained his position to me in these words: "I just had to be married again. My first wife was destroyed last year, and if I have no wife who will help me in the fields? I cannot pay wages for labour." He pointed to the bride and asked me what I thought of her. My comments were, I hope, extremely tactful; he told me: "She is a very strong woman." Most of the women who contract a second marriage have been divorced. Although there is no bar to widow remarriage, widows do not often marry again. One reason is the existence of a modified form of fraternal polyandry. A woman is permitted to have sexual relations with her husband's younger brother, and in the event of her husband's death it is his younger brother's duty to marry her. Even where the conditions are not favourable to such an arrangement, she is usually welcome to stay on in the home of her late husband. She probably does a good deal more than earn her own keep by her share in the work of the household, and where she has children they belong to the clan and family of her husband and make a bond between her and the rest of the family.

Cases of polygamy are rare. The most frequently recognized cause of a polygamous marriage is the absence of children by the first wife. Such a wife may be divorced or leave, but sometimes she prefers to remain with her husband, who takes another wife in order to beget children. The only case known to me where a man had three wives was exceptional in another way, for he was one of the few Santals of the area who was a prosperous landowner-cultivator. In all that has been said the assumption has been made that the family is patrilocal. The only exception to this rule arises when a man has no sons but has daughters. In this event one at least of the daughters remains at her own home after her marriage, and her husband, known as a "house son-in-law", comes to live there. This arrangement is common to all agricultural communities in Bengal. Among the Santals no bride price has to be paid, and in some instances the marriage ceremony is postponed till the end of a trial period during which the youth lives in the home of his future father-in-law and works for him without wages. He is accepted as the girl's husband when he is known to be a good worker, and thereby he also establishes his claim to receiving a portion of the land when his father-in-law dies. He does not change his clan, for this he cannot do, but he and his heirs can inherit from his wife's father. Hence this form of marriage furnishes the only exception to the rule that land must not pass out of the possession of the clan.

The term for divorce comes from the symbolic act that accompanies it. It is *sakam orec'*, or "leaf tearing". There are two sufficient reasons for a man to divorce his wife. The first is infidelity and the second is witchcraft. As marriage is a contract that involves two villages, representatives of both villages are summoned to sanction the divorce. The bride's father is compelled to return the bride price and the husband makes formal declaration of the divorce. He takes a *sarjom* leaf between his hands and tears it down the centre in token of the dissolution of the marriage tie. Then he has to provide a meal for those who have been summoned to the council. Owing to the fact that the bride price has to be repaid to the husband's family, the parents of the bride frequently object to the action, and where the guilt of the wife requires to be proved the proceedings may drag on for several months. If her parents can show that some blame attaches to the husband they can retain the bride price, and this they usually wish to do even when they do not desire their daughter to be reinstated in her husband's home. Until the bride price has been repaid the formal dissolution cannot take place.

A wife cannot formally divorce her husband, but she can, and sometimes does, refuse to continue to live with him. The problem of the runaway wife is one that is continually exercising the Santal village community, a fact that suggests the existence of many underlying strains. The mother-in-law is frequently blamed. In one family well known to me the wife of the younger son ran to her own home during the cultivation season in several successive years. At that time her presence was greatly needed to help with the fields, and she asserted her rights by running away. Her own explanation was that her mother-in-law made her work too hard and did not give her enough to eat. She remained with her own parents, who were not unwilling to feed her while she could be of service to them, but would return her to her husband after a lapse of two or three months. They settled down to normal married life after the mother-in-law had become aged and enfeebled by rheumatism. Sometimes a wife who suffers from continuous fever refuses to stay in her husband's home, and if there are other causes of discontent her refusal may become permanent, in which case her father has to return the bride price and she becomes free to marry elsewhere.

Although the standards of Santal morality allow for a wide variety of sexual behaviour, once those standards have been flouted society can be fiercely intolerant. In the spring of 1939 a daughter of the village priest at Barikul who was married to a "house son-in-law" was discovered in the act of having sexual intercourse with a young man of the same village in the adjoining forest. There was some delay in taking action, for the headman from the aggrieved husband's village was asked to attend the council. The elders meanwhile extorted a preliminary fine of ten rupees from the guilty man, at which the young men were enraged. One of them said: "When we are guilty of small faults you fine us five rupees; in future you should take only five annas from us." When the council met, the amount of the fine was raised to sixty rupees. This was raised within two hours by the man selling all the livestock that he possessed. Of this sum, five rupees was for the villagers of Barikul, five rupees for the fellow villagers of the aggrieved husband, and the balance was paid to the aggrieved husband to enable him to find another wife. He was also allowed to collect from the home certain things that he had earned while living there—a spade, an axe and the brass cooking utensils. Ordinarily when a home is broken up such things are divided between the husband and the wife. On the same evening a party of the villagers accompanied him to a neighbouring village and completed a marriage ceremony for him with a new wife. Most of the usual formalities were omitted, but a bride price was paid and the marriage sealed. The guilty man was required to take the wife into his own home, but when next day the villagers found that this had not been done they went to the priest's home, where they found the young woman lying on the floor seriously ill. In spite of her condition, they took her down to her paramour's home, only to be met by his irate wife and mother brandishing axes. She was taken back to her own home and the council was again summoned. The elders by now had become seriously alarmed by the possibility of violence, and were relieved rather than otherwise when word was brought that the girl had died. Evidence showed that she had that morning taken poison in the form of oleander seeds, which furnish an easy means of taking poison. Their efforts were now directed towards the necessity for deciding how to report her death. In every village there is a *chowkidar*, or village policeman, appointed by the government, one of his duties being to report births and deaths. The villagers solemnly debated with him whether they should report the truth and trust to the possibility of bribing the *daroga*, or police inspector, in order to escape further inquiry, but they decided in the end to suppress the truth and save trouble. The girl was buried deep in the forest without ceremony, and her death was later reported as being due to fever. The council then decided that they would inflict the traditional penalty for adultery on her paramour. This is twofold. Images of the two guilty persons are made and carried through the village; and, in addition, heavy stones are attached to the genitals of the man, who is then made to walk through the village. In this case he took the remedy into his own hands by summarily leaving the village, to which he did not return till the lapse of several months had served to cool the general indignation.

CHAPTER 12
DEATH

It is far easier to describe the actions of the Santals in the face of death than to reduce their beliefs concerning death and the destiny of man's soul to any system. Under the stress of bereavement the behaviour of the men is stoical, in somewhat marked contrast to the behaviour of the majority of the peoples among whom they live. The women, however, give full vent to the expression of their grief and voice their lamentations in words that are poetical in form and content. As soon as a death has occurred, preparations are made for the burning. Cremation is the almost universal rule, although there are certain significant exceptions. Children who die before puberty are buried with little ceremony in shallow graves on the edge of the forest, and though thorns are placed over the grave to protect the body from wild animals, such graves are often disturbed. Men and women who have died from certain diseases are buried in the same manner, a fact that accounts for the often unsavoury condition of the patch of jungle that adjoins the compound of the Mission Hospital at Sarenga. This is particularly true of those who die from tuberculosis, which is known to the Santals as *khok' ajar*, or "cough fever", and leprosy, which is called the "great disease". When deaths occur in the village from these causes or from some other infectious disease such as smallpox, the living avoid contact with the dead bodies as far as possible. The body of the dead person is fastened to a rude stretcher made with *sarjom* saplings, and the stretcher is then yoked to a pair of bulls which drag it out of the village. There the body is left after a token burial with a few handfuls of earth, and the task of corpse disposal is left to the vultures and jackals. In some villages burial is the custom because of the difficulty of obtaining sufficient firewood.

In the usual course of events the *goḍet'* goes through the village calling on every house to contribute its share of the wood for the burning. From each house one of the men takes a stick for the burning to the bereaved home, while one of the women takes along a small amount of oil and turmeric for anointing the body, and, if the dead person be a married woman, some vermilion in addition. When all have gathered, the corpse is washed and rubbed all over with the oil and turmeric; in the case of a married woman fresh vermilion is put on her forehead and in the parting of her hair. Next, all the articles required for the cremation are collected. These include a spade, an axe, parched rice, an old winnowing fan, a water pot, a handful of straw from the roof of the house, cotton seeds, a small earthen pot containing turmeric paste, flour made from sun-dried rice, and a hen. The body is carried out from the courtyard feet first on a string bed that is borne by four men. When the end of the village street is reached the bed is set down for a minute and those who wish to do so anoint the body once more for the last time. The women folk do not accompany the body beyond the confines of the houses. When the last anointing is over, the bed is picked up and carried to the regular cremation ground, which is by the side of a stream or a lake. At Sarenga, where both Santals and non-Santals live, they share the same cremation ground. The pyre is known as the *sara*; it is constructed from north to south and the body is placed upon it with the head pointing to the south, this being the general Hindu custom as well. The foundation is made with large logs on which kindling wood and smaller pieces of firewood are laid, and the four corners are marked by driving stakes into the ground. Before the pyre is set alight all clothing is removed from the body, including the piece of string that has been fastened round the waist since a string was first placed there at the time of the *janam chaṭiạr*. Leaves and small pieces of wood are placed over the body to "cover the shame". When the body is in position the hen is sacrificed. It is transfixed to one of the upright corner stakes with thorns. "The reason", said a Santal, "is this. One life has gone, and to save that life in the next world we send another life. By giving this other life we please *Jom Raj* (the king of the underworld according to Hindu mythology)."

When a married woman has died her husband has to apply fire to the corpse. In the case of a man the duty is performed by his eldest son, and failing a son it falls to the lot of the senior kinsman on the male side who is present. He takes in his hand a thin stick to the end of which a rag has been tied. This end he dips in the oil vessel and it is then set alight. Then, suported by two of his neighbours, he walks round the funeral pyre three times, after which he puts the burning cloth to the mouth of the corpse, looking in the opposite direction as he does so. Even in cases where the corpse is buried, fire must be applied to the mouth. When this has been done, the two men who have been supporting the chief mourner set fire to the two southern corners of the pyre, while one of them watches to see that the fire takes proper hold. It remains his duty to see that the fire burns properly until the corpse has been thoroughly consumed. When it is over the onlookers begin to search among the embers for the *jaṅbaha*, literally the "bone-flower". I have never met a Santal who has been able to explain the meaning of the term. Three pieces of bone are collected, two from the skull and one piece of the collar bone. The turmeric paste and the sun-dried rice flour are mixed together and used to clean the bones; the small earthen pot in which the turmeric was carried is cleaned in the fire, and when it is dry the inside is again cleaned with some of the paste, after which the bones are put into it. The mouth of the pot is then stopped up with a fragment of earthenware and is sealed with some of the same paste; a small hole, however, is left in the centre of the lid "to enable the dead one to breathe". The remains of the fire are put out with great care. One of the men brings water from nearby, using the water pot brought from the house for this purpose; others sprinkle water and one man scatters the ashes with the winnowing fan. If the fire should rekindle it is thought to be a great misfortune. Men would have to be collected to put it out once more and the bereaved family would be made to pay a fine to the rest of the village. When the fire is out the ashes are brought together in a small space and the rest of the site is cleaned with a plaster of cowdung and water. The parched rice is then sprinkled over the cleaned space, and this is known as "sowing" the rice, the same term being used as for the similar procedure during the marriage ceremony. Finally, the corpse bearers and the one who saw to the fire have to cross the ashes from south to north. The remaining ashes are covered over with the winnowing fan, and each of them in turn then leaps over with his left hand lightly resting on the fan as he does so. The party then leave the cremation ground and the pot containing the bones is buried at the base of a tree.

The members of the funeral party then bathe, after which they return to the end of the village street, where they light a small fire, using the straw from the roof of the house. They burn the cotton seeds together with some resin and oil cake, and holding their hands into the thick smoke they rub it all over themselves. On completing this operation they collect once more at the bereaved home to comfort the family and to drink beer. On this occasion no one who belongs to the same clan as the dead person and his family may partake of the beer.

The next phase in the ceremonies is known as *tel nahan*, or "oil washing", and alternatively it is spoken of as *umul ader*, or "bringing in the shadow". If the people of the house are very poor a modified form of this ceremony can take place on the evening of the cremation; in any event, the particular day seems to be dictated by considerations of convenience, and it takes place also on the third and on the fifth day after death. All the villagers gather in the courtyard, where the senior member of the family kills a young hen by dashing its head against the lintel of the door into the house. One of its wings and one leg are tied to a stick and the remainder of the flesh is cooked. One portion of the cooked food is taken out to a cross-roads at the end of the village street, where a small thatched-roof "house" is constructed. The food is placed under this roof, the "house" is circumambulated three times in the same way as the funeral pyre and is then set on fire. A second portion is deposited in a basket, which in turn is placed in a rope sling and suspended from a rafter over the spot on the veranda, or it may be in the house, where the dead person expired. The remainder of the food is set on a plate made from *karam* leaves instead of on the usual leaf plate made from *sarjom*, and it has to be eaten by the chief mourner, the one who applied fire to the mouth of the corpse. He takes only a few mouthfuls, raising the food to his mouth with his left hand, this being the only occasion when a man uses his left hand for eating. The food that he leaves is taken to the cross-roads at the end of the village street and thrown away together with the implements in which it was cooked. When the people who took it are returning to the house they pass by an *ukhur*, or mortar, in which water has been left for the purpose, and each person dips the big toe of his left foot in the water as he walks past. They are accompanied by the chief mourner, who on his return to the courtyard takes the leg and the wing of the hen that were tied to a stick and throws them over the house. At this stage also, in some cases, the vessel containing the bones is dug up and brought to the house, where it is slung from a rafter: though in other cases it seems that the bones are left outside the village to await the time of their final disposal. Memorial stones are not set up at this or any other time.

When the food has been served to the chief mourner and to the spirit of the dead person, the rest of the villagers are feasted. If possible, the meal consists of a goat meat curry with rice, and there is a plentiful supply of rice beer. Before the villagers eat, one of the young men is possessed by the spirit of the dead and another is possessed by *Maraṅ Buru*. These two sit side by side on the ground holding in their hands a new winnowing fan in which grains of rice are placed. These grains are both whole and broken and separate out when they are shaken up. The possessed youths utter the guttural-sounding grunts which are typical of persons in their condition, shake their heads from one side to another and jerk the winnowing fans up and down. When the spirits are fully in control they are addressed by one of the relatives. He calls on the name of the deceased and says: "Now, *Gõsãẽ*, we have given you this rice, speak well to us. Tell us, how did you die and how did you fall? Did you leave us at your own wish, or was it through some disease or through someone's enmity?" On the answer to this question will depend in most cases the subsequent proceedings of the mourners. Questions are asked until the mourners are satisfied that there is no more information to be gained. The spirit of the dead man is cautious in making accusations, and imputations of witchcraft or spirit activity in causing death are usually couched in general terms, for his relations will have recourse to the *ojha* and the *jan* for confirmation if they deem it necessary to do so. At the end of the conversation the spirits go from one to another of the assembled company, and addressing them by name they ask for a drink of water. In return they are supplied with beer to drink, after which they return to normal consciousness. Next, the animal for the feast is offered to the spirit of the departed. A sacrificial square is marked out with flour in the courtyard and in it the animal is fed on sun-dried rice. Vermilion is applied to it in the usual manner of sacrifices, but the animal is slain with a blow on the back of its head. This animal is provided by the bereaved household, but in addition each of the houses in the village provides a hen to contribute to the feast. The invocation with the offering is as follows: "Take this, *Gõsãẽ*; we are giving this to you in order that you may be freed from *Jom Raj Haḍuṛ Raj*,[1] from the house of the *Suṇḍi* and the *Haḍi*." The *Haḍi* are the Haṛi caste, outcasts who tend the cremation grounds of the Hindus, and it may be that the *Suṇḍi*, who are now the sellers of drugs and liquor, have also been associated with the disposal of the dead. When all the food is ready for the feast it is divided into three portions. One of these is for the people of the village, one for the bereaved household and one for their relatives, who have gathered whether they belong to the same village or have come from a distance for the occasion. As the food is being served to each person, the server tells him: "This piece is from the wing" or "This piece is from the leg"; all the meat is cut into small

[1] *Haḍuṛ Raj*, another name for the king of the underworld.

pieces to make for convenience in eating with the fingers, and it is a point of etiquette to serve each guest with a variety of delicacies from different parts of the bird or animal being eaten, but the flesh from the head is reserved for the chief mourner and his kinsfolk.

With this ceremony one part of the final rites has been completed. The villagers who assisted at the cremation have been safeguarded against the dangers that are inherent in handling the corpse of a dead person and the village is again clean. The mourners have received much comfort from the display of village solidarity and from the sympathy of their kinsfolk and they are free once more to resume their daily work. They have also re-established contact of a kind with the spirit of the departed and so satisfied one of the most persistent longings of the human heart. He has spoken with them and explained from his present knowledge the reason for his death. The presence of the bones within the house or at least at the base of a tree just beyond the village acts as a continual reminder of his nearness to them. So far as the funeral rites are designed to compensate the living for their loss, all that can be done has now been done, but something still remains to be done before the departed spirit will be at rest. The bones have to be taken away to the river, where they will be floated away on the tide. The river in question is the Damodar,[1] which is known to them by the name *Nãĩ*, or River (all other rivers are called *gaḍa*); it lies from eighty to one hundred miles away from the farther villages—a considerable journey. The time for undertaking this expedition is dictated by the claims of work and other social obligations, and it usually happens that a party from a group of neighbouring villages set out together in the short period of comparative leisure which follows the transplanting of rice during the rains. An animal is set aside at home to be used at the final feast that will take place on the return of the travellers. Before they leave home an ear of the animal is pierced and the blood which falls is mixed with some sun-dried rice that is placed in the earthen pot with the bones. The ceremony at the river is carried out at one of several traditional cremation grounds that abound on its banks. These are Hindu sites, and the attendants, who are usually of the *Haḍi* and *Dom* castes, receive a fee from the Santals—a cloth and some money. The ceremonial reminds one of the procedure followed at the "water marriage" celebrations by the village tank. The site has to be bought, and upon it cowrie shells are placed in a circle

[1] See Chapter 3, p. 28.

within which three vermilion spots are made. The one who floats away the bones should be the one who placed fire to the mouth of the corpse at the burning. He changes his clothes and walks forward until he is quite covered by deep water. He then faces towards the east and releases the bones into the current together with the blood-besprinkled grains of rice. When he comes out of the water a further offering is made of earth from the river bank. This is placed on leaves and floated away with an invocation to the ancestors asking them to receive the spirit of the dead person. This done, the members of the party take a meal by the river bank, eating flattened rice and cakes that they have brought with them. They leave some of the food for the attendants and set out on their homeward way.

Babulal gave an account of the return of the Barikul party on August 18, 1939. He records that it was a hot day and the maize in the homestead fields was fast ripening. "Very early today those who had gone to the river returned to the village. We could hear them cry out '*Horibol, Horibol*'. When they arrived, the *mạṅjhi* and the *goḍet'* called everyone together and we washed the feet of the travellers. One person from each house went to wash their feet, and in return they received a gift of sweetmeats from a parcel that the travellers had brought home with them. When the washing was finished each one went to his own house to drink beer, and then the mothers asked their sons: 'O my boy, at which place did you float away your father?' They replied saying: 'At the *Tel kupi* and *Tirio ghats.*' So all the people asked for news of their dead kinsfolk and took a meal, and then in the afternoon they went about their work." *Ghaṭ* is the Bengali word for a landing place on the side of a river, and Babulal names in his account two of the places to which the Santals of the area go. *Tel kupi* is a small earthenware pot used for carrying oil, and *tirio* we have met before, as it means a flute, but I have not obtained any explanation of the names. The former name is a hybrid expression, for *tel* is a Bengali word, while *kupi* is Santali; the ordinary Santali word for oil is *sunum*.

The final feast takes place after the return from the river. It is known as *bhaṇḍan* and is in accordance with the means of the family concerned. When the guests have come together, three of the young men are possessed by the spirits of the dead person, the founder of the village and *Maraṅ Buru* respectively. On this occasion the spirits are asked if they are satisfied with all that has been done, and they are expected to give their assent. The animal set aside for the *bhaṇḍan* is offered to the spirit of the dead person, and when it is slain the side on which the animal falls is retained by the giver, while the upturned side is retained by the villagers. The expression used for the side on which the animal falls is *gur lotom*, and this term is also used for any animal that has been reserved for a forthcoming festival and then could not be used because of a death in the family during the interval. When the feast has been prepared, the guests are called to sit down by the host, who calls out three times: "Come along, all. It is time for the *bhaṭ* and *bosṭom* to eat the rice." *Bhaṭ* and *bosṭom* are the names of two beggar castes.[1] After all have eaten, a conversation takes place between the villagers on the following lines. A spokesman of the villagers speaks to the assembled company: "In virgin soil and uncut forest, O fathers, such and such a headman cut the trees and made a level plain where he put up huts to dwell in, O fathers. Things went well with them, O fathers, their numbers increased, they gathered together like a flock of doves, O fathers. Now in this house there has been a death and the people in it have been cleansed from defilement, O fathers." Next he addresses the headman: "O father headman, allow us to go to our homes, for all things have been completed." The headman replies: "Fathers, you may go. Go to Sikaṛ[2] and bring from there Modon the washerman and Kisṭo the barber." The villagers ask the headman: "And what will they get from us?" To which he replies: "They ought to get from you a basket of rice and an uncastrated goat." Then the villagers ask to be excused: "O father, Sikaṛ is a long way off and who is able to go? Let us be our own washerman and our own barber. Let it be said that from today all the work is finished for this world and the next." When they have been excused, those who carried the corpse to the burning ground have their say: "O fathers, O five, we gave and burnt some wood", whereupon they are given small pieces of burnt wood in exchange. Similarly, they speak of the spade which was used, in return for which they receive some meat. They tell how their eyebrows were singed in the fire and for this receive some beer in a new pot. They take these things away from the house to consume later.

So end the death ceremonies. Most of the living are thereby freed from their obligations to the dead one and also from the dangers to which this period in their lives has exposed them. As far as they could, the rites have ensured the future happiness of

[1] *Bosṭom* is a form of *Vaishnava*. Cf. reference in the *Karam* festival myth in Chapter 9, p. 118.

[2] A country in which the ancestors once dwelt, according to tradition.

the departed spirit who has now taken his place with the ancestors. His son remains under an obligation to name him at the time of the family sacrifices, and his widow owes to him and to herself certain marks of her widowhood. She wears no flowers or vermilion in her hair and she leaves off the iron bangle given her in marriage. Now, however, the family is free to resume normal relations with the world of men and of spirits, for once again they can marry and give in marriage.

Death is essentially an interruption of the normal processes of living. In the conditions under which the Santals live it is often sudden in its onslaught; it descends upon a house unexpectedly and usually as a cruel visitant, for the number of those who live to enjoy a peaceful old age is small. It is never due to accident, for this is a concept beyond the range of Santal philosophy, and the living take pains to discover the cause of every death that occurs, for their own protection. Unless steps are taken to prevent a recurrence it is common belief that at least three deaths will take place in quick succession. But it remains wrapped in mystery. In one of the folk-tales it is told how a woman craved a boon from a holy man: "Give me this boon, to know where the *jivi* goes when we die and by what road does it depart, through the mouth or through the nose, and having departed where does it go? Give me to see what happens. Tell me also when I shall die and when I have died where will my *jivi* go?" Man is compounded of two different substances, *hoṛmo*, or body, and *jivi*, or soul; these are sometimes separated in dreams, and the final separation in death is a fact that none can deny, but what happens then? Death figures in many sayings that express the sense of the unknown. "In this life", runs one saying, "there is eating and drinking and the wearing of clothes. In the next life who knows what there is?" Some will tell that on death the soul of man enters into a large lizard, the *ghinni*.[1] One story that has a wide currency tells of two men who lay down to rest at the foot of a tree. One of them fell asleep and the other was amazed to see a large lizard coming out of the mouth of his sleeping companion. When the latter awoke he said that in his dream he had been led to a place where treasure lay buried. Yet another common saying expresses scepticism concerning this belief. "Whether after death I shall become a common lizard, *kakṛa*, or a large lizard, I know not." This saying is used to give expression to the ancient materialist principle of behaviour: "Let us eat, drink and be merry, for tomorrow we die."

[1] Probably *Tiligua rubriventris*.

When a person is dying inside a house a great effort is made to remove him into the open before the *jivi* departs, for otherwise it will have difficulty in leaving the house, but the concern felt in this case is probably more on behalf of the living than the dead. The road by which the soul leaves the body is not known with certainty, for in addition to the nose or mouth it may depart through the ears, or, as I was informed in a case where a girl had died with her eyes staring wide open, "Her *jivi* went out through her eyes." Some of the ideas current about the future life have a moral content. There is at least an aspiration that the inequalities of this life will be rectified in the next. In the folk-tale quoted above[1] the boon was granted, and to the comfort of the woman who asked the questions she saw the soul of a poor man being treated with great respect, while the soul of a rich man, in this case her own father-in-law, was very roughly handled. Many such stories are told about the souls of Brahmins and men of low castes. Ideas are also held about punishment in the future life. This is reserved for those who have gone scot-free in this world. Those who were greedy are made to carry baskets of dung on their heads. Special tortures are also in store for those who wilfully shirk the payment of their debts, and above all for those who transgress the tribal code of sexual morality as well as for those who fail to show the traditional tribal marks on their bodies.

It would be surprising if any people in India did not show some trace of belief in reincarnation. The Santals accept it in a general way, but it has no great hold on their thinking. Hutton has inferred that the belief in reincarnation in India is a development from the theory of soul-matter or material life-substance of which he has found evidence through examining the cult of the dead among the hill tribes of Assam.[2] There is no need to hark back to such origins to account for the vague belief in reincarnation that is held by Santals at the present day. Every Indian village is able to furnish stories of recognition and memory which "prove" to the satisfaction of the villagers the assertion that men return to this earth in a different form after death, thus popularizing the doctrine of *karma*, which is one of the few beliefs universally accepted by Hindus and is one of the great achievements of Hindu thought. The Santals are surrounded by this atmosphere; accepting it, they repeat the stories which they hear and add others to the common stock. The

[1] See page 158.
[2] J. H. Hutton, *Census Report of India*, 1931, Vol. I, Ch. xi.

custom of naming is not directly related to the belief in reincarnation, for the names of grandparents and others are bestowed on children even though they are still alive. As we have seen, the spirits sometimes make their wishes known when they want a particular name to be given. This appears to be due to the fact that one of them feels that he has not been duly honoured rather than that the dead person in question has actually been born again in the person of the child.

The nature of the tie that binds *jivi* and *horm̥o* together remains obscure. *Jivi* is in a sense identified with the breath which departs from the body at death, but the identification is not complete, for the *jivi* may also leave the body during sleep and unconsciousness. In grammar the Santals distinguish between the animate and the inanimate. Bodding states: "One might be tempted to define the animate as that which has a 'substance' with something living, a living force, inside this, that makes it capable of acting and moving; a combination of 'matter' and a spirit or spirit force is demanded."[1] This cautious and tentative statement by the greatest authority on the Santali language illustrates the difficulty encountered when we try to reduce Santal belief to a system. When the word *jivi* is used alone with a predicate it is constructed as inanimate; on the other hand, anything possessed of *jivi* is regarded as animate.

Ancestor worship serves to keep the memory of the dead alive and welds the community of the living into one with those who have lived in the past. The dead go on a journey; but although they join the ancestors they are not far away and their welfare is bound up with that of the tribe even as the welfare of the tribe is bound up with theirs. At the end of life people look forward to reunion with their loved ones. I well remember an old woman who was sunning herself one cold morning outside her house. I was passing through the village and stood to talk with her for a few moments. "Where is your husband?" I asked. "He is gone", she replied, indicating the sky; then she added: "I shall soon join him. He is building a house for the two of us, and when it is ready he will call me." Had she, I wondered, had a dream in which her dead husband had appeared to her? I did not ask and I have never learnt.

[1] P. O. Bodding, *Materials for a Santali Grammar*, Pt. II, p. 29.

CHAPTER 13

THE IMPACT OF CHRISTIAN MISSIONS

WHEN "Brother Noyes" in the year 1838 "came to a small village in the heart of a dense jungle"[1] somewhere on the borders of Bengal and Orissa, a new factor was introduced in the history of the Santals. Those pioneer missionaries, American Baptists of the early nineteenth century, seem to have felt early the charm of the Santals. The following extract from the journal of Jeremiah Phillips for February 10, 1841, is typical of the attitude pervading the first reports: "Spent the morning in making up a vocabulary of Santal words. Obtained about 150 words. *P.M.* Hearing that there would be a large dance some three or four miles off, and as most of our villagers had gone, we determined to go also. On our way we overtook a company of men, women and children, dressed in their nicest cloths, singing and skipping about in the most delightful manner. On arriving at the spot, we found some six hundred people assembled in a circular enclosure, in the centre of which a few leaves of the *sarl* tree were placed upon some rough images of elephants, horses, crocodiles, etc. Around these were some two hundred women, while in the outer part of the circle a large company of musicians, followed by the men, were marching round at a varied pace, the weaker sex in the centre more leisurely. The scene was pleasant to witness; it is so seldom that we see anything like activity, that we delight to gaze even upon a dance. The highest bliss to which an Oriya aspires is to stuff himself till he can eat no more, and then lie down to sleep in the sun. This constitutes his happiness here, and in his opinion will constitute his happiness hereafter. But here appears to be a very different people. Wherever we have been, we have found the women mingling with the men, in their labours and in their recreations; and they do not appear to be considered inferior. The consequence is they look like human beings—they respect themselves."[2] The American Baptists at work in the Midnapore district of Bengal as well as in Orissa were the first to give the Santals some literature, and as soon as possible they developed an extensive system of primary educa-

[1] See Chapter 1, p. 3.

[2] This extract occurs in the Eighth Annual Report of the Freewill Baptist Foreign Missionary Society, read and accepted at the anniversary meeting at Topsham, New England, on October 7, 1841. Other passages also have been published in a paper entitled "Early Records concerning the Santals", *Man in India*, Vol. XXV, 1945, by the present writer. See also footnote 1 on page 4.

tion without losing sight of their main objective, the presentation of the Christian Gospel. One of their missionaries wrote in 1865: "We have by no means lost sight of the all-important fact that secular education without heart culture is of very little consequence. Hence, we have ever made the spiritual instruction of the people as prominent as possible. . . ."[1]

The main missionary effort developed in the north after the tragic rebellion of Santals had directed public attention to their affairs. The Santal Mission of the Northern Churches published its Seventy-Fifth Annual Report in 1941 and reported a total community of over 25,000 Christians. This mission, with supporting committees in Norway, Denmark and America, grew out of the pioneer work of a remarkable Norwegian, Lars Olsen Skrefsrud, and his Danish companions, Mr. and Mrs. Boerresen. Resigning from the Gossner Lutheran Mission, they began work independently and established a mission station at Benagaria in 1867. Skrefsrud, who was in every sense a giant of a man, prepared an *Introduction to the Grammar of the Santali Language*, which was published in 1873. It is to his enthusiasm and interest that we owe the account of the Santal traditions published in Santali in 1887. His linguistic work was carried forward and developed by the great scholar P. O. Bodding. To their efforts more than to any other cause the Santals owe the fact that Santali has developed a literature. The first efforts of the missionaries were aimed at providing the scriptures, song books and reading primers, for which purpose the Roman script was adapted, but a great stimulus to the study by the Santals of their own institutions was provided by the publication of the traditions.[2] This mission also publishes the only Santali periodical, which is now in its twenty-sixth year. Other societies that have made notable contributions to missionary work in the Santal Parganas and neighbouring areas are the Church Missionary Society and the Church of Scotland, the latter being particularly noted for the excellent service of medical missionaries at Bamdah. The Santal members of the different Church bodies are brought together in the meetings of the Santal Christian Council, a body that was established in 1934 and is the only organization of any kind that brings together Santals

[1] Stacy, *Life of Otis Robinson Bacheler*, p. 318, quoted from *Primary Education among Santals of Midnapore*, 1931, A Survey with Proposals, by Lewis Clayton Kitchen, Calcutta.

[2] *Mare Hapramko reak' Katha*, Dumka (1st ed., 1887). An English translation by P. O. Bodding was published in Oslo in 1942, entitled *Traditions and Institutions of the Santals*.

from different provinces in India for mutual consultation. Through the influence exercised by its members in their several localities it has done not a little to heighten the community consciousness of the Santals in many places.

One of the constituent bodies of the Santal Christian Council has been at work among the Santals of the Bankura district for about sixty years. Before that date the American missionaries based on Midnapore made long tours which included the south-western areas of the Bankura district, but they would seem to have had little effect on the lives of the people. After the Methodist mission was established in the headquarters town of the Bankura district, the Americans withdrew and missionaries from Bankura began to tour the same area. Little progress was made until after the mission stationed its first missionary at Sarenga in the year 1888, though the first Santal converts were baptized near the town of Bishnupur. The missions established among the Santals are all evangelistic in intention. Their agents not only proclaim the Gospel, but they do so in the hope that non-Christians will accept the Christian Faith in Baptism and enter into the membership of the Christian Church. In the Bankura district the number of Santals who have responded to the preaching in this manner is not much more than a thousand. Although progress has been relatively more rapid in some areas than in others, it remains true everywhere that only a small proportion of the Santals has entered the Christian Church; on the other hand, in comparison with the non-Christian communities who are their immediate neighbours, the Santals have proved responsive. By describing here some aspects of the work in the Bankura district with which I have been intimately associated I do not wish to convey the impression that what is true for one area is true for all. In fact, it is impossible that such should be the case. Many factors make for differences. The Christian Church among the Santals is of greater age and maturity in some places than in others; in some areas work has been concentrated almost exclusively with Santals in view, whereas elsewhere it has formed one among many activities of the mission in question. The various traditions from which the missionaries, and in particular the pioneer missionaries sprang, made for differences in emphasis and attitude towards Santal institutions and culture. Nevertheless, it is my belief that the description of a local situation in the context of the Santal culture of the area may help to throw some light on the general problem of missionary work among the Santals.

The missionaries at Sarenga became familiar at a very early stage with the facts of exploitation of the Santals. One result of this is that missionaries have been foremost in bringing and keeping the facts before the notice of the authorities. The evidence of missionaries is recorded in McAlpin's report.[1] Further direct measures have been taken to better the condition of the Santals both as tenants and as cultivators. During the period when the law was of little use as a safeguard of the rights of cultivators it seemed that the only way in which they could be helped was by acquiring landlord rights over the Santals and so assuring them of a square deal. In the Santal Parganas and elsewhere the Santal Mission of the Northern Churches has acquired a large *zemindari*, or estate, which includes a tea estate in Assam, as many of the Santals in its area migrated to the tea gardens. At Sarenga during the twenty years following the establishing of the mission, landlord rights in a number of small properties on which there were Santal tenants were acquired in order to save the Santals from eviction or from having to pay greatly enhanced rents. A later generation of missionaries has frequently had cause to wish that it could be freed from the burden of these commitments, but it is difficult to see how they could have been avoided if the people were to be helped in the one matter which affected their living more than any other. Though the situation today is very different, the tradition then established still leads Santals to look to the Christian Church for advice and protection. "As the hot season proceeded", we read in one report, "the hunger situation became serious for many people. We were occupied with building work in the compound and a young men's confirmation class which we had for some weeks, but our thoughts were also taken up with the problem of getting famine relief of some kind or other. And anxiously looking for some efforts to be made by government to meet the tremendous need, we finally got information about the loan arrangement (the Land Improvement Loan Fund) advancing money for buying seed and thus giving hopes of a harvest the following autumn. Before the rains started this loan money was realized from the police stations, and every landowner was supposed to have a chance to receive some. But just returning from the hills we had the Santals coming into the compound in large numbers every day complaining that they were refused the loan help. After much consultation a deputation of some elected villagers

[1] M. C. McAlpin, *A Report on the Condition of the Santals in the Districts of Birbhum, Bankura, Midnapore and North Balasore*, Bengal Government, 1909.

was sent to the Sub-Divisional Officer with a petition. The result was negative. After still more deliberation we went to Dumka and with our Secretary's help placed the petition before the Deputy Commissioner. This was immediately granted. A few days after this nearly two thousand more of the population in this area, 80 per cent. of which is stated to be Santals, got their little share of the promised loan."[1]

At Sarenga as elsewhere the necessary preoccupation with the problem of daily bread led to other developments in policy. In addition to becoming a landlord the mission also became a cultivator and employer of labour, thus being in a position to introduce improvements in farming methods to the people in a practical manner and not merely by preaching. Furthermore, something had to be done about the problem of debt that was crippling the Santals. Loans were granted to individuals, and in this matter, too, a later generation of missionaries, which is wise after the event, is inclined to question the wisdom of what was done. An attempt was made in the early years to give loans to cultivators at reasonable rates of interest through the organization of a grain bank, but most of the beneficiaries, unaccustomed to any but the most overbearing and unscrupulous behaviour from their moneylenders in the past, did not see the urgency of loan repayment, and in later years there has been an attempt to establish co-operatives on a sounder basis. Some of the loans given in the early years in order to save land for a family were on a scale that a subsequent generation that has had to try to realize them can only regard as inordinately lavish. The need for this kind of help has been greatly diminished since protective legislation came into force.

If missionaries were compelled to work for economic justice often against their will, they found other spheres open to them which they were eager to enter. Everywhere they have been the pioneers of education for the Santals; until recently they were almost the only agencies in the field. In the district of Midnapore the American Baptist Mission has, by a delegation of authority by the government, been almost solely responsible for the administration of funds and the supervision of schools. These range from the village primary school with a single teacher to a Santal High School for boys where they may sit for the matriculation examination of Calcutta University. In the Bankura district a missionary has always been a member of the Santal Education

[1] *The Seventy-Fifth Annual Report of the Santal Mission of the Northern Churches*, 1941, pp. 46–47.

Board of the district, and from the beginning the mission sought to establish primary schools in the villages. Openings were found in centres either where some people had been baptized or where some of the influential villagers desired to see a school for the education of their children. The early period corresponded with an awareness, at least among a section of the Santals, that their boys should learn to read and write in order to be able to protect themselves; they were frequently discouraged by caste Hindus, most of whom in country areas may have felt quite sincerely that they were actuated by the highest motives. An old Santal related: "The *Deko* say to us, 'You cow-eaters, if you learn to read and write you will go blind', and many of our people, being simple, believe them." And so they turned readily to the missions who wished them to be educated. The government also found it convenient to rely on the help of missions and has made extensive educational work possible through grants. In the Bankura district Santal children can pass from their village schools to middle schools at Sarenga, and some have subsequently been able to go to High School and a mission College in the district town. At Sarenga a training school for village teachers trains the young men who staff the primary schools of the area. In spite of these efforts there has been disappointingly small progress towards literacy among the Santals. They remain largely indifferent to the type of education provided, for even in the remotest village the idea that the village school is merely a stepping-stone to further education has become deep rooted, and so the majority of the villagers cannot discover that the school is relevant to their needs. It is thought sufficient if two or three of the villagers are literate, for they can be relied on to help their illiterate companions. In the Bankura district the number of non-Christian girls who have attended the schools is very small, and none at all have so far attended the boarding school at Sarenga, although Christian and non-Christian boys mingle happily in the boys' school.

Medical work has likewise been prominent. The churches, which report to the Santal Christian Council, are responsible for seven general hospitals, five leper hospitals and a number of clinics. At Sarenga the arrival of a doctor in 1914 heralded the development of a hospital that now occupies a commanding site and brings healing to many thousands of patients, both Santal and non-Santal, every year. It is the centre of a nurses' training school where a number of Santal girls have qualified as trained nurses. While the hospital receives as many patients as can be dealt with, it is probable that the chief limitation to its usefulness is still to be found in the ideas of the people, who regard it too often as a last resort. A further handicap is that it is a great upheaval in the life of a family if they have to take a patient to hospital, involving themselves in severe economic loss. Nevertheless, the influence of the hospital grows steadily and chiefly by the advocacy of those who have themselves been patients.

One significant movement of reform within the Santal community showed clearly how the influence of missions has been working. It was an apparently spontaneous movement among the Santals of Midnapore and Bankura, but it coincided with a period of nationalist activity in the Civil Disobedience movement of 1930, from which the Santals held aloof. In spite of their detachment, they were ripe to listen to propaganda. In the Sarenga area the three most prominent leaders had all received their education at the boys' boarding school and they had subsequently been trained there as village school teachers. At the time none of them was a Christian and neither in public nor in private did they indicate that their thoughts had ever turned towards accepting the Christian faith. These three men gathered round them a small band of helpers who, with great enthusiasm and at considerable sacrifice, went round the countryside and summoned mass meetings of the Santals to hear them. At some of the gatherings the missionary at Sarenga was invited to preside and to speak, largely it seemed because they were anxious for the government to realize that the movement was in no way directed against established authority. They urged the following reforms: firstly, a general tightening of the authority of the village officials in order to safeguard the basis of family life and reduce the number of broken marriages—the officials were urged to set the tone of Santal life by their example; secondly, abstention from drinking spirits and from drinking rice beer, except for ritual purposes and at festivals; thirdly, the prohibition of the large gatherings where women danced in public so that many Hindus gathered to watch them. Dancing should be carried on only in their own villages. This modest programme roused considerable excitement and opposition. The reformers discovered that the elders did not like to be told what was their duty, and the mass of unthinking youths became resentful. For the most part the reformers relied on persuasion, and at several meetings they succeded in having resolutions passed in favour of the reforms. They were goaded into direct action when they saw that in spite of resolutions public opinion did not favour the cancellation of the great Lakshmi Puja gathering at Sarenga. They put out pickets and for one year by this means they secured its abandonment; the following year it took place with small numbers attending, which have since increased. The one permanent memorial of the movement, however, is in connection with this gathering, for whereas formerly it used to continue throughout the night, it now starts earlier in the day and the crowds disperse as evening comes on. In every other respect the reformers were disappointed. Two of the three leaders became disillusioned about the possibility of reform from within; their teaching took on a new note. One of them in a speech pointed to the example of the Karen people of Burma of whom he had been reading, and in due course these two presented themselves for Baptism.

The proposed reforms were "puritan" in character. There was nothing specifically Christian about them, and indeed they were exactly similar to those advocated by many movements among Santals and others that have been influenced by Hinduism. A dislike of puritanism is one of the reasons why Christianity has not made more headway. Santals frequently object that when they become Christian they have to give up their *ṛaskạ*. An old preacher wrote: "It would be good if people kept their daughters at home, for then dancing at festivals would come to an end and words of religion could enter people's ears and stick. I have visited many villages and still do so. Folk do not wish to enter the new Way because they will have to give up sin. They say: 'Yes, religion is good, but there is no pleasure in it. There is no joy apart from drinking beer and spirits; whether at births or marriages there could be no jollification.'" Unlike some other missions, we in Bankura have not asked for a pledge of total abstinence as a prerequisite of Baptism, but in practice many of the Christians tend to talk as though drunkenness is the greatest sin as it is certainly the most conspicuous failing of the Santals. Apart from the rights and wrongs of total abstinence propaganda among primitive people, Christians are normally debarred from sharing in the village festivals that afford the chief opportunities of communal revelry with its accompaniments of drinking and dancing. Although there has never been any preaching against dancing in the area, its association with the festivals and the tribal cult is sufficient to discourage it among the Christians. It is not surprising, therefore, that the lives of the Christians, who are cut off from sharing in the traditional manifestations of tribal rejoicing, appear colourless to the heathen

Santal, who is not friendly disposed towards puritanism in any shape or form.

Another type of objection to Christianity arises out of what may be termed the "marginal teaching", largely unintended, of those who propagate the faith. "I shall never become a Christian", said an old man. "What should I do with a pair of shoes?" This remark was greeted with evident amusement on the part of the bystanders. He had been more impressed by the garb of the preachers than by their words. Many of the younger men and women of the Christian community drift away to employment in the towns, and when they return home they are not slow to display their superior material culture. Shoes, fountain-pens and wrist-watches are symbols of prosperity, and it is natural that in the Santal village they should at times be confused with the fruits of Christianity. The Santal who has no desire to change his lot or who sees no possibility of doing so is content with the old way of life.

Undoubtedly the most deep-rooted objection, however, arises from the fact that the individual Santal knows of no security apart from his clan and tribe, and he sees in Christianity something that threatens to become a disintegrating influence. This awareness has developed its own mythology in beliefs which appear to the Christian missionary to be entirely without rational foundation and which seem to have been deliberately invented by persons maliciously disposed. What, for example, can be made of the commonly repeated assertion that the ritual of Baptism is accomplished by means that revolt the sensibilities of Santals, such as the transfer of spittle from the mouth of the officiating minister to that of the convert? Yet it is likely that the stories have grown without deliberate intent. Santals affirm that mixed marriages are actively encouraged by Christians. This belief, though mistaken, is not without foundation. One of the early converts related that he held back because he was not married. According to his own account he had some difficulty in making the missionary understand his attitude, for if he had married after Baptism the only alternatives before him would have been to marry someone who was related to him or to marry a non-Santal, and quite naturally he could bring himself to do neither. The most usual response to the appeal of the preacher is expressed in the words: "Yes, your religion is good and some day we shall all become Christians: but—we shall wait until all of us can do it together." Less commonly one hears the reply: "If the headman became a Christian, all in this village would do so."

The attitude of the community towards the family or the individual who has become Christian is a complex of tolerance and incomprehension. Becoming a Christian is not in itself an offence for which there is an established penalty in tribal custom: the village council does not act and there is no formal outcasting of the offender from the community as there is, for example, when a Santal has married outside the tribe. The denial of tobacco and drinking water, two of the common manifestations of "separateness", are rarely used in the area, though sometimes found elsewhere. Thus, in the early days of the mission at Benagaria, Skrefsrud found that Christian converts were being cut off from social intercourse; by a process that sounds very like intimidation he invited all the leading Santals of the neighbourhood to a feast with the converts and informed them that having eaten with the converts they must now receive them back into the tribe.[1] Where social ostracism does occur it does not last long. There is rarely any need for a family to change their residence on becoming Christian so far as their fellow villagers are concerned, though some Christians do so because there are occasions when an isolated Christian family is put to grave inconvenience. This is particularly the case when a death occurs, for the non-Christians will have nothing whatever to do with the disposal of a corpse after the strange manner of the Christians. Such predicaments occur only when the degree of isolation is great. With the individual convert it happens sometimes that he has to eat his meals separately from the rest of the family for a time. It is served to him out in the courtyard rather than on the verandah or in the house, but this signifies contempt rather than any other emotion and it does not last. Sometimes the members of the family show signs of genuine grief. There is no reason, from a Santal point of view, why non-Christian Santals should not marry Christians, although such marriages are not popular. The chief discouragement to them and the only discipline against them is exercised from the Christian side. And while relations between a convert and his kinsfolk and distant relatives do become strained, the old friendly relations are often resumed and it is customary for Christians to pay visits to the homes of non-Christian relations and *vice versa.* No attempt is made to dispossess or disinherit Christians who continue to enjoy the fruits of their toil in the fields.

This tolerance of Christians in the midst alongside the dis-

[1] My authority for this statement is a small life of Skrefsrud in Santali, published by the Santal Mission of the Northern Churches.

approval of much in the Christian message is perhaps due to the fact that Santal society is not sufficiently aware of danger. In the area, very few conversions of village officials have taken place. During the first decade of the present century a *parganath* with his family became Christian, and the reports of the time speak of hoping that his example would be followed by many others. In fact the Church has made practically no progress in that *pargana* since; a brother of the convert became *parganath* in his place. In a more recent example which occured in 1940 in the Midnapore district, a baptized *parganath* retained his office, but his example in becoming Christian was not followed. The only cases of village headman and village priest accepting Baptism have occurred in one village where the mission had become landlord. The large majority of converts have come from the rank and file of Santal society.

Individual religious experience plays a comparatively insignificant part in the first approach of the Santal to the Christian faith, though it is a strong motive in isolated cases. Dosoroth Hãsdãk', baptized in 1916 at about the age of thirty-five, was such a case. During the years when the mission was in its infancy he was growing up in a small village eighteen miles from Sarenga. He was sent to a village school by his father, and his first knowledge of Christianity was gained when he sat for the final examination, and this knowledge supplied him with a faith at a later crisis in his life to take the place of his former belief in the spirits. Here are his own words: "From that time (when he had gone to sit for an examination) I used to question in my mind the customs of the Santals. For a long time I went on drinking and dancing and I used to reverence the spirits in tree stumps, stones and trees, but all the time with growing dissatisfaction. As my sins increased, the Heavenly Father led me into more and more temptation and trouble. Two boys and two girls died at childbirth, and believing only in the spirits I ran to all the *ojhas* round about, but none could do anything. Then my wife and I talked together and decided that as the spirits had never been able to do anything we would no longer heed them but depend on God alone. So we tried to learn more about Him, and after awhile we heard of the mission at Sarenga. I went there a few times and got understanding; then I was baptized when Spencer Sahib paid his first visit to Samadi. From that time, believing in the One God and by His mercy, all my children and all of us have remained well."[1] Dosoroth died in 1940, being

[1] Quoted from a MS. in my possession written by Dosoroth at my request.

bitten by a snake as he slept on his verandah one night. He did not rouse until it was too late to apply any effective remedy. His relatives who were present subsequently told a story of sublime self-command and faith. He bade them farewell: "Do not be concerned about me, but always believe in God; although my body is being destroyed, my spirit cannot be destroyed. And follow the example of my brothers and myself, who never had a quarrel." He read to them from his New Testament. In the words of a nephew who wrote me a letter shortly afterwards: "Many people came from round about when they heard of his death to show their grief. My uncle preached the name of Jesus right up to the time of his death."

Dosoroth ascribed his freedom from the molestation of spirits to his belief in the One God. The heathen Santal considers that the process of transferring allegiance from one to the other is fraught with grave dangers. Christians put themselves beyond the pale of the tribe and so they do on the whole escape from the attention of the malevolent powers to whom Santals as a whole are subject, but when a recent convert meets with misfortune it is because the spirits have been able to get at him. A young man in Barikul died from typhoid about six months after his Baptism, and the common verdict was that the *bongas* had taken their revenge.

Many of the early converts were first drawn to the Church in order to gain some freedom from oppression. From time to time examples occur of people who wish to escape trouble which they have reason to fear from their own people. Families have been baptized when the mother has been accused of witchcraft and they have been persecuted accordingly. In the early period a family became Christian through the man having married a cousin. Although cross cousin marriages are not entirely prohibited, they are frowned upon as they serve to complicate relationships. This couple were subjected to local persecution, and at one stage, I am told, they feasted their fellow villagers in an effort to be reinstated in society. Ultimately, however, they sought the refuge of the Christian community. Their home was within two miles of Sarenga and so they were near to other Christians. Others sought relief from harassing landlords and their agents. They thought that the right way to deserve the help of the missionaries was to do first what the missionaries asked them to do in matters of religion. For although missionaries did relieve much distress, they proclaimed that what they really wanted to see was a change of heart in the people. There has always been a danger when we wish to afford relief to individual cases that we should take as a criterion the attitude of the individual to Christianity, for there has to be some line of demarkation when it is physically impossible to help all who are in need. It may be that in some instances Santals concealed their real motives and pretended to a religious feeling that they did not possess, but if so, such cases were rare. When I first lived in the area it was still common for people to come to the mission house with their financial and land troubles in the hope of obtaining help, and not infrequently they offered to become Christians if it was my wish.

Many became Christian as a result of their first contact with Christian teaching in school. Birsingh Hembrom became a Christian when he was about thirty. His first wife had borne him no children and so his father had arranged for him a second marriage, and he was unable to enter the Church until the issues raised by his bigamy had been settled. Fortunately, perhaps, in his case, his first wife left him and returned to her own home when she heard talk of his becoming Christian. But like many others he used to say: "I knew Jesus for what He was from before my marriage because I had been in the hostel for four or five years and we used to study the Bible for an hour every day." One of the three leaders of the reform movement in 1930 was Dubraj Mạrnḍi, who has since died of tuberculosis. His approach to the faith was that of a thoughtful nature which weighs every step. He said once in my hearing: "I have been puzzled by the fact that in this country (area) God is saving the Santals and not the others. We are only rat-eating drunkards. But He is doing it because if others see that He can save us it will show His glory in a way that would not otherwise be possible."

The great difference between the first period of mission activity and following stages is the existence of a Christian community. A community of Christian Santals with a social life of their own introduces a new factor into the situation. The influence of kinsfolk which often serves to hinder a person from entering the Church now operates at times in the opposite direction. "We have seen that our cousins in such and such a village are happy", say inquirers, "and we want to join them." On one occasion when a Christian was urging his non-Christian relatives mullow his example he received the reply: "All right, nephew; where the head goes the tail will follow." If in some of its aspects the social life of the Santal Christian community places a stumbling-block in the way of the non-Christians, it also acts as the most influential attracting force. Converts today do not have to step out into the unknown as the first converts did. Cutting themselves off, as they must, from many aspects of their old community life, they find themselves not alone but members of a new community.

CHAPTER 14

THE NEW COMMUNITY

THE Santal Christian community is more than an aggregate of individuals who have broken off from the tribe or have been born of parents who did so. It possesses a social life of its own; the individuals and families who compose it have opened their lives to a new influence and with it to a system of ideas that is capable of establishing a pattern of social behaviour distinct from the old. The new pattern will not be different in every respect from the old, which has much of value to contribute and which still exercises a powerful influence in certain directions. By examining the main trends in the present life of one particular community we may not be able to forecast what the pattern will be when Santals in far greater numbers have entered the Church, but we should be able to see the outlines of development in the years immediately ahead.

The great majority of the Santal Christians in the area have retained their status as villagers and cultivators. Their economic interests and activities are the same as those of their non-Christian neighbours. They toil for their daily bread and have to rely on the same aptitudes, skill and intelligent foresight and they earn respect according to the degree in which they display them. They maintain the traditional division of labour between men and women. The men plough the fields and repair their houses; they cut the trees of the forest and cart timber to the railway station. As the long lines of bullock carts enveloped in a cloud of red dust bump over the country roads, one finds here and there in the line a Christian man urging on his pair of bullocks. In bad years when a crowd of men are thronging round the office of the local police station to receive their cultivation loans from the government the Christians take their turn with the rest. The women do the work of the house and take the customary share in the cultivation of the fields and in the food-gathering activities of the village women. The men play their part in the annual hunts and the heads of the household sit with the rest of the villagers in the councils of the village and the tribe.

In spite of the common interests and activities which bind the villagers together irrespective of religious allegiance, the Santal Christian is immediately aware of certain tensions which issue progressively in a breaking away from the old way of life.

The most important cause of tension is the acceptance of a theology—a new myth, as it may be called—that results in a new ordering of religious activities and social obligations. The shadowy figure of the Supreme Being is invested with personality and comes into the centre of consciousness. He is not merely the Creator to whom little is ascribed except a vague reference as the dispenser of good and bad weather; He is vitally concerned with human conduct. The stories of Genesis are grafted on to conceptions that are already held and affect the latter. The story of the Jews is appreciated as that of a people who suffered through a long history from oppression, and the story of the wanderings appeals to the Santal. It is altogether fitting that the One Saviour of all mankind should be born of a people with whom the Santal feels that he has much in common. The traditional story of the origin of mankind is held to supplement the biblical narrative. In preaching, the Santal constantly refers to Adam and Eve as *Pilcu Haṛam* and *Pilcu Buḍhi*; *Marań Buru*, on the other hand, is equated with Satan, and the cult of worship that he instituted is regarded as a deception imposed on the Santals. To the Santal who has been led in any degree to appreciate the Christian teaching about God, the identification of *Marań Buru* with Satan seems to be obvious. He led the first human pair into sin and revealed to them the secret of sexual intercourse, for which the polite name among the Santals is always *baṛic' kạmi*, or evil work. He caused their ancestors to wander through the forests and finally foisted on them the cult of the spirits centring in the worship of himself. It follows that there are certain things which a Christian may not do. They are cut off from any activity that savours of worship of the tribal spirits. They do not contribute in cash or in kind to the offerings associated with the village festivals. This in turn excludes them from the communal rejoicing, the dancing and the feasting which take place during the festivals. At such times they are frequently the only sober persons in the village. It is impossible to live in a village at the time of the great Spring and Harvest festivals without becoming acutely aware of the gulf which divides the Christians from their neighbours, and without realizing that the Christians are themselves deeply conscious of the gulf. The same is true of the clan sacrifices; but it is interesting to observe that rules of behaviour which are linked with the mythology of the clans still regulate the conduct of the village Christian to a very large extent. A Murmu who has a clan taboo against building a house with four sloping sides to the roof continues to live in the style of house enjoined by custom. Food taboos and those relating to dress and ornament are respected and the rules governing clan exogamy are accepted without question. The reason underlying these facts is probably that even when the myth has been discredited the code of behaviour is charged with emotions that continue to enforce it as long as the village environment has been little affected.

In their attitude to the ancestor cult many of the Christians have evolved a compromise. Some families known to me started their Christian life on the basis of a bargain with the spirits. In one village in particular where there are now eight Christian households in a community of twenty-eight families, at least three of the original families to be converted left one of the brothers outside the Church. The unbaptized members of these families were charged with the responsibility of maintaining the fellowship of the family with their ancestors. As one of those concerned said: "If the offerings had not been continued, then the ancestors might have shown their displeasure at all the children becoming Christian." Others who have become Christians continue to make offerings. In no case have I ever been able to discover evidence that Christians make any animal offerings, but during the festival which takes place at the end of the month of *Pus* many Christians make the cakes that are traditionally associated with the festival and make offerings of them to their immediate forbears. The family, represented by the living and the dead, continues to be a focus of powerful sentiments, and the Christians are evidently aware of a void in the teaching that they have received in regard to it.

The identification of *Marań Buru* with Satan incidentally provides a mythological foundation for propaganda in favour of total abstinence, for it was he who taught the first parents to brew beer. It is difficult to estimate the extent to which such propaganda has had the desired effect among the Christian community. Some of its members are known and respected as total abstainers, a fact that illustrates the introduction of a changed standard of values. On the other hand, the majority of village Christians certainly drink beer. The attitude of the community towards the older people who indulge is tolerant, and the habit is explained largely by the fact that the provision of beer is important in showing hospitality towards visitors. Drunkenness, however, is not condoned and it is certainly no longer a form of communal rejoicing. Drinking to excess, where it occurs, has become a private habit surrounded with secrecy.

The second main factor in producing tension is that the Christian becomes a member of a community that is different from the tribal community into which he was born and different from any other within his experience. He may know of one or two Santals who have been influenced by the Bengal form of Vaishnavism and have adopted some strange customs in consequence, and he is familiar with the semi-secret society formed by the *ojha* and his disciples, but neither of these provides any analogy with the society of which he now becomes a member. The preaching of the Christian Faith has been pioneered by European missionaries, and up to the present the direction of the affairs of the Christian Church has remained in the hands of missionaries to a greater extent than in many other parts of India. Their apparent superiority tends to make the village Christian belittle his own ideas and institutions. Their superior wealth and beneficence tempt him to rely on their help, and sometimes produce resentment when the help is withheld for a reason which he is quite unable to appreciate, the desire to make him "independent". Furthermore, Santal Christians are linked through the Church with Christians who come from other communities. This fusion of diverse elements produces strain at times. There has been no difficulty from the first in taking common meals, and this has safeguarded the witness of the Sacrament of Holy Communion to the unity of believers in Christ. On the other hand, many Christians shrink from contact with the corpse of a non-Santal Christian. Near the village of Samadi there used to be one household of Christians who were of Bhuiya stock. I was on tour in the area when the old grandmother died. She was buried in the Christian burial ground, here, as in most villages, a piece of wasteland within the holding of one of the Santal Christians, but none of the local Santal Christians would touch the corpse. The persistence of such ideas varies, one might say, in inverse proportion to the degree of contact which the local community enjoys with other Christians. Samadi is in a far corner of the area and such an incident would not occur nearer to the centre. This can be further illustrated by the fusion that has been gradually taking place in the Christian community through intermarriage. Although the village Christian abhors the thought of intermarriage, a few individuals have ignored the rule of tribal endogamy and have contracted marriages against which there are no Christian sanctions. Those who have done so would not find it possible to continue to live in the village community, and they are usually men and women who are already divorced from village life. A Santal who has been educated to University standard and subsequently obtained government employment has already been almost completely detribalized. He has little contact with his kinsfolk after early childhood, and if he chooses to marry a non-Santal wife he is strong enough to ignore the sentiment of other Santals. He has to suffer the knowledge that the majority of the Santal Christians as well as the non-Christians are extremely critical of his action and no longer regard him as one of themselves. It also happens sometimes that boys and girls who have been away from home in the mission boarding schools either persuade their reluctant guardians to agree to mixed marriages or force the issue on the community by their own action. The opposition aroused by such marriages usually abates with the passage of time.

While it is convenient to regard education as the third of the factors producing tension in the life of the Christian community, it is in some senses the key to all the rest. To some extent it has been responsible for strains felt through the whole range of tribal life, and this will become increasingly evident in the future with the spread of education. The problems created in the life of the Christian community are the more acute because its members have been eager to grasp at the advantages that accrue from education. Boys and girls in Christian families are sent to the local village school without any question. Immediately they are brought in touch with a new world. In accordance with government regulations they begin to learn to read and write Bengali. Attempts that have been made to give to Santali a more prominent place in the curriculum are not popular, for it has no commercial value. After completing the course at the village school the majority of the children pass into the life of boarding schools at Sarenga, where they remain for an average period of four years. The majority of the teachers at these schools now are themselves Santals and products of the same community, but the type of life is far removed from that of the village, and Santal culture is at best an "extra". The main emphasis of the schooling, accepted by teachers, parents and boys alike, is that the latter should be fitted for higher education or industrial training. Two-thirds of the pupils are Santals, but their language is banished from the classrooms except for about two periods in the week. Prayers are conducted in Santali alternately with Bengali. Although they are encouraged to learn and practise their tribal dances, the activity takes on a self-conscious quality which is quite unable to stand up to the general assumption of the Bengali community that these dances are fit only for the uneducated and "simple" villager. The education of girls follows a somewhat different pattern. For many years the Christians were slow in taking advantage of facilities for girls' education and the numbers in the girls' school were comparatively small. To a former generation girls were destined to the life of village housewives, and the education provided was not only irrelevant but it positively endangered the success of their daughters in marriage. Many of the older generation and some of the younger express a preference for illiterate wives who need less clothes and become proficient in house and field work by living at home. In school the girls live a sheltered life. Although agricultural training is given both to boys and girls in school through the care of gardens and through work on the rice fields belonging to the mission, such activity is regarded as an extra and some parents have voiced the view that it is a form of exploitation! In recent years, however, a change has come over the general attitude towards girls' education owing to the growth of a small number of economically independent unmarried women whose earnings are valuable to their families and also to the rise of a demand for educated wives by a section of the men. The changing attitude was illustrated by the fact that when in 1937, as a result of a change in policy, the girls were housed in cottages constructed as nearly as possible on the lines of a Santal village, there was considerable opposition from the parents. They objected that the girls would have too much housework in addition to their studies.

A new class of Santal Christians has been created which sets the tone for changes in the community. The more intellectual members are lost to village life; they pass to High School or to other training and many of them retain only slender links with their village homes. They follow a wide range of occupations unknown to Santals of the older generation, in government service, as paid mission agents, and in recent years they have begun to enter the ranks of industrial workers in the city. Girls have become nurses and teachers. The local leaders of the Church are largely salaried members of the mission staff who are "compound" centred rather than village minded. Their small but regular wages have made them better off than the great majority of the peasants among whom they work; and one result is that the latter do not invariably follow the lead they are given.

From time to time the local Church courts have to consider matters of discipline for moral offences. The only kind of "sanction" that is effective in such cases is a social and economic boycott of the offender by other members of the community. This type of boycott is familiar enough in village life, and the leaders in the Church courts do at times seek to impose it. They are frequently discouraged by the fact that the Christian villager declines to obey the resolution of the meeting in which he doubtless feels he should have a greater voice. The comparative impotence of the Christian community to deal with offenders does encourage moral laxity in certain individuals. The further inference that some offences are more common in one section of the community than in another, or among Christians than among non-Christians, does not follow. When village Christians are themselves faced with the necessity of taking disciplinary action they fall back on tribal practice as nearly as possible. On one occasion a Santal Christian man died at his home about seven miles from Sarenga and the local "catechist" came to ask me to conduct the funeral. This request was unusual, for in the normal way he would have conducted the funeral himself. The dead man, however, had left his home fourteen years before and had lived in the "east" with a non-Christian woman, for which reason his name had been struck off the rolls; so far as the local Christian community was concerned, they understood by this that he was to be to them "as a heathen and a publican". Shortly before he died, knowing himself to be seriously ill, he had desired to return to the scenes of his childhood and he had come back to the home of his aged and widowed mother. The dilemma faced by the local Christians when he died was a very real one. No one else would dispose of the body; but if they did so, how was it consistent with the fact that the man had been thrust out of the community? Unwilling to face the alternatives, they wished me to do so. My advice to the catechist was that he was to carry out the wishes of the majority of the members of the church in the place. Later I learnt that they had decided to make the widowed mother pay a fine of five rupees, a considerable sum for her, and in return they agreed to bury the corpse without holding any prayers over the grave. Half the money was paid to those who dug the grave, and the balance was deposited in the "poor fund" of the local church.

The danger of a cleavage between the leadership and the rank and file can be seen also in the attitude of many of the former to their own language and culture. They have benefited materially from their aptitude at school in mastering the subject matter of their Bengali education and they are all too conscious of the early handicaps arising from bilingualism. They entertain a very natural ambition to give their children a better chance than they themselves have enjoyed, and so a number of them have banished the use of Santali from their homes. This is done not only to give their children a start in school, but also because they feel that if their children learn Santali first they will speak Bengali with a Santal, and therefore an uncultured, accent, on account of which they themselves have experienced the shafts of derision. In any case it is probable that owing to their education they find the Bengali language more adequate for the expression of many of their own needs. They are therefore predisposed to turn their backs on Santal culture and adopt modes of behaviour that are alien to the Santal village. The moral standards of individualism and those of a society where the individual counts for little have clashed in their lives and have not yet resulted in an equilibrium.

Nevertheless, as we have seen in the previous chapter, the Christian Church is making some contributions of real significance to the whole community through the new educated leadership which is also responsible for elements of real value in the life of the Christian Church itself. Among the leaders, as also among the rank and file, there is much genuine religious experience and sincere piety that issue in unselfish service to the village as a whole and to the Christian Church in particular. Chuneram Hembrom, a pensioner of the mission, wrote: "Now because of my age they have pensioned me on seven rupees a month. However, God and Jesus the Saviour of men have not deserted me. The spirit of my mind is cool (i.e., it is at peace). I believe that if we unite body and mind in prayer and ask anything in the name of Jesus it will be granted to us. All of us pray to Jesus Christ. Although my wife can neither read nor write, she prays with knowledge every evening and we are content. By our deeds and by our words we bring pain to God, but through Jesus we ask for forgiveness."[1] Many members of the second generation of Christians are active in a hundred local situations, serving their fellows. Some are revered by many generations of school children and are themselves proud of those whom they have helped to go farther on the road of learning than they themselves have travelled. In time of famine and sickness they spend themselves on behalf of their fellows and are trusted by all.

Corporate life in the Christian community finds expression in

[1] From a manuscript in my possession.

a new symbolism and is fostered by a new ritual. The central act of corporate worship on Sunday, springing from a tradition that is more sabbatarian than sacramental, has taken hold of the imagination of the people. Babulal describes the visit of a missionary to Barikul on a Sunday: "At about two in the afternoon the bell sounded for the Christians to praise the Holy Name of the Heavenly Father. Everyone knew that our *mạñjhi haṛam*[1] had arrived, or the bell would not have been sounded so early. A second bell followed according to custom. All the Christians gathered, and first as we entered the church we prayed in our minds for strength. The *mạñjhi haṛam* read out a song and we all sang it together, after which we all knelt and followed his prayer. When there was something in the prayer with which we heartily agreed we said to ourselves: 'Heavenly Father, let it be!' Then we heard the Sixteenth Chapter of St. Mark's Gospel, and from it he spoke many words for strengthening us and gave us good advice. At the end we sang again and after prayers we came out of the church. As we stood on the verandah we greeted the *mạñjhi haṛam* and had sweet conversation together. He asked some of us elders a few questions: 'What is the state of mind of the villagers? Why do they not accept Jesus?' He also asked: 'What is the state of the evening daily prayers in the village and how goes the Class Meeting?'[2] We told him: 'The people of the village are only drunkards, and as to that we are also at fault, for we have had one or two drunkards amongst us and we have not tried to work hard for Jesus Christ. As for the second thing, evening prayers are being held in a different house each evening; it is not possible for us all to gather every evening. The Class Meeting is going very well. We are hoping that by its influence we shall be able to get rid of drinking and other evils amongst us. We have made a rule amongst ourselves about drinking. If anyone is found drinking we shall fine him five *siki*.[3] If it happens three times we shall fine him five rupees. Then if he continues we shall bring it to the notice of our *marañ naeke* or *mạñjhi haṛam* and drive him out from us. We shall not sit with him no matter what he wishes to do, whether at a birth or *chaṭiạr* or marriage; nor shall we go to his house. Then we shall be

[1] Babulal uses a curious phrase here for the missionary. It is not in general use. Literally the "old headman" or "chief headman", the term is in general use to designate the original founder of a village. A missionary is generally *padri Sahib.*

[2] This Methodist term occurs in the manuscript. It is familiar to the community.

[3] A *siki* is equivalent to four annas.

able to drive out all evil from amongst us and the work of Jesus Christ will progress.' "

In some parts of the Santal Church many of the hymns sung are translations of ancient and other Christian hymns set to western melodies, but in this area nearly all the hymns are the product of the community. In the hymnbook now in use[1] there are one hundred and forty hymns, of which one hundred and twenty are original compositions of Christians in the area. Half the remaining twenty have been borrowed from Santali hymn-books published elsewhere. All these have been set to folk-melodies, and the book is a best seller at markets and fairs through the whole area. The words show clearly the stamp of their environment and at the same time they are full of biblical imagery:

> Come, come, merciful Jesus,
> Come, come, to the house of my mind.
> Seeing Thee, in a moment of time
> My mind breaks up.
>
> Life Thou art and Truth,
> And the True Way art Thou,
> Help of the helpless, Jesus,
> That is why I seek Thee.
>
> Among sweet-scented flowers Thou the parrot,
> A dark jewel art Thou.
> In whose mind Thou art the jewel
> He alone is truly rich.[2]

In one hymn Jesus the teacher of the Truth is likened to the bright evening star in the night sky. In another they sing:

> The star of morning has risen and shines,
> The gentle morning breeze is blowing,
> The day of salvation has come to us.[3]

Some of the hymns owe not a little to the fact that the writer knew hymns in Bengali or more remotely in English, but the sentiments have been popularized by being set to Santal melodies. One of the most popular of the evening hymns, set to a haunting melody belonging to the *heṛhet'* or weeding songs, is

[1] *Dhorom Seren Puthi*, 3rd ed., Sarenga, 1936.
[2] See Appendix B, No. 28.
[3] See Appendix B, No. 29.

little more than a translation of the familiar words of "Abide with me":

> The sun has set, O Jesus stay with me,
> I have no other friends but Thee.
>
> Life does not stand, and swiftly it is gone,
> On earth I nothing find but Thee alone.
>
> Nor hardship nor trouble nor death shall I fear
> If Thou grantest mercy and stayest near.
>
> Thy Cross I hold, forgive my sins I pray,
> Give heavenly light, be with me night and day.[1]

Whether the coming of Jesus is thought of as the shining of a bright star in the sky of a dark night or as the light that heralds the approach of dawn and a glorious day, in all circumstances the devotion of the Santal Christian Church is centred in Him as the Light of the world.

The festivals of the Christian year are becoming landmarks in the lives of the people. This is particularly true of the Christmas season. The communal feast when all the Christians eat together on Christmas Day is a natural expression of the spirit that animates the day. Various activities are arranged for the children. The type of celebration followed in the area has been created by the tradition established over a number of years in the central mission station. A Christmas tree is erected in the church and a party held there for the children on Christmas Eve. Originally, the gifts on the tree came from England, but for several years they have been found largely by the local community. Father Christmas is now a familiar figure. The young men of the church remain awake all night and set out soon after midnight to sing carols outside the homes of the members of the community, leaving off when they have completed the round soon after daybreak. A large proportion of full members attend a service of Holy Communion in the morning, but the main body of worshippers gather in large numbers for a service beginning soon after noon. All are dressed in new clothes, and the body of the church, which is bare of furnishings except for sitting-mats, is well filled for a service in which singing predominates. At the close of the service the youths begin a dance in the church, and going out through a side door they dance round the building. On

[1] See Appendix B, No. 30.

this occasion they make use of *sarpa*, and the Christmas songs that they sing are set to *Sohrae* tunes, as Christmas falls into the harvest season. During the afternoon of Christmas Day sports are held. These attract large numbers of spectators, and the final item in the sports, an archery contest, has become established as one of the events of the countryside. The interest and enthusiasm of spectators and competitors, who gather year after year to display their skill, is out of all proportion to the value of the prize that is offered. When the sports end the people disperse, the Christians to feast in their own homes.

Good Friday is observed with great solemnity, and the majority of the adults fast until after they have attended church. The services are very well attended, and on the initiative of the people themselves new forms of celebration are frequently being introduced. In most of the local churches the three-hour service has established itself in the customs of the people. On Good Friday in 1946 at the village of Barikul the people decided to follow the service by a silent procession through the village street. They filed behind a "standard bearer" who carried a rude cross fashioned from two *sarjom* saplings. At Easter it is customary for the dawn to be greeted by bands of young men singing in the village and also at the local Christian burial ground. The day is also characterized by large and enthusiastic gatherings of worshippers. Little has been done in this area to "baptize" the magico-religious practices connected with agriculture, and although Harvest Festivals are celebrated by the bringing of thank-offerings to church and the decoration of the church buildings, they have not become times of community rejoicing and remembrance as have the historic occasions associated with the Incarnation, Death and Resurrection of the Saviour.

In the customs that surround life's crises one sees the blending of old and new concepts and symbols. Pregnancy taboos are widely observed, and steps have to be taken by Christians to remove the uncleanness resulting from birth. The practice of "churching" women was not introduced to the people at the beginning and it has never been put in the forefront, but the Christians carry out the bathing and naming and the feasting of neighbours. In this they are joined in many cases by non-Christian villagers, though no two Christian occasions are alike in this respect. In some places most of the villagers gather, in other places all the women come, while at other villages only Christians collect. Something depends on the strength and persistence of ties that have been maintained with kinsfolk and something on the general regard for the individuals concerned. The same variety is found in the degree to which precautions against *bhut* and other unseen adversaries are observed, but a new element has been introduced in the prayer offered on the occasion by the local leader of the church. Infant Baptism follows usually during some part of the first year of the child's life. Very young children are withheld from Baptism as a rule, and this may be partly due to a feeling that the ceremony is in some way dangerous to the new-born infant. Among some people it is sought in connection with the time when the child first begins to eat rice; among others it is customary for them to offer their children in Baptism on Christmas Day. When the child is taken to church to be baptized both the parents and the child are dressed in new clothes and relatives and neighbours are invited to a feast in the home of the child.

Many pre-Christian elements remain in the preparations made for marriage. The choice of marriage partners is still largely in the hands of the parents of the bridegroom and the bride. The services of a go-between are engaged and ceremonial visits take place during the course of which the bride price is negotiated and paid. During the early years of the mission the custom of bride price was actively discouraged, but a fuller understanding of its importance has led to a tacit acceptance by the authorities; in the meanwhile it is now often referred to by Christians under the name of "mutual help". The rise of economic standards in the Christian community is reflected in a tendency among parents of Christian girls to demand a bride price higher than the rate current in the non-Christian community. From time to time Christians have met to discuss means by which the bride price may be fixed and excessive demands restricted. On the eve of the religious ceremony which is central in Christian marriage the traditional anointing is observed in the homes of both parties to the marriage and many of the traditional songs are sung. A Christian explained these ceremonies by saying that they are regarded as a way of saying to the bride and bridegroom: "From now you are separate." It cannot be denied that they are an effective way of emphasizing this truth.

The marriage ceremony, which has to be conducted in accordance with the provisions of the Indian Christian Marriage Act, is held either in a church building or, where there is no church, in the courtyard of the bride's home. The last occasion on which I was present at a Santal Christian marriage was in February 1945.

The service took place in the church at Barikul; the month is significant, for Christians observe the same times and seasons as others. The bride, whose home was in the village, had been away to boarding school and was sixteen years old. For her wedding she was dressed in a red *saṛi*, and her head and face were covered by one end of the garment. The bridegroom was a village schoolmaster whose home was in a village some eight miles distant. He too was dressed in "respectable", i.e. Bengali, fashion, with a silk cloth thrown over his right shoulder. Many non-Christian women and girls crowded into the church with the Christians to watch, though non-Christian men stayed outside and peered through the windows. The service is according to the Order in the Book of Common Prayer, and the bridegroom presents the bride with a ring. The fact that the bride was holding in her left hand an iron *jaṇti*, or betel nut cracker, led to somewhat complicated shufflings when the ring was being placed in position. The mutual vows involve the repetition of the personal names of the bride by the bridegroom, and *vice versa*, a definite departure from tribal custom. When the Benediction had been pronounced a maternal aunt of the bride tied one end of the latter's *saṛi* to the end of the bridegroom's silk cloth, and this was followed by the signing of the register, an act that is always regarded with great interest by the non-Christians who observe it. While the register was being signed the men and women in the church sang alternate verses of a marriage song. Before the main party had left the building the rest of the congregation went out and the door was locked. No one else was allowed to leave the building until the bridegroom had promised to pay a fee to the old women whose duty it was to sweep the church, a building of mud walls with a thatched roof that was used also as a day school. The bride, the bridegroom and the officiating minister were garlanded.

At the bride's home after the ceremony we saw some of the mock garlands which the *lumti*, or bridesmaids, had made for the bridegroom and his father. They were of plaited coco-nut fibre decorated with tamarind fruits and pieces of the hard outer shell of the *sinjo* fruit. The groom and bride arrived back at the home still tied together; they were being led by the wife of the local "catechist", who held the bridegroom's right hand in her left, and the small procession was completed by an unmarried girl walking close behind the couple, holding an umbrella over their heads. The knot in their clothing was now untied and they were both carried into the house on the hip of a stalwart married woman to partake of their first meal together, the only time when they would sit and eat together. The feast took some time to prepare; the bride's relations—her parents were dead and she was married from the home of a paternal aunt, a blind widow—had provided a goat, but as they were in poor circumstances the Christian villagers had contributed the rice from their homes. While the guests waited for the food there was a good deal of singing, the songs being both traditional and Christian. Here are some examples noted at the time:

> Two bows and six arrow shafts I kept in store.
> The arrowheads have been sent ahead to *Radha*;[1]
> The money also has been sent ahead to *Radha*.[2]
>
> You who should have come yesterday at noon,
> Why, sons, did you arrive in the evening?
>
> Three headmen from three villages
> Wrangled over the marriage booth;
> They did not want to let go the vermilion giving.[3]
>
> The daughter bids farewell and goes;
> The house is forlorn, father, the house is forlorn.
> The rice in the straw bundle has been pushed out;
> Its wooden platform is forlorn, father, its wooden platform is forlorn.[4]

The following song struck a Christian note:

> My life (Jesus) and your life,
> Two lives (Jesus) are bound together;
> Like the *alak* creeper and the *bando*[5] creeper,
> Like the spider web in the palmyra tree,
> Two lives (Jesus) are bound together.[6]

On this occasion I was unable to remain to witness the final farewell and homegoing, but these follow closely the traditional Santal way.

In the death ceremonies there is little trace of pre-Christian modes of thought. This is not surprising in view of the fact that Christian teaching not only gives a new significance to the individual but also has something definite to say about the destiny of the human soul after death. The difference is emphasized for

[1] The name of the bridegroom's village.
[2] See Appendix B, No. 31.
[3] See Appendix B, No. 32.
[4] See Appendix B, No. 33.
[5] Two forest creepers.
[6] See Appendix B, No. 34.

the Santal Christian by the fact that the Christian custom—so far as he is aware—is burial. When a death has occurred the interment follows as soon as possible, but not before the corpse has been anointed with oil and turmeric. For this service the Christians are dependent upon each other; non-Christians keep themselves strictly away from the house of death. The grave is always dug lengthwise from east to west and the head of the corpse is placed towards the west. Whenever possible the body is draped in a new cloth, but in any case the clothes worn at the time of death are also buried. Coffins are a sign of affluence; usually the body is laid on a bed of leaves at the bottom of the grave and covered gently with leaves and sticks before the earth is filled in. Small treasures are laid in the grave, personal possessions of the deceased; and it is not uncommon to bury a New Testament or a Bible with the body. The subsequent mourning and funeral ceremonies of the non-Christian are altogether absent; in their place we find that on the day after the funeral, which is also usually the day after the death has taken place, the Christians gather at the bereaved home, where they sing and pray together and hear the Scriptures read. The dead person is praised and the living are comforted; and no passages are more used at these occasions than the familiar words of the Twenty-third Psalm and the Fourteenth Chapter of the Gospel according to St. John. They share the Christian hope and in expressing it they are giving a new content to the word *ṛaskạ* that is so often on the lips of the Santal, for they speak of *jaejug ṛaskạ*, eternal joy.

APPENDIX A

SANTAL KINSHIP TERMS

THIS list of terms is added in the hope that it will assist in the comparative study of Indian kinship terms that may one day be undertaken. A list of terms current among the Santals of Mayurbhanj is found in *The Santals*, by Charulal Mukherjea, and reveals no significant differences. Many of the terms in use among the Santals are the same as those found among the Bengalis.

(1) *Speaker's own Generation*

Brother	Boeha
Elder brother	Dada
Eldest brother	Marań dada
Younger brother	Bokoń
Youngest brother	Huḍiń utạric' bokoń
Sister	Misera
Elder sister	Ạjiń
Younger sister	Bokoń kuṛi
Mother's elder brother's daughter	Mamoń hopon era
Mother's younger brother's daughter	Mamoń hopon era
Father's elder brother's son	Goṅgoń hopon
Father's younger brother's son	Kakań hopon
Father's elder sister's son	Hatomiń hopon
Father's younger sister's son	Hatomiń hopon
Mother's sister's son	Kạkiń hopon
Mother's brother's son	Mamoń hopon
Husband's elder sister's husband	Ajnariń jāwāẽ
Husband's elder brother	Barhońhar
Husband's younger brother	Erweliń koṛa
Wife's elder sister's husband	Saḍge
Husband's younger sister's husband	Erweliń koṛa jāwāẽ
(Man's) Elder sister's husband	Teńań
(Woman's) Elder sister's husband	Teńań
(Man's) Younger sister's husband	Bokoń kuṛi jāwāẽ
(Woman's) Younger sister's husband	Bokoń kuṛi jāwāẽ
Wife's younger brother	Erweliń koṛa
Wife's elder brother	Barhońhar
Husband	Jāwāẽ / Hereḷ

Son's wife's father	Balań
Daughter's husband's father	Balań
Wife	Oṛak' gomkeń
Husband's elder brother's wife	Ńatań era
Husband's elder sister	Ajnar
Husband's younger sister	Erweliń kuṛi
Husband's younger brother's wife	Huḍiń ńatań era
Wife's elder brother's wife	Barhońhariń renic'
Wife's younger brother's wife	Erweliń oṛak' gomket'
Father's elder sister's daughter	Hatomiń hoponera
Father's younger sister's daughter	Hatomiń hoponera
Father's elder brother's daughter	Gońgoń hoponera
Father's younger brother's daughter	Kakań hoponera
Wife's elder sister	Ajnar
Wife's younger sister	Erweliń kuṛi
Younger brother's wife	Bokoń bạhu
Elder brother's wife	Hiliń
Son's wife's mother	Balań era
Daughter's husband's mother	Balań era

(2) *Generation next above Speaker*

Father	Ạpuń
Father's elder brother	Gońgoń
Mother's elder sister's husband	Gońgoń
Father's younger brother	Kakań
Stepfather	Kakań ạpuń
Mother's younger sister's husband	Kakań
Father's elder sister's husband	Kumạń
Father's younger sister's husband	Kumạń
Mother's elder brother	Mama
Mother's younger brother	Mama
Husband's father	Hońhar
Wife's father	Hońhar Nạihar
Mother	Enga Ayo Go
Stepmother	Kạkiń eńga
Father's elder brother's wife	Gońgo ayo Marań ayo
Father's younger brother's wife	Kạki Huḍiń ayo

Mother's elder sister	Gongoń era ayo
Mother's brother's wife	Mạmi hatom
Mother's younger sister	Kạki
Father's sister	Hatom
Wife's mother	Hanhar
Husband's mother	Hanhar

(3) *Generation next below Speaker*

Son	Hopon Babu Beṭa
Elder brother's son	Bhacań
Wife's elder sister's son	Gongoń era hopon
Husband's elder brother's son	Bhacań
Wife's younger sister's son	Erwelin kuṛi hopon
Husband's younger brother's son	Erwelin koṛa hopon Bhacań
Husband's younger sister's son	Erwelin kuṛi hopon
Woman's elder brother's son	Homonin
Woman's younger brother's son	Homonin
Man's elder sister's son	Bhagnań
Man's younger sister's son	Bhagnań
Husband's younger sister's son	Bhagnań
Wife's younger brother's son	Erwelin koṛa hopon
Woman's elder sister's son	Ạjin hopon
Daughter's husband	Jãwãẽ gomkeń
Man's elder brother's daughter	Bhacań kuṛi
Husband's elder brother's daughter	Bhacań kuṛi
Woman's elder brother's daughter	Homonin kuṛi
Husband's younger sister's daughter	Erwelin kuṛi hopon
Man's elder sister's daughter	Bhagnań kuṛi
Woman's elder sister's daughter	Ạjin hoponera
Husband's elder sister's daughter	Ạjnarin hoponera
Man's younger sister's daughter	Bhagnań kuṛi
Wife's elder brother's daughter	Barhońharin hoponera
Wife's younger brother's daughter	Erwelin koṛa hoponera
Woman's younger sister's daughter	Bokoń kuṛi hoponera
Man's younger brother's daughter	Bhacań kuṛi
Wife's younger sister's daughter	Erwelin kuṛi hoponera
Son's wife	Kiminin
Daughter	Hoponera

(4) *Third Generation from Speaker*

The characteristic name for this relationship is the word *goṛom,* which is used both for grandchildren and for grandparents, with the addition of descriptive adjectives drawn from the table of relationships to define the relationship more precisely.

Examples

Son's daughter's husband	Goṛomiń kuṛi jāwāē
Sister's son's son	Ạjiń goṛomtet'

APPENDIX B

SANTALI TEXT OF SONGS

(1) *Chapter* 1, *p*. 10

Sohrae

Kuṛi kuṛi kuṛiạreko gitic'a,
Koṛa koṛa goṛareko gitic'a.

(2) *Chapter* 1, *p*. 10

Sohrae

i. Mạńjhi daraekan hõ dildạl dildạl,
Paranike daraekan hõ kaṭabe kaṭap,
Goḍet' daraekan hõ haka ḍaka.

ii. Mạńjhi belaepe sutạm parkom,
Paranik belaepe ṭenḍar mạci,
Goḍet' belaepe topak' parkom.

iii. Mạńjhi nemaepe hõ taṅ hạṇḍi,
Paranik nemaepe hõ dul hạṇḍi,
Goḍet' nemaepe hõ boḍoc' hạṇḍi.

iv. Mạńjhi nemaepe hõ piṭha cakna,
Paranik nemaepe hõ leṭo cakna,
Goḍet' nemaepe hõ lac' kaṭa.

(3) *Chapter* 4, *p*. 45

Doṅ

Kolkata bajarre bibi lain gạḍi
Rel do ńurakan hõ;
Khoborakope Siuṛi hoṛ
Aguiako.
Hir hor khir khor kupi kol
Bibi lain gạḍi rel hõ,
Ṭhelao rakap'.

(4) *Chapter* 4, *p*. 45

Lagṛe

Asansolre
Bijli bạti,
Sebel, sebel.

(5) *Chapter* 4, *pp.* 45 & 46

Lagre

Bonero pakhia kande
Bhinu bhinu kande piar'
Mach kande ghumure ghumur piari,
Pran kande tomari lagi.

Car konia pukhuri
Nana roṅger pakhir basa he
Khanek nuṛe khanek bose
Basa nạhi pae basa nạhi khujiya pạe.

(6) *Chapter* 4, *p.* 46

Porob

Jolke ba gele biṭi
Kene ba biṭi pallum?
Ki ba mai bolibo
Ki ba mai kohibo?
Rajaram bagane
Phula phuṭilo,
Se o phul ṭuṭite amae topol holo.

(7) *Chapter* 4, *p.* 46

Lagre

Nạdite hoilo ban
Par koro, Bhogovan
Par koro, Bhogovan re.

(8) *Chapter* 4, *p.* 46

Jhika

Manuser o jonom jhinga phuler koli,
Ki na lagi ele re soṅsar;
Aro ki pabe durlob jonom
Ses jibon Kisṭo odhikar.

(9) *Chapter* 4, *p.* 46

Sohrae

Kaera kõẽare do cele menaea,
Kaera kõẽare do kunkạl menaea,
Kaera kõẽare do kunkạl menaea.

Am do re kunkạl cakem ạcura,
Iṅren eṅga apa bạnuk' kina,
Iṅren eṅga apa benaokakinme.

Benao do re bachaṅ benaokakin ge,
Benao jiwi do re bacha ohoṅ emle,
Benao jiwi do re bacha ohoṅ emle.

(10) *Chapter* 4, *p.* 47

Dāsāē

Tokare do guru hõ, gạiko janamlen,
Tokare do cela hõ, mạnwiko busạṛlen.

Hihirire guru hõ gạiko janamlen,
Pipirire cela hõ mạnwiko busạṛlen.

(11) *Chapter* 4, *p.* 47

Jhika

Holud pukur aila
Manilal raja hõ,
Chatur puri aila,
Jadob Siṅ rani.

Sunile he Durjon Siṅ,
Tuṅ bhũiyer raja hõ,
Maro maro
Komore bandho.

(12) *Chapter* 5, *p.* 62

Kahini

Toṛegor pukhuri Bahagor bandelare
Engaṅ goe janamlediṅ
Ạpuṅ goe hoborlediṅa.

Utạr dạkhin purub pạchim hende rimil doe rakap'akat'
Iṅ do go jonome ṭuạr
Iṅ do go okateṅ senok'a.

Muṅga dareṛeṅ japak'lena muṅga mayam do laṭhaadiṅ,
Sate umulreṅ teṅgolena
Sate dak' ho joṛoadiṅa.

(13) *Chapter* 5, *p.* 62

Jare jare siṅ cando, jare jare ṅinda cando,
Jib dan dom emadiṅ
Cok dan do bam emadiṅ.
Mit' biṭa lac' lągit'
Sotok' sunum jivi lągit'
Des disom goṅ caṛcao baṛaekan.

(14) *Chapter* 5, *p.* 63

Kaera tole jonom dilo
Ason pate ḍhaka dilo je.
Giḍi giḍi soner giḍi,
Giḍi giḍi rąila giḍi,
Pusaloṅ de go
Mąi go bhik de.

(15) *Chapter* 8, *p.* 95

A Dāsāĕ song

Tokoe guruaṅ rupe dąnṭic' dai na dai,
Tala nąi Kasaire dai na dai,
Rupe dąnṭic' jhamare jhumure.

Dhorom guruaṅ rupe dąnṭic' dai na dai,
Tala nąi Kasaire dai na dai,
Rupe dąnṭic' jhamare jhumure.

(16) *Chapter* 9, *p.* 105

A Baha song

Hesak' ma coṭere
Tude doe ragele;
Des ṁa nąturen
Disom ma bihuren.

The above words are followed by these as a kind of chorus:

Naejom jomme naeke ere!

(17) *Chapter* 9, *p.* 105

A Baha song

Sokṛare haṭ baha daina,
Sokṛare haṭ baha daina,
Gutuialaṅ jhamka jakur daina,
Bahaealaṅ, dalae dalae.

(18) *Chapter* 9, *p.* 107

A Baha song

Halańalań ṇajiń matkom,
Bahaealań ṇajiń sarjom baha
Ńuilań ṇajiń matkom rasa.

(19) *Chapter* 9, *p.* 108

A Baha song

Ne tora nepe tora
Murum pańja;
Ne tora nepe tora
Sosań pańja.

Toka birte boloena
Murum pańja;
Toka birte soṛoena
Sosań pańja.

Man birte boloena
Murum pańja;
Siń birte soṛoena
Sosań pańja.

(20) *Chapter* 9, *p.* 110

A Baha song

Dol calaoen kuṛi pata daṛakan,
Phirphiri do kuṛi kirińatape.

Kuṛikoak' panḍere hende ḍumur chata,
Phirphiri do kuṛi kirińatape.

(21) *Chapter* 9, *pp.* 116, 117

A Karam song

Hạnuman jo maribere puta ki na he karabe
Hạnuman jo maribo go ayo cam chulabo.

Cama jo chulabere puta ki na he karabe
Cama jo chulabo go ayo madole chawabo.

Madol jo chawabere puta ki na he karabe
Madol jo chawabo go ayo karame gaṛabo.

Karam jo gaṛabere puta ki na he nacabe
Karam jo gaṛabo go ayo goḍet' niphur ḍanḍahi mathayet'.

(22) *Chapter* II, *p*. 136

(*a*) *Question:* Ehõ raebaric' timin saṅgiṅrem sągunkeda?
Answer: Ạḍi saṅgiṅ hõ buru parom
Cando boṅgageye likhonkeda.

(*b*) *Question:* Ehõ raebaric' bạhu kuṛi doe timin maraṅ?
Answer: Bae maraṅa bae huḍiṅa,
Jonok' mutire jhumka raca jojok' kan kheṛec' kheṛec'.

(23) *Chapter* II, *p*. 136

Sateate babu ṅelkediṅ
Ṭhepkate babu rukedaṅ,
Kunkạl bhajan bachaokate babuṅ aguama.

(24) *Chapter* II, *p*. 136

Bor dekho ghor dekho
Puạl kuṛ tule dekho.

(25) *Chapter* II, *p*. 137

(*a*) *Question:* Ehõ raebaric' jãwãẽ oṛak' do timin saṅgiṅ?
Answer: Bae saṅgiṅa bae sora,
Hane ṅelok'kạn kaera bakul.

(*b*) *Question:* Ehõ raebaric' jãwãẽ koṛa do timin maraṅ?
Answer: Bae maraṅa bae huḍiṅa,
Kạsi ghuṭure gạiye gupi,
Tirioe oṛoṅa riyo royo.

(26) *Chapter* II, *p*. 141

Ạcure bihure seṅgele titi do,
Berhale ṅamele kuili gại noṛak' do.
Suc' dak're hosoren soner goṛ sikri do,
Ḍạḍi dak're hosoren ruper goṛ paini do.
Tokoe coe halaṅket' soner goṛ sikri do,
Tokoe coe tumạlket' ruper goṛ paini do?
Kạru ge halaṅket' soner goṛ sikri do,
Kạru ge tumạlket' ruper goṛ paini do.

(27) *Chapter* II, *p*. 141

Tokoeak' racare dak' bhumbhuk'en
Dak' bhumbhuk'en hale dak' bohilen?
Hembromkoak' racare dak' bhumbhuk'en
Dak' bhumbhuk'en hale dak' bohilen.

(28) *Chapter* 14, *p*. 184

Bapla

Dela dela daya Jisu
Dela dela moneń oṛak're
Tuṛi ghuṛi ńelat' lemkhan
Mone ińak' ṛapudok'a.

Amge jivi amge sotya
Sạri hor hõ amge ho
Nisạrtiren sạrti Jisu
Jivi khojme onatege.

Akaṛ baha amge kiya
Mulạn munihõ amge ho
Mone muni jãhãẽic' am
Sạri kisạṛ do unige ho.

(29) *Chapter* 14, *p*. 184

Sohrae

Bhurkae rakapenhõ ḍigi migi
Setak' hoe doe hoyet' hiside hiside
Totrạu din do hale seṭerakan hõ.

(30) *Chapter* 14, *p*. 185

Heṛhet'

1. Beṛadoe hạsurena tahenme Jisu sãõte,
Am bańkhan eṭak' gate bạnuk' kotiń okoehõ.

2. Jivi saṭ saṭge calak' kan bań teńgona,
Otreń ńel ar cet'hõ ge bạnuk' anań am begor.

3. Harket' saset're dayaem emań khan do
Gujuk' guruk' bań bora sãõtem tahen khanhõ Probhu.

4. Sap'edań amak' krusge ikańme sanam dos khon
Siń ńinda sãõtekate emańmehõ serma marsal.

(31) *Chapter* 14, *p*. 189

Bapla

Ak' barea ḍol turui goṭen doho oṭokadań
Sar kodo Radhare kol laha akana
Poesa hõ Radhare kol laha akana.

(32) *Chapter* 14, *p.* 189

Bapla

Hola tikinre hijuk' hoṛ
Cedak' beṭape singaṛena?

Pea atoren pea mąńjhi
Mąṛla lągit' ko repec'kana
Sindra dange coṅ baṅko aṛag.

(33) *Chapter* 14, *p.* 189

Bapla

Hoponera bidąi oḍok'
Oṛak' nisunen baba oṛak' nisunen.
Bąndi hoṛo ṭhelao oḍok'
Ḍhula nisunen baba ḍhula nisunen.

(34) *Chapter* 14, *p.* 189

Bapla

In reak' jivi Jisu am reak' jivi
Jivi jivi Jisu tolakan do
Alak jąṛi bando nąṛi
Tale dare bindi ganak'
Jivi jivi Jisu tolakan do.

APPENDIX C

GLOSSARY OF SANTALI WORDS OCCURRING IN THE TEXT

Abge boṅga: Sub-clan spirit.
Ader: To bring in.
Adwa caole: Sun-dried rice.
Ajar: Fever.
Alak: Two parasitic plants: *Cuscuta chinensis*, Lamk., and *Cassytha filiformis*, Roxb.
Atnak': A tree, *Terminalia tomentosa*, W. and A.
Baha: A flower.
Bakheṛ: Invocation.
Banam: A fiddle (see illustration, p. 42).
Bando: A plant, *Spatholobus Roxburghii*, Benth.
Bapla: Marriage.
Bǫric': Evil.
Bǫsiǫm: Time of breakfast: left-over food.
Batol: Unwholesome.
Bir: Forest.
Boṅga: Spirit that is worshipped.
Buaṅ: Musical instrument (see illustration, p. 41).
Buḍhi: Old woman.
Bul: Drunken: saturated.
Buru: Mountain: also spirits.
Bhanḍan: Final funeral feast.
Bhitǫr: Inner room.
Bhitri: Inner.
Bhut: Ghost.
Caco: Toddler.
Cando: Month: also the Supreme Being (*siṅ cando*, the sun: *ṅinda cando*, the moon).
Cela: Disciple.
Cikhnǫ: Mark, sign.
Curin: Female ghost.
Chǫṭiǫr: Ceremonial cleansing.
Dak': Water.
Dare: Tree.
Dãsãe: Month, September-October.
Deko: Hindus.
Dihri: Hunt priest.
Dipil: To carry on the head.
Doṅ: A kind of dance.
Doṅgeṛ: Ditto.
Dul: To pour.
Duṛup': To sit: a council meeting.
Dhubi: A common grass, *Cynodon dactylon*, Pers. Reg.
Ḍǫn: Witch.
Ḍhãk: A drum (see illustration, p. 44).
Ḍhǫi: Midwife.

Ende: Ind festival.
Enec': Dance: play.
Era: Woman.
Erba: A gram, *Setaria italica*, Kunth.
Gaḍa: River.
Gelbar: Twelve.
Girą: Knotted string.
Goḍet': Village messenger.
Gonoṅ: Bride price.
Gõsãẽ: "Lord", a title used in addressing the *boṅga*.
Guą: Betel nut.
Gur loṭom: Side of animal falling to the ground when killed at *bhanḍan*, q.v.
Guru: Teacher.
Ghinni: Large lizard.
Halaṅ: To lift.
Hąnḍi: Rice beer.
Haṛam: Old man.
Hą̃s: Goose.
Hą̃sil: Gander.
Hąsli: Woman's neck ornament.
Heṛe: Husks.
Heṛhet': To weed.
Hesak': A tree, *Ficus religiosa*, L.
Hesel: A tree, *Anogeisses latifolia*, Wall.
Hili: Elder brother's wife.
Hoṛ: Man: a Santal.
Hoṛmo: Body.
Horok': To put on.
Hotrin: Deer.
Iṛi: A millet, *Panicum crusgalli*, L.
Itąt': Left-over food.
Jaejug: Everlasting.
Jaher: Sacred grove.
Jan: Witch finder.
Ją̃nti: Betel nut cracker.
Jaṅ: Bone.
Jiu: Life principle: soul.
Jivi: Ditto.
Jogmąṅjhi: Guardian of morals.
Jom Sim: A clan festival.
Jhiką̃: A kind of dance.
Kakṛa: Common lizard.
Kąmi: Work.
Kãṛã: Blind.
Karam: A tree, *Adinia cordifolia*, Hook.: festival associated with this tree
Kikir: Kingfisher.
Kudąm: Back of the house.
Kupi: Small earthen pot.
Khoda: Tattooing.
Khok': Cough.

Khũṭ: Sub-clan.
Lagṛe: A kind of dance.
Leḍha: The lame one.
Leṛda: A kind of drum (see illustration, p. 42).
Liṭa̧: The chief tribal spirit of Santals.
Lumti: Bridesmaid.
Madol: Portion of animal slain in hunt.
Mak' Mõṛẽ: Sacrifice to the "Five".
Maloṭ: Epidemic.
Mańjhi: Village headman.
Marań: Great.
Matkom: The *mahua* tree, *Bassia latifolia*, Roxb.
Mayam: Blood.
Met': Eye.
Mokor: Festival in mid-January.
Murum: A buck, *Portax tragocamelus* (*nilgae*).
Nahan: To bathe.
Nãi: Damodar river.
Naeke: Priest.
Nij: Own.
Ńinda: Night.
Ńutum: Name.
Ojha: Magician.
Orec': To tear.
Paranik: Deputy headman.
Pargana: Group of villages.
Parganath: Headman of a *pargana*.
Pa̧ris: Clan.
Pa̧ura̧: Distilled liquor.
Peṛa: Kinsman: neighbour.
Pilcu: First.
Poa̧ti: Pregnant woman.
Poita: Sacred thread.
Pon: Bride price.
Porob: Festival.
Pret: Ghost.
Ran: Medicine.
Ra̧ska̧: Pleasure.
Rot: A tree, *Ougenia dalbergioides*, Benth.
Rua̧: Sickness.
Rum: Spirit possession.
Sada: White.
Sakam: Leaf.
Sara: Funeral pyre.
Sarjom: *Sal* tree, *Shorea robusta*, Gartn.
Sarpa: A percussion instrument (see illustration, p. 40).
Sendra: Hunt.
Sidup': Erect.
Sika̧: Cicatrization.
Sim: Fowl.
Sindur: Vermilion.
Sinjo: A tree, *Ægle marmelos*, Correa.

Sin: Day.
Sirom: A grass, *Andropogon muricatus*, Retz.
Sohrae: Harvest festival.
Sunum: Oil.
Tirio: Flute.
Tok: Pestle.
Tumdak': A drum (see illustration, p. 42).
Turuk: Moslem.
Than: Place: usually Sacred place.
Ṭamak: A drum (see illustration, p. 42).
Ṭaṇgi: Sacrificial axe.
Ṭunki: Small basket.
Ṭhakur: The Supreme Being: also spirit.
Ukhuṛ: Mortar.
Umul: Shadow.

APPENDIX D

BIBLIOGRAPHY

Archer, Mildred:

THE FOLK-TALE IN SANTAL SOCIETY, *Man in India*, Vol. XXIV, 1944.

Archer, W. G.:

SANTAL POETRY, *Man in India*, Vol. XXIII, 1943.

BETROTHAL DIALOGUES, *ditto*, Vol. XXIII, 1943.

AN INDIAN RIDDLE BOOK, *ditto*, Vol. XXIII, 1943.

FESTIVAL SONGS, *ditto*, Vol. XXIV, 1944.

MORE SANTAL SONGS, *ditto*, Vol. XXIV, 1944.

THE ILLEGITIMATE CHILD IN SANTAL SOCIETY, *ditto*, Vol. XXIV, 1944.

THE FORCIBLE MARRIAGE, *ditto*, Vol. XXV, 1945.

THE SANTAL REBELLION, *ditto*, Vol. XXV, 1945.

Bodding, P. O.:

ON THE DIFFERENT KINDS OF SALUTATIONS USED BY THE SANTALS, *Journal of the Asiatic Society of Bengal*, Vol. LXVII, Pt. III, 1898.

ON TABOOS AND CUSTOMS CONNECTED THEREWITH AMONG THE SANTALS, *ditto*, Vol. LXVII, Pt. III, 1898.

A NOTE ON THE "WILD PEOPLE" OF THE SANTALS, *ditto*, Vol. XXVII (New Series), pp. 141–263.

SANTAL TRADITIONS, *Journal of the Bihar and Orissa Research Society*, Vol. II, 1916.

SOME REMARKS ON THE POSITION OF WOMEN AMONG THE SANTALS, *ditto*, Vol. II, 1916.

Materials for a Santali Grammar, Benagaria, 1922.

Studies in Santal Medicine and Connected Folklore, *Memoirs of the Royal Asiatic Society of Bengal*. In three parts. Pt. I: The Santals and Disease, 1925; Pt. II: Santal Medicine, 1927; Pt. III: How the Santals live, 1940.

A Chapter of Santal Folklore, Kristiana Ethnographical Museum, 1924.

Santal Folk-Tales, three volumes, Oslo, 1925–9.

A Santali Dictionary, five volumes, Oslo, 1932–6.

Santal Riddles and *Witchcraft among the Santals*, Oslo, 1940.

Traditions and Institutions of the Santals, being a translation of *Horkoren mare Hapramko reak' Katha*, Oslo, 1942.

Bompas, C. H.:

Folklore of the Santal Parganas, London, 1909.

Bradley Birt, F. B.:

The Story of an Indian Upland, London, 1925.

Buchanan, F.:

An Account of the District of Bhagalpur in 1810–11, Patna, 1939.

Campbell, A.:

SUPERSTITIONS OF THE SANTALS,

THE TRADITIONS OF THE SANTALS,

SANTAL LEGENDS,

Campbell, A.:
DEATH AND CREMATION CEREMONIES AMONG THE SANTALS, and SANTAL MARRIAGE CUSTOMS. All being articles in Vol. II of the *Journal of the Bihar and Orissa Research Society*, 1916.

Carstairs, R.:
Harma's Village. A Novel of the Santal Rebellion, Pokhuria, 1935.

Chatterji, S. K.:
THE LINGUISTIC PROBLEM, *Oxford Pamphlets on Indian Affairs*, 1943.

Crooke, W.:
Religion and Folklore of Northern India, Oxford, 1926.

Culshaw, W. J.:
SOME NOTES ON BONGAISM, *Journal of the Royal Asiatic Society of Bengal*, Vol. V, 1939.
SOME BELIEFS AND CUSTOMS RELATING TO BIRTH AMONG THE SANTALS, *ditto*, Vol. VII, 1941.
LARS OLSEN SKREFSRUD, 1840–1910, *International Review of Missions*, Vol. XXXI, 1942.
THE "FOLK-CONSCIOUSNESS" OF THE SANTALS, *Essays in Anthropology presented to S. C. Roy*, Lucknow, 1942.
EARLY RECORDS CONCERNING THE SANTALS, *Man in India*, Vol. XXV, 1945.
THE SANTAL REBELLION, *ditto*, Vol. XXV, 1945.

Dalton, E. T.:
Descriptive Ethnology of Bengal, Calcutta, 1872.

Dutta, K. K.:
The Santal Insurrection, Calcutta, 1940.

Gausdal, J.:
Contributions to Santal Hymnology, Bergen, 1935.
THE KHŬṬ SYSTEM OF THE SANTALS, *Journal of the Bihar and Orissa Research Society*, Vol. XXVIII, 1942.

Ghurye, G. S.:
The Aborigines—"So-called"—and Their Future, Poona, 1943.

Guha, B. S.:
RACIAL ELEMENTS IN THE POPULATION, *Oxford Pamphlets on Indian Affairs*, 1944.

Hunter, W. W.:
The Annals of Rural Bengal, London, 1868.

Hutton, J. H.:
Census of India, 1931, Vol. I. Pt. I, Report; Pt. II, Tables; and Pt. III, Ethnographica.
PRIMITIVE TRIBES, *Modern India and the West*, Oxford, for the Royal Institute of International Affairs, 1941.

Kitchen, L. C.:
Primary Education among Santals of Midnapore, Calcutta, 1931.

Macphail, J. M.:
The Story of the Santals, Calcutta, 1922.

Man, E. G.:
Sonthalia and the Sonthals, London, 1867.

McAlpin, M. C.:
A Report on the Condition of the Santals in the Districts of Birbhum, Bankura, Midnapore and North Balasore, Calcutta, 1909.

Mukherjea, C. L.:
The Santals, Calcutta, 1943.

Naqavi, S. M.:
SANTAL MURDERS, *Man in India*, Vol. XXIII, 1943.

O'Malley, L. S. S.:
Bengal District Gazetteers: Santal Parganas, Calcutta, 1910.
Bengal District Gazetteers: Bankura, Calcutta, 1910.

Risley, H. H.:
The Tribes and Castes of Bengal, Calcutta, 1891.

Skrefsrud, L. O.:
Introduction to the Grammar of the Santali Language, Benares, 1873.

Skrefsrud, L. O., and Craven, C. H.:
NOTES ON FRATERNAL POLYANDRY AMONG THE SANTALS, *Journal of the Asiatic Society of Bengal*, 1908.

Sutherland, H. C.:
Report on the Management of the Rajmahal Hills dated June 8, 1819, Deputy Commissioner's Record Room, Dumka.

INDEX

Where there are several references, italics indicate that the subject is dealt with in full.

ANCESTOR Worship, *82*, *83*, *84*, 102, 113, 120, 158, 160, 177
Baha festival, 103 ff.
Betrothal, 138
Bhitar, 83 f.
Birth, 10, 39, *120* ff.
Burial, 149, *150*, 178, 190
Cando (Ṭhạkur), 53, 60, 65, 86, *90*, *91*, 93, 117, 120, 128
Cattle-baiting, 112
Charms, *102*, 121, 126
Cicatrization, 72, *132*
Clans, 2, 11, *67* ff.
Dancing, 35, *39* ff., 69, 94, 103, 105-7, 113-17, 130, 141, 167, 168
Death and cremation, 10, 22, 28, 92, 114, 120, 123, 129, 132, *150* ff., 181
Dihri, 33, 34
Divorce, 73, *147*
Drink, 29, 31 f., 35, 41, 68, 81, 107, 111, 113, 130, 140, 143, 152, 167, 168, 177, 183
"Five", The (see also Mak' Mõṛẽ), 80, 81, *82*, 102, 103, 106, 114, 157
Future life, 89, 92, 132, *158-160*
Goḍet' (bailiff), *10*, 104, 105, 111, 112, 142, 143, 150, 156
Gõsñẽ Era, 81
Headman (Mạñjhi), *7*, 34, 64, 82, 83, 98, 111, 113, 114, 143, 144, 156, 157
Hindus, relationship with, *15* ff., 21
Houses, construction of, 30, 48, *71*, *72*, 76, 99, 176
Initiation (caco chạṭiạr), 64, *129*, *130*
Jaher (sacred grove), *80*, 103, 105
Jaher Buḍhi, 80, 81, *82*, 103, 105, 106
Jan (witch-finder), *99*, 100, 154
Jogmạñjhi, *9* f., 111, 112, 130, 138, 139, 142, 143
Joking relationship, *12*, 35, 128
Jom Sim festival, 64, 72, 74, 91, 123 (note)
Karam festival, 64, 114, *115-18*
Land tenure, 3, 6, 8, 11, 17, 147
Liṭạ, see Marañ Buru
Mak' Mõṛẽ festival, 18, 114
Mạñjhi than, 82
Marañ Buru (Liṭạ), 31, 66, 67, 68, 80, *81*, 86, 88, 89, 90, 103-7, 109, 115, 128, 140, 153, 156, 176, 177
Marriage, 8, 10, 22, 33, 37, 39, 41, 47, 67, 69, 71, 76, 120, 129, 130, 132, *134* ff., 169, 179, 187-9
Medicine, 11, 22, 93, 97, 98, 113, 121
Midwife, 123-27, 130
Mokor festival, 83, 87, 112
Names and name-giving, 12, 127
Ojha, 80, 93, *94-99*, 101, 113, 114, 125, 128, 154, 171, 178
Ornaments, *48*, 71, 133
Paranik (deputy headman), 9
Pargana, Parganath, *11*, 32, 79, 81, 171
Pata (hook swinging), 110, 113
Pilcu Haṛam, Pilcu Buḍhi, *66* f., 115, 176
Polyandry, 146
Polygamy, 121, 146
Priest, 10, 22, *78*, *79*, 85 ff., 103-5, 110, 111, 113, 139, 141
Co-priest, *79*, *80*, 97
Purification (Janam Chạṭiạr), *126*, 151
Raebaric' (go-between), *135*, 142, 187
Sacred Places, 80 ff.
Sacrifice, 18, 22, 33, 71 ff., 79-89, 103, 123, 151
Salutations, 12, 13
Santali language, 2, *21*, *22* ff., 48, 179, 182
Santal rebellion, 6
Sohrae festival, 10, 18, 72, 74, 75, *110-12*, 186

Spirits, Boṅgas, 23, 71, *78* ff., 112, 113, 128, 156, 160
Evil spirits, Bhut, Pret, Curin, 24, 33, *92* ff., 121, 122, 125, 154, 171, 172, 187
Taboos, 2, 28, 33, 71, 73 ff., 89, 102, 176, 177, 186
Tattooing, 72, 74, *132*
Time, divisions and calculations of, 25 ff., 33, 139
Totem, 2, 11, 70
Villages, 4, 7, 8
Widows, 12, 73, 145, 146, 158
Witches and Witchcraft, 93, 97, 98, *99-101*, 147, 154, 172
Women, position of, etc., 29 ff., 84, 89, 99, 180